ID0835782

Compromising
THE Classics

Compromising THE Classics

ROMANCE EPIC NARRATIVE IN THE ITALIAN RENAISSANCE

Dennis Looney

 WAYNE STATE UNIVERSITY PRESS DETROIT

99   98   97   96   5   4   3   2   1

Library of Congress Cataloging-in-Publication Data

Looney, Dennis.
    Compromising the classics : Romance epic narrative in the Italian Renaissance / Dennis
Looney.
        p.   cm.
    Includes bibliographical references and index.
    ISBN 0-8143-2600-5 (alk. paper)
        1. Epic poetry, Italian—History and criticism.   2. Romances, Italian—History and
criticism.   3. Italian poetry—15th century—History and criticism.   4. Italian poetry—
16th century—History and criticism.   5. Ariosto, Lodovico, 1474-1533—Criticism and
intrepretation.   6. Boiardo, Matteo Maria, 1440 or 41-1494—Criticism and interpretation.   7. Tasso, Torquato, 1544-1595—Criticism and interpretation.   I. Title.
PQ4117.L66   1996
851'.03209—dc20   96-12085

FOR *Joanna*

Yet his classicism was classicism with a difference.
The classics were there—the five positions, jumps, beats,
turns and perfect feet—but so were heels, turned-in legs,
protruding hips, contractions in the torso and arms in new
configurations not found in any ballet dictionary.

NOTES ON GEORGE BALANCHINE'S APOLLO,
PITTSBURGH BALLET THEATRE PROGRAM,
NOVEMBER 1991

Contents

Contents

Acknowledgments

*I*n a book about sources it is proper to acknowledge one's debts. I would like to thank the many friends ("ariostofili" as Croce says of Giraldi Cinzio) who helped me give definition to this book: David Brumble, Karin Gleiter, William Kennedy, Rita Lizzi, Ronald Martinez, the late Raymond Prier, Amedeo Quondam, Giovanni Pozzi, Charles Ross, Deanna Shemek, Michael Sherberg, Elissa Weaver, and Sergio Zatti. In particular, I thank Albert Ascoli and Lawrence Rhu, readers for the press, who went over the manuscript with a thorough skepticism that has made it much better. Ascoli made countless corrections and suggestions, most of which I have accepted gladly, while Rhu helped me see the forest for the trees. I would also like to thank Daniel Javitch for encouraging me graciously from the beginnings of this project. My teachers at Boston University and the University of North Carolina at Chapel Hill, will, I hope, be pleased. In any case, it pleases me to name them: Dennis Costa, William Mullen, Aldo Scaglione, Philip Stadter, Sara Mack, and D. S. Carne-Ross. To say that Carne-Ross prepared me for "learned Italian things and the proud stones of Greece" is no exaggeration: I first heard of Ariosto in his elementary Greek course and was inspired to learn more of both.

Institutions, too, have helped me. The University of Pittsburgh has been generous in its support. I received summer stipends from the Dean of the Faculty of Arts and Sciences (1987, 1988), and a grant from the Central Research Development Fund (1991), as well as grants for travel from the Newberry Library Committee, the Medieval and Renaissance

Studies Program, and the West European Studies Program. My colleagues in the Department of French and Italian, especially Clare Godt, Francesca Savoia, and Daniel Russell, have made the daily rigamarole bearable, even pleasurable. So has Mark Possanza in the Department of Classics. It's hard for me to imagine a more congenial setting in which to have begun my career.

I enjoyed the largesse of the National Endowment for the Humanities during three summers. Franca Nardelli and Armando Petrucci taught me much that I have been able to put to use in this book at the NEH Summer Institute on Italian Archival Sciences, Newberry Library, Center for Renaissance Studies, 1988. Giuseppe Mazzotta conducted a lively colloquium on the medieval and Renaissance recovery of antiquity at the NEH Summer Institute on Petrarch and Petrarchism, Yale University, 1989. Albert Ascoli and David Quint gave generously at the NEH Summer Institute on Ariosto and Tasso, Northwestern University, 1990. I also learned much from the many colleagues with whom I shared those summers.

I owe a debt of thanks to the following libraries and their staffs: Beinecke Library, Yale University; Biblioteca Ariostea, Ferrara; Biblioteca Estense, Modena; Biblioteca Nazionale, Florence; British Library, London; Folger Shakespeare Library, Washington, D.C.; John Hay Library, Brown University; Hillman Library, University of Pittsburgh; Newberry Library, Chicago; Vatican Film Library, Saint Louis University; and Wilson Library, University of North Carolina at Chapel Hill. At the Newberry, Paul Gehl came to my rescue more than once with sources, references, and good judgment. Werner Gundersheimer, director of the Folger, kindly shared with me needed books, from the library's collection and his own.

I acknowledge the help of the staff at Wayne State University Press, a diligent, competent, and pleasant crew: Mary Beth O'Sullivan, Ann Schwartz, Lynn Trease, Stacy Lieberman, Jonathan Lawrence, and Arthur Evans, the director of the press. Let me add the usual caveat about the final product by slightly adapting the prefatory remarks to a sixteenth-century translation of Achilles Tatius: "Mistakes occur in all our actions as if of necessity, but I cannot imagine any endeavor more prone to a greater diversity of errors than publishing a book." The translator, Francesco Angelo Coccio, then compares himself correcting his manuscript to Hercules hacking away at the Hydra's heads. I, for my part, have applied all the Herculean energy I could muster to this book, but there probably still are some undecapitated snakes lurking within these pages. For whatever errors you may find, stern reader, I take the blame.

I thank my extended family. Looneys and Herberts in Tennessee, Thorntons in England have hosted me on numerous occasions. Most of all I thank my wife, Joanna Thornton. She as well as any Renaissance poet has perfected the art of compromise, for which I am truly grateful. I may make an "ariostofila" of her yet, but if I don't, it doesn't matter.

The third section of chapter 1 appeared in a slightly different version, "Ariosto the Ferrarese Rhapsode," in *Interpreting the Italian Renaissance: Literary Perspectives* (Stony Brook: Forum Italicum, 1990); chapter 4 appeared in a slightly different version in *Countercurrents: The Primacy of the Text in Literary Criticism* (Albany: SUNY, 1992). I thank the publishers for permission to reprint.

At the first encounter with a text in translation, I note the translator and edition I follow. If I do not specify otherwise, translations are my own.

Introduction: Sources of Compromise

> Only begetters, however, are a romantic convention: poems don't have only begetters.
>
> MARTIN AMIS ON PHILIP LARKIN[1]

*T*his is a study of literary compromises in three of the major poems of the Italian Renaissance, the romance-epics of Boiardo, Ariosto, and Torquato Tasso. The term "romance-epic" is itself indicative of a critical compromise, suggesting, as it does, a hybrid genre that combines elements of medieval vernacular romance with elements of classical epic. Although the term is problematic, I use it as a point of departure because it delimits the boundaries of my inquiry. In this study I consider how narrative artists in the Renaissance renovated the popular genre of romance through their imitation of classical epic. I also consider how the classical genres of pastoral, satire, history, and, to a lesser extent, comedy and tragedy affected their adaptation of romance. In the poems of Boiardo, Ariosto, and Tasso, a new kind of narrative arose from this process of imitation. I examine most fully those features of the narrative design of Ariosto's *Orlando Furioso* that suggest an affiliation with classical models. Ariosto's allusions to certain classical works shaped the narrative patterning of his poem, so that from one perspective it resembles a classical work, while from another it resembles a medieval romance. Subsequently, Ariosto's allusions to classical sources often promoted a reevaluation of those models in terms of his own vernacular tradition.

I focus on how the three poets compromised classical models by incorporating them into the narrative structures of their vernacular poems. I use the notion of compromise to counter what I perceive to be a bias in most studies of the narrative poems of Boiardo, Ariosto, and Tasso. The bias depends on the rigid dichotomizing of the poets' sources into two groups, classical and medieval, each of which, in general, critics have associated with a specific kind of source: with the classical sources, verbal and stylistic allusions; with the medieval sources, themes and images. In the introduction to the single most important book on Ariosto's sources, Pio Rajna proposes to attend to the *Furioso*'s medieval underpinnings because its classical allusions are merely "le imitazioni di singoli versi, immagini, similitudini, che non importassero per il concepimento [of the *Furioso*]" (*Le fonti* IX). (the imitation of single verses, images, similes, which were not important for the conception [of the poem].) He opts for those thematic allusions that reveal the medieval imagination at work—"invenzione" is his word to describe this type of source over those of classical *elocutio* or verbal style. But Ariosto (and Boiardo and Tasso) do much more with classical texts than allude to a simile here or borrow a nice turn of phrase there. They also borrow thematic material from classical texts—"invenzione" in Rajna's phrasing.[2] Moreover, and more to the point for the thesis of this study, the narrative dispositions—to use the technical term from rhetoric—of their respective poems bear the imprint of classical narrative design.[3] Throughout this study I shall focus on the part of rhetoric known as disposition or arrangement to counter the dichotomy of sources promoted in positivist studies—classical versus medieval, with its concomitant division of verbal art (elocution) and themes (invention).

Part of my thesis considers how these three poets understood and then to some extent overcame the distinction between classical and medieval, especially in the construction of their respective narratives. I use the term "to compromise" to examine the process of literary historicization that engaged the creative energies of Boiardo, Ariosto, and Tasso as they confronted this distinction. I use the verb in two specific ways, to denote distinct moments in the incorporation of allusions into the text. First I intend that it keep its basic sense of exposing something to suspicion. Ariosto's allusions to the classics, for example, encourage a reader to return to the authorities to whom he alludes with a raised brow, to read them anew. This literary-historical phenomenon, which contributed to the reception of the classics in Italy, is not, however, my primary concern. I am more interested in what effect compromised classical allusions might have (or might have had) on individual critical interpretations of the poems in question.

This focus on practical criticism suggests "to compromise" in its second sense. "To compromise" is derived from Latin *mittere*, "to send," and the prefixes *cum* and *pro,* suggesting the sending of one thing forth (*pro*) among (*cum*) others.[4] The narratives of Boiardo, Ariosto, and Tasso regularly draw attention to a single, specific model, which may be either classical or vernacular, setting it forth, as it were, among other sources.[5] This may happen for any number of reasons: aesthetic, ideological, or poetic, for example. Usually the privileging of a certain source is only momentary; subsequent developments in the narrative undercut the source, so that it is compromised in the term's first sense. The process of compromising a source, then, involves highlighting it in some way, singling it out to be undercut so that the reader's perception of it is affected. To be sure, the basic narrative models for the romance-epics of the Italian Renaissance are vernacular; however, our poets frequently compromise classical sources in adapting their vernacular models. Hence my focus as reflected in this book's title, *Compromising the Classics: Romance Epic Narrative in the Italian Renaissance.*

I consider how these poets and their readers (and the poets themselves as readers) reinterpreted certain classical authors from Boiardo's lifetime through Tasso's, a span of approximately one hundred years from the late fifteenth century to the end of the sixteenth. One of the effects of this reinterpretation of the Greek and Roman classics was the move to canonize a set of new classics written in the vernacular. In a recent study of Ariosto's critical fortune in the sixteenth century, Daniel Javitch examines the extratextual processes of literary assessment and propagandizing that led to the widespread recognition of the *Furioso* as a vernacular classic on a par with, or even surpassing, the acknowledged masterpieces of antiquity.[6] Critics, editors, publishers, and readers aggressively campaigned to identify Ariosto as the Ferrarese Homer or Vergil. Many motives lay behind this promotion: political, economic, and literary-theoretical, among others. The barrage of essays written from the 1540s into the next century on the nature of the *Furioso* records the various arguments made for the contemporary poem's canonical value. These are the documents that determine Javitch's reconstruction of this moment in the literary history of Italian culture. In fact, these essays and the debate they record mark the beginning of the definition of the modern literary canon in the West.

While Javitch addresses the extratextual forces that contributed to the legitimation of the *Furioso,* he does not consider another equally important factor in the canonization of the poem, namely, "that the *Furioso* possessed particular features that enabled it to be deemed a classic" (*Proclaiming a Classic* 4). By focusing on the role classical allusions play in the *Furioso,* I examine precisely the intrinsic or internal aspects of its narrative design that may indeed have enabled its readers to see it as a classic. I treat the poems of Boiardo and Tasso similarly, although their critical fortunes were different from Ariosto's. No one in the sixteenth century proclaimed Boiardo's *Orlando Innamorato* a classic, and it was Tasso himself who had to assert the classicism of the *Gerusalemme Liberata* in his critical writings. I consider the three poems' narratives from the same point of view, on the assumption that both Boiardo, in the generation before Ariosto, and Tasso, two generations later, employed similar narrative techniques. I assume, however, that Ariosto's chronological position in the literary history of Ferrara was crucial. Falling between Boiardo and Tasso, he learned how to construct a classically inspired vernacular narrative from the former and passed on the legacy, much of which subsequent generations accepted, to the latter. That is, in studying Ariosto's narrative we are also considering paradigms that were available in differing degrees to Boiardo and Tasso. Although these three poets shared a family of patrons—the Este of Ferrara—and an intellectual heritage associated with a revolutionary school at the Estense court, an even greater bond linked the three: the compositional habit of alluding to classical authors in the spirit of compromise.

There are, however, noticeable differences in the allusive poetics of the three Ferrarese artists, differences that can be attributed to the degree to which popular Ferrarese culture had assimilated the classical tradition. Boiardo, writing during the latter decades of the Quattrocento, was uncomfortable, I believe, with making his classicism too apparent in the *Innamorato,* his one poem most designed for public consumption. In his imitation of Vergil's *Aeneid,* for example, he seems reluctant to display his familiarity with Vergilian narrative lest it impinge on the expectations of an audience steeped in romance. Ariosto, for his part, had to solve a problem that was very different from Boiardo's: he had to make his poem's classicism known to that small audience of his humanist peers whose opinions mattered most to him, without denaturing its vernacular characteristics. During the opening years of the Cinquecento, a humanistically trained poet needed to be "classically correct" in his poetic language and, to a lesser extent, in the subject matter and design of his poem. Ariosto's genius was, we shall see, in working out brilliant compromises between the strictures of a burgeoning classicism and Ferrara's local version of literary romance. Tasso, too, had problems negotiating the proper degree of classicism in the *Liberata,* but for him, writing in the post-Tridentine decades of the Cinquecento, the problem was very nearly opposite Boiardo's. The classical requirements of poetry had become the subject of theoretical debate with doctrinal ramifications. Thus, Tasso had to broadcast a doctrinally sound classicism in his poem, while at the same time taking care not to write the romance out of it. He coped with the pressure, much of which was institutionalized but some of which was brought on by his own punctiliousness, by elaborating a theory of compromised classical sources in his poem.

Phrases such as "the compromised source," "the source of compromise," and "compromising the classical source" require some substantive explanation from the appropriate texts. Those texts, however, will be most meaningful if preceded by several examples of sources of compromise, which I now provide.

Midway through Ariosto's *Orlando Furioso,* the poem's titular hero goes mad, in a scene that contains a figurative representation of the compromising of sources.[7] The author portrays Orlando's psychological disintegration by bringing together a series of allusions to classical pastoral, comedy, epic, and satire, on the one hand, and to vernacular lyric and romance, on the other.[8] The scene of Orlando's madness remains essentially unchanged over the course of the poem's three editions, although the third highlights the scene by shifting it to the poem's center.[9] In the editions of 1516 and 1521, which contain forty cantos, the scene occurs at the end of canto 21; in the definitive edition of 1532, increased to forty-six cantos, the restructured narrative has Orlando go mad right at the poem's center, at the end of canto 23. In the third edition the poet brings the first half of the narrative to its conclusion and begins the second half with the focus steadily on Orlando's descent into madness—the "furore" proclaimed in the poem's title and in its opening programmatic stanzas.

From the end of canto 23 and continuing through 39, Orlando wreaks havoc upon the countryside and its benign inhabitants, plucking a shepherd's head off, tearing a woodcutter in half, kicking a donkey from one hilltop to another: the list of superhuman feats of destruction is long. The violence begins at the site of its inspiration, at the grove that reveals that the woman to whom Orlando has dedicated his life, Angelica, has fallen in love with another man. Not that she was ever really in love with Orlando, at least not in Ariosto's version of their story. She used him to her advantage at various times, as when, for example, he escorted her from Cathay to Europe, but she never professed to love him, nor any other of her many suitors for that matter. Now, however, at the point in the narrative that catapults Orlando into madness, things are different. Angelica has consummated her love for a young Saracen, Medoro, whom she discovered wounded and nursed back to health with her oriental charms. The site of consummation resembles a Renaissance garden, a pleasance, with a grotto watered by a crystal fountain that shelters the lovers from the midday heat. They, in their comfort, have left a visible record of their pleasure: on no less than one thousand trees Angelica has carved their names in calligraphic configurations dubbed "coitograms" by a recent critic (19.36.4);[10] and Medoro has decorated the walls of the grotto with a pastoral poem in Arabic on his sexual conquest. The poem makes it clear that the lowly Medoro is well aware of the magnitude of his achievement. He knows that he has been where no man has been before, although many of the poem's greatest characters, Christian and Saracen, have tried to go there.

Orlando's first reaction to this place is disbelief. He tries to convince himself that Angelica has not been unfaithful to him, that what he knows to have happened there did not really take place. But seeing through his delusions, Orlando finally breaks down, losing his appetite, suffering insomnia, crying, screaming, fleeing. He inadvertently stops to seek lodging at the very house where Angelica and Medoro had stayed. After several hours of fitful sleep, Orlando flees again and spends the night wandering through the woods, only to circle back ruinously the next morning to the grotto, the very place that brought on the onslaught of grief. This time, as soon as he sets foot in it, he begins to attack the secret garden with all the force of Christendom's greatest warrior (23.130–31.1–4):[11]

> Tagliò lo scritto e 'l sasso, e sin al cielo
> a volo alzar fe' le minute schegge.
> Infelice quell'antro, et ogni stelo
> in cui Medoro e Angelica si legge!
> Così restar quel dì, ch'ombra né gielo
> a pastor mai non daran più, né a gregge:
> e quella fonte, già sì chiara e pura,
> da cotanta ira fu poco sicura;
>
> che rami e ceppi e tronchi e sassi e zolle
> non cessò di gittar ne le bell'onde,
> fin che da sommo ad imo sì turbolle,
> che non furo mai più chiare né monde.

[He] slashed at the words and the rock-face, sending tiny splinters shooting skywards. Alas for the cave, and for every trunk on which the names of Medoro and Angelica were written! They were left, that day, in such a state that never more would they afford cool shade to shepherd or flock. The spring, too, which had been so clear and pure, was scarcely safer from wrath such as his; / branches, stumps and boughs, stones and clods he kept hurling into the lovely waters until he so clouded them from top to bottom that they were clear and pure never again.[12]

First Orlando destroys Medoro's eclogue inscribed on the stone walls of the cave, then he goes after the trees on which Angelica has carved their names.[13] Having razed the grotto, he proceeds to dump all the rubble into the spring at the center of the landscape where fate has led him. The heap of rubble includes the slashed rock-face (the "sasso" of lines 111.8 and 130.1) on which Medoro had inscribed his bucolic poem back in canto 19, which we read for the first time in canto 23. Somewhere among all the fragments of stone, there must be one piece bearing Medoro's verse or some portion of it, "Liete piante, verdi erbe, limpide acque" (108.1). (Happy plants, verdant grass, limpid waters.) With supreme, if subtle, irony, Medoro's poem on the clear waters contributes to the muck. The spring is denatured forever once its clear, pure, beautiful, and cleansed waters—four adjectives occurring over six lines—become a muddled confusion.[14]

I take the muddied source and Orlando's contamination of it to stand generally for Ariosto's intertextual poetics.[15] While I am wary of reading into the poem my own concerns, Ariosto, I believe, does provide substantial textual grounds for interpreting the scene as emblematic of this aspect of his poetics. I have referred to Orlando's act as "contamination" not only because it is one of the technical terms used in the Renaissance to characterize a mode of literary imitation that blends models;[16] "contaminare" is also the verb that the poet himself used in the first and second editions of the *Furioso* to describe Orlando's treatment of the spring. In the first edition (1516), the text of the verse in question reads "che sì cōtaminò, che sì turbolle" (21.131.3). In the second edition (1521), the line, altered only slightly, bears no diacritical marks, but the key verb remains: "che si contamino: cosi turbolle" (21.131.3). In both texts the verb in the third person singular agrees with "Orlando" mentioned in the previous line (131.2). The definitive verse from the 1532 edition, given in context above, is "fin che da sommo ad imo sì turbolle" (23.131.3). "Contaminare" is exchanged for a conjunction, "fin che," and an adverbial phrase, "da sommo ad imo." The rather bland commentary, "from top to bottom" (lit., "from the highest point to the lowest") may seem like a poor substitute for the verb with its theoretical connotations. And yet the adverbial phrase for all practical purposes is synonymous with "contaminare." Borrowed from Horace, translated into the vernacular, and charged with meaning, "da sommo ad imo" is, in the economy of this poem—like Ariosto's first choice, "contaminare"—a gloss on intertextuality. Just how such a small phrase can bear so much weight will become clear later in the chapter: for now we need to plumb the spring's murky waters.

Catching a glimpse of the rock Orlando shattered as it sinks into the muck suggests two ways of interpreting the *Furioso* and its literary sources: the poem generates meaning both horizontally and vertically, as it were. On the one hand, words, phrases, themes, characters, even entire episodes, accrue meaning as the narrative unfolds from its beginning toward its end in a horizontal—one might say, intratextual—movement. The repetition of "sasso," for example, at key points in the first half of the narrative culminates with Orlando's destruction of Medoro's poem.[17] Olimpia, watching Bireno's sails slip over the horizon, is "petrified" with grief (10.34.7–8), much as Orlando is "stone-faced" when he finally realizes Angelica has given herself to another man (23.111.7–8).[18] On the other hand, the rock fragments also suggest an interpretive possibility that we may associate with a vertical movement: the reader fathoms the text for its literary precedents, its sources. Orlando's enraged destruction of the pleasance becomes more meaningful if the reader realizes that Medoro's pastoral poem is literally part of the mix that our hero stirs up. The narrator helps the reader in this regard by reminding him of the connection between cantos 23 and 19 with a verbal pointer to the earlier passage: "Questo era un di quei lochi già descritti" (23.102.5). (This was one of the spots described earlier.) In a gesture of auto-citation that is a feature of Ariosto's narrative, canto 19 becomes an internal source for the scene in 23.

One can extend this image of reading the poem vertically to include its many external sources as well. In canto 23, as happens throughout the poem, Ariosto alludes to a literary chronology and suggests the position of his poem in it, only to collapse that literary-historical time frame by straddling several different traditions in his poetics of allusion. In the fiction of the poem, Medoro's eclogue reflects several literary (and linguistic) traditions: composed in Arabic, the *Furioso* tells us, it purportedly is translated into Ariosto's Italian via Bishop Turpin's French.[19] Here is the text of Medoro's poem within the poem (108–09):

> Liete piante, verdi erbe, limpide acque,
> spelunca opaca e di fredde ombre grata,
> dove la bella Angelica che nacque
> di Galafron, da molti invano amata,
> spesso ne le mie braccia nuda giacque;
> de la commodità che qui m'è data,
> io povero Medor ricompensarvi
> d'altro non posso che d'ognior lodarvi:
>
> e di pregare ogni signore amante,
> e cavallieri e damigelle, e ognuna
> persona, o paesana o viandante,
> che qui sua volontà meni o Fortuna;

ch'all'erbe, all'ombre, all'antro, al rio, alle piante
dica: benigno abbiate e sole e luna,
e de le ninfe il coro, che proveggia
che non conduca a voi pastor mai greggia.

Happy plants, verdant grass, limpid waters, dark shadowy cave,
pleasant and cool, where fair Angelica, born of Galafron, and loved
in vain by many, often lay naked in my arms. I, poor Medor, cannot
repay you for your indulgence[20] otherwise than by ever praising
you, / and by entreating every lover, knight, or maiden, every
person, native or alien, who happens upon this spot by accident
or by design, to say to the grass, the shadow, the cave, stream, and
plants: "May sun and moon be kind to you, and the chorus of the
nymphs, and may they see that shepherds never lead their flocks
to you."

Medoro's address to the natural setting in catalog form and his verbal
elegance are characteristic of the genre of pastoral, filtered through the
vernacular lyrics of Petrarch,[21] while his concern that the oasis not be
violated sounds a theme from Vergilian bucolic poetry.[22] It is not the first
time in the *Furioso* that one of Angelica's admirers has waxed Petrarchan.
Sacripante strikes similar chords in his reflections on the virgin as rose
(1.41–44). In canto 23, once Medoro has culled that particular rose
(Ariosto's way of putting it at 19.33.1–2), he adopts the tone of Petrarchan
lyric to praise the garden (108.8) before he shifts to the Vergilian request
(still cast, however, in Petrarchan language) that it be protected (109.1–
8). He means the literal garden where he and Angelica made love,[23] but
earlier in the text the narrator has described Medoro's physical act of
love, in its turn, as "setting foot in that garden" (19.33.4). Medoro has
already invaded one garden, "that garden," and now in a Vergilian mode
he worries about the sanctity of the place where he repeated that act time
and again.

The Petrarchan/Vergilian reverie is interrupted momentarily by the
verses "de la commodità che qui m'è data, / io povero Medor ricompen-
sarvi" (108.6–7). "Commodità" (or the Latin form *commoditas*) is not
found in the typical pastoral lexicon, either in its Vergilian beginnings
or in its Petrarchan reception. The word derives ultimately from the
combined forms *con* and *modus* in Latin, which together mean "propor-
tionate measure," its semantic family including the adjective *commodus,*
"comfortable," a word one would expect to encounter in pastoral. Indeed, elsewhere in the *Furioso,* Ariosto describes a sylvan setting as a
"solitario e commodo boschetto" (11.2.4).[24] But the substantized form
of the adjective, *commoditas,* hardly has a bucolic heritage; rather, it

is straight out of Roman comedy. Plautus and Terence depend heavily on the noun to signify: (1) timeliness; (2) convenience or advantage; and (3) obligingness.[25] Many passages in Ariosto's plays suggest an awareness of these connotations of "commodità."[26] This comes as no surprise, since Ariosto, who declares his familiarity with Plautus and Terence on more than one occasion, played a large part in the revival of Roman comedy in Ferrara.[27] Why then did he use the word at this seemingly uncomic moment in the *Furioso*?

As many commentators note, Medoro is referring to the comfortable pleasures of the body the place has afforded him.[28] At the same time, however, Ariosto surely heard in "commodità" the comic notion of "timeliness" or "opportunism,"[29] which is, in fact, the word's basic meaning in classical Latin and the sense most common in Plautus and Terence.[30] This meaning of "commodità" casts Medoro's poem in a light that commentators have not seen heretofore, with the word underscoring the timeliness of his encounter with Angelica. To be sure, their chance meeting was timely in that it saved his life, but, in an even more opportune manner, it allows Ariosto to remove Angelica from the narrative. The union of Angelica and Medoro resolves the entanglement of plot threads around Angelica and consequently sets up the next major segment of the poem, cantos 24–39, on Orlando's madness. In other words, the "commodità" given to Medoro in that special place is a ticket to the Far East (Angelica's home) and a way out of the poem. Resolving the plot in this manner is comic not only in its unexpected timeliness but also in its promotion of the lowly Medoro as beneficiary of such an opportunity. And while he goes from the bottom to the top of the scale of being, from "povero" to son-in-law of the king of Cathay, Galafron, his good luck sends Orlando in the opposite direction, from Charlemagne's right-hand man to bestial lunatic. To couch this double trajectory in terms of genre, one could say that the intervention of rules associated with comedy instigates Orlando's tragic decline. And let us not forget that this has occurred in the context of a pastoral. To sum up, Ariosto alludes to the dynamics of the classical comic plot in a pastoral scene inspired by Petrarchan poetry weighted with the foreboding of Vergilian concerns. This extensive mixing of sources is typical, we shall see, of Ariosto's (and Boiardo's and Tasso's) art. The sources are brought together, or compromised in the etymological sense of the word, and subsequently one source—in this case the allusion to *commoditas*—is momentarily singled out. In canto 23, the pastoral-romance is compromised by the threat associated with Vergilian bucolic poetry, a threat, however, that is realized through the operations of a comic mechanism. And in compromising the pastoral-romance, comedy opens up the narrative to the inevitability of tragedy—a prospect anticipated from the moment we read the poem's title, with its calque on Seneca's *Hercules Furens,* and hear of Orlando's madness in its opening stanzas.[31]

In encapsulating several key texts of the pastoral tradition from Petrarch to Vergil and in mixing them with Plautus and Terence, Medoro's poem compromises all those sources and encourages the reader to reconsider the vernacular and classical works in terms of each other and to reconsider them in relation to the *Furioso.*[32] The appropriation of such a wide variety of seemingly incompatible sources creates the ambiguous generic status of the *Furioso*—Is it romance? Is it epic? What is it? Thus it happens that the romance-epic misfit, Orlando, invades the pastoral oasis, which timely comic resolution turns into the site that marks the beginning of the knight's private tragedy. The jostling of genres within the elastic framework of the *Furioso*'s narrative turns Orlando into a kind of Frankenstein monster—a character of neither romance nor epic nor pastoral nor comedy. In an idyllic setting where shepherds rest their flocks, Orlando (no shepherd he) is metamorphosed into a beast, thus annulling Medoro's prayer that the place be preserved from any intruding animals. It is, in fact, the destruction of Medoro's pastoral poem that marks the irreversible turning point in Orlando's transformation. But the character's change does not signal a simultaneous transformation of the narrative from pastoral or romance or comedy to epic or tragedy. Nothing is that clear-cut in the design of the *Furioso.* Even as the poem approaches the epic conclusion of its final cantos, to choose one of many possible examples, Rinaldo can still wander off on an extended adventure more suitable to the genre of romance (42–43). Here, in what could have been a pastoral interlude in canto 23, amidst a fullness of sources from different genres, we witness another, perhaps even more important, example of a compromised generic model: the epic.

Ariosto registers the *Furioso*'s epic pretensions by paraphrasing the beginning and end verses of the *Aeneid* at his poem's beginning and ending—but the reader who expects to find the poem full of the stuff of epic will be disappointed. As we have seen, the titular hero, who carries much of the poem's epic burden, goes mad at the narrative's middle and, therefore, cannot move inexorably toward the completion of his appointed task in the manner of an epic hero. Is it a sign of romance, then, for the protagonist to wander off his literal and mental course into madness? To be sure, the characteristics of romance defy the straightforward teleology of epic: deviation, diversion, and digression are typical of the romance narrative.[33] And there is at least one notable romance precedent for Orlando's madness: Yvain (more on whom below) also deviates from the typical behavior of a proper knight. Orlando, however, exists in a netherworld somewhere between the two generic possibilities offered by epic and romance. He sets out on a quest for Angelica like a good knight of medieval romance (9.7.6), zigzagging inevitably along the way. But despite occasional detours like the episode of Olimpia (9–11) or Atlante's castle (12), his application to the quest has an epic seriousness about it. The narrator draws our attention to the heroic expansiveness of Orlando's task in an unusual classical allusion that likens his search for Angelica to Demeter's for Persephone (12.1–4).[34] And just before he comes upon the site of Angelica's betrayal (as he sees it), a simile of Homeric inspiration describes Orlando in heroic terms.[35] When Orlando finds himself in the pastoral-romance setting at the end of canto 23, whereas the romance knight in him should defer the quest and indulge momentarily in this place of pleasure, the epic misfit goes berserk.

Ariosto's treatment of Orlando as a creature who moves between two genres, two traditions, two kinds of narrative, depends on his immediate predecessor, Boiardo. Orlando, a traditional figure in medieval Franco-Italian literature, is associated with the *chanson de geste,* the heroic war poetry of the Middle Ages. In that literary tradition he fights and dies nobly as befits Charlemagne's most heroic knight. For later Italian writers, however, Boiardo's treatment of Orlando is the prism through which prior literary representations of his heroism are refracted. A recent critic puts it well: "In blending the 'Matter of Britain' with the 'Matter of France,' Boiardo heaped upon Orlando, the *preux* of the *chanson de geste,* the unfamiliar responsibilities of the *courtois* of courtly romance."[36] Boiardo has his version of the traditional character do something heretofore inconceivable, as his title broadcasts: *Innamoramento d'Orlando,* "Orlando's Falling in Love."[37] In such condition he is hardly the stuff of literary heroism. Add to this mix the resurgent classical humanism that was coming into its own at the beginning of the Cinquecento in Ferrara, and one can see that Ariosto had his hands full (not to say tied) when he began to sketch his own picture of Orlando. His version recalls the figure of medieval legend and bears a slight resemblance to Boiardo's courtly lover, but at the same time there is much to suggest that his Orlando is a creature of the new classicism. Perhaps, as has been suggested, Ariosto's Orlando plays the part of a "burly male Dido," if not exactly that of a new Aeneas.[38] In other words, the reception of the classical tradition is compromised by the other traditions that Ariosto's chronology requires him to hold in the balance. Here the intervention of medieval romance contributes to turn Ariosto's would-be Aeneas into an imitation of Dido in a compromise of the Vergilian epic model.[39] In chapter 3, I explore this dynamic further in examining how counterclassical epic narrative from antiquity, especially

Ovid's *Metamorphoses,* which bears some resemblance to medieval romance, contributes to Ariosto's compromise of the Vergilian narrative
ideal. In chapters 3 and 4, I also discuss briefly Ariosto's dependence
on Ovid's *Fasti,* another classical work that encourages the Renaissance
poet to compromise the standard classical canon.

Roman satire, too, is incorporated into the mix, precisely at a point
in the narrative that requires it to be understood alongside medieval
sources. A verbal allusion to a passage from Horace's *Satires* 2.3 on
human folly suggests that Ariosto intended this poem to provide a gloss
on Orlando's behavior at the center of the *Furioso.* To my knowledge no
commentator has addressed the complexity of this allusion to Horace,[40]
while many commentators, following Rajna, have linked Orlando's madness to various madmen from chivalric literature: Tristan, Lancelot, and
Yvain are the most frequently cited medieval antecedents. The parallel
Rajna sees between Orlando and these characters, in fact, is crucial to
his interpretation of the poem and to his understanding of Ariosto's
poetic interaction with the medieval literary world.[41] The critic writes
of penetrating the origins of Orlando's actions, as if singling out the
appropriate source will reveal the mysteries of the poem to him.[42] But
the multitude of possible medieval madmen—in addition to the three
already cited, Rajna finds Merlin in *Vita Merlini,* the Bon Chevalier Sans
Paour and Daguenet in *Palamedès*—causes a problem for the critic. In
regard to the climactic passage at 23.133, he laments in jest: "Peccato
che i pretendenti alla paternità di quella povera ottava siano parecchi"
(406)! (It's a shame that there are several [sources/authors] who claim the
paternity of that woeful stanza!) Underlying the playful irony of Rajna's
tone is an anxiety in the critic's discovery that there is an unwieldy number
of influences at work. Rajna, however, is an accomplished reader who
can cope with such intertextual fullness. The tally of sources leads him to
articulate a more sensible position: "Anzi, qui, come in vari casi consimili,
bisogna proprio ammettere la pluralità dei padri" (406). (On the contrary,
here, as in other similar cases, one must admit outright the plurality of
fathers.) I could investigate Rajna's rhetoric for its dependence on paternal
language or on the biological impossibility of multiple fathers,[43] but that
would lead me astray from my assignment, which has more to do with
the issue of plurality. Indeed, what I am proposing is more like Rajna's
project of source criticism than it is different from it. But let us move on.
There is a "father" Rajna has ignored: Horace.

Orlando, in dumping the rubble of the grove into the spring, stirs
up its limpid water "from top to bottom." Earlier in the chapter we saw
how the phrase "da sommo ad imo" (131.3) replaces "contaminò" in the

definitive, third edition of the poem. Caretti was the first critic to hear in the Latinate ring of the added locution Horace's *ab imo / ad summum* (*Satires* 2.3.308–09). But neither Caretti nor Bigi, who also mentions the allusion, points out that Ariosto borrows the tag only to invert it: not "from bottom to top" as Horace has it, but "from top to bottom." Granted, the inversion may seem too obvious to require comment, but the context of Horace's phrase suggests that Ariosto's allusion to it is especially charged.

Horace's *Satires* 2.3 is an experimental literary piece in which the poet utilizes the dialogue form within the poem's narrative to descant on the follies of mankind. The subject matter of the poem leads us into what we may justifiably call Ariostan territory. Damasippus reports to Horace a conversation he had with Stertinius on the follies of avarice, ambition, self-indulgence, love, and superstition. The piece ends as Damasippus suggests that even writing is an activity of the mentally unbalanced. In keeping with the generic restrictions of satire, there is a light tone to much of the discussion, which manages to touch repeatedly and with entertaining variety on the topic of madness. No fewer than thirteen different expressions are used for madness, including an adjective that may have caught Ariosto's attention, *furiosus* (207).[44] An entire section of the satire discusses the madness induced by love (247–80), a madness that can lead to the death of both the lover and the beloved (276–78). The guiding metaphor for madness throughout the satire, which is established early in the narrative, has a decidedly Ariostan ring about it:

> velut silvis, ubi passim
> palantis error certo de tramite pellit,
> ille sinistrorsum, hic dextrorsum abit, unus utrique
> error, sed variis illudit partibus . . . *Sat.* 2.3.48–51

> Just as in a forest, where some error drives men to wander to and fro from the proper path, and this one goes off to the left and that one to the right: both are under the same error, but are led astray in different ways . . .[45]

The Horatian phrase to which Ariosto alludes at 23.131 occurs near the end of the satire, when Damasippus responds to Horace's question, "From what mental failing do you think I suffer?" (307). According to his interlocutor, Horace has several problems: he is obsessed with a building project described as an attempt to imitate the big boys "from bottom to top." Equally problematic are his writing of poetry, his temper, his passion for youth, and his tendency to live beyond his means. The list might continue, but Horace, in a feigned fit of temper, interrupts his friend's catalog, and the poem ends on a humorous note. It is significant that the phrase Ariosto rewrites refers to imitation: "longos imitaris, ab imo / ad summum totus moduli bipedalis" (308–09). (You try to imitate the big boys when you only measure two feet total from bottom to top.)[46] The remark, with its emphasis on construction and imitation, has literary overtones, comparable to other passages in his work where Horace refers to writing as a kind of building activity.[47] It is as if Horace were being told, "You are not big enough to challenge the models before you, whether architectural or literary." One could take this to be a criticism of Horace's attempts at changing the genre of the satire. In other words, through Damasippus's comments Horace may be alluding to an unfavorable reaction to the experimental satires of his second book in contrast to the reception of the first book, which respectfully and duly imitates the standard model for satiric poetry, Lucilius.

Ariosto, for his part, accepts the challenge of imitation. He utilizes the phrase in its new, inverted order, giving it his own accent. Moreover, he alludes to the Horatian satire in its entirety, rather than simply adducing a portion of it out of context. Ariosto's allusion to Horace's Stoic meditation on madness gives a classical underpinning to the theme of madness in the *Furioso,* which is acted out time and again in what most critics read as a medievalizing allegorical wood of error.[48] But Orlando is not merely Tristan, Yvain, Lancelot, and company, nor is the forest at the center of the poem's actions simply medieval; the paladin is also a character moving through a Stoic world full of entrapments, who eventually is caught and goes mad.[49] One wonders if the Renaissance poet heard in *ab imo ad summum* a classical version of his thematic signature, the prepositional phrase "di su di giù," which often glosses the mad erring of characters in the poem.[50] Moreover, did Ariosto align the traditional medieval wood of error with Horace's *silva* to highlight his own program of imitation? Let us not forget that Ariosto's allusion occurs as his narrative describes the confused and muddied waters of the pastoral pool, which stand for the mixing of different literary sources. To replace Horace's "from bottom to top" with Ariosto's "from top to bottom" in this context stirs up the waters, as it were.[51] Or we could say that Ariosto's adaptation of the Horatian passage compromises the classical work by increasing its meaningfulness through its association with various medieval texts that also focus on mad erring.

I have lifted a tiny phrase from a gigantic narrative and made much of it because I believe that this inverted allusion to Horace gives us a glimpse of Ariosto's poetics of allusion. It is a "spy," in the terms of Spitzerian rhetorical criticism, that bespeaks a much larger issue:

Ariosto's creation of meaning by incorporating other poems into his own.[52] This phenomenon is part of a poetic process that is common in humanist poetry. Poetry that is based on *imitatio,* the poetics of imitation, develops by building a new poem around an old poem or poems that become the center of the new one. The humanist poet Poliziano, in the generation just before Ariosto, engaged in a similar kind of *contaminatio,* which one critic has called the "dismemberment" of the past.[53] Sources need to be taken apart, undone, "deconstructed," or, in the imagery of Ariosto's allusion to Horace, turned upside down, before they can be reassembled and incorporated into the imitating poet's poem.

Nearly a century ago, Giulio Bertoni, a Romance philologist who studied the literary and cultural history of Ferrara, observed that Ariosto's poem exhibited a "perfect fusion of romance and classical elements." Therein, he claimed, lay the *Furioso*'s originality.[54] In the chapters that follow I examine at length the contraposition of the medieval and classical, in the *Furioso* as well as in the *Innamorato* and *Liberata.* I come, however, to a conclusion that differs from Bertoni's: the fusion of sources that one encounters in all three poems—not only in Ariosto's—is deliberately confusing and, consequently, more imperfect than not. Yet this imperfection is fruitful. The fusion of sources in the poems of Boiardo, Ariosto, and Tasso is such that at times it is impossible to distinguish the romance and epic origins of the poems of the three Ferrarese poets. This kind of confusion, symbolized by the hyphenated generic tag, romance-epic, invites the critic to consider not only the texts themselves but also the generic boundaries between them and the generic possibilities they encompass. In what follows I develop the notion of compromise as a heuristic device to explore these problems in the three major poems of the Italian Renaissance.

CHAPTER 1

Compromising Criticism

Fontes non sunt multiplicandae praeter necessitatem.

BOETHIUS OF DACIA[1]

"Renovate This Poet's Tomb!"

*I*n 1881, Aldo Gennari, a concerned citizen of Fer-
rara, requested that the city council grant funding to refurbish Ariosto's
sepulchral monument in the public library. The monument, housed in the
library since 1801, had fallen into disrepair and was virtually ignored
by the townspeople.[2] Gennari argued that Ariosto, not to mention the
reverential visitors who came from around the world to pay homage to
the poet, deserved better. A refurbished monument was the least the town
should do. In addition, he proposed that all the objects still in existence
that could be traced with certainty to Ariosto's possession some 350
years earlier be gathered around the monument. The tomb would become
a literary shrine; indeed, its location in the library had already made it
into much more than merely a repository of the poet's bones. The shrine
would include the poet's chair, his inkwell, and some editions of his works
(Gennari mentions the 1516 *Furioso* and two copies of the 1532 edition,
as well as a copy of the *Satire* and a collection of his letters). Finally, to
lend the ensemble a saintly credibility, there would be a digit from one
of the poet's fingers that somehow had been separated from the skeleton
when the body was exhumed and reinterred in 1801.

There are more details to Gennari's plan—the type of tiles for the floor surrounding the monument, the color of paint for its bookshelves, what kind of tapestry to drape over the tomb—but I can make the point I want to make about his project without describing it in its entirety. Gennari's project reflects two trends in the intellectual life of Italy in the latter decades of the nineteenth century: positivism and nationalism. Both trends leave their mark on literary studies in that period, and both, consequently, affect the criticism of the poems of Boiardo, Ariosto, and Tasso.

The campaign to unite the separate city-states and territories of the Italian peninsula and its neighboring islands into a confederated nation— that moment in Italian history that historians call the Risorgimento—had been successfully completed for around a decade when Gennari sought to refurbish the tomb of his city's most famous native son. These years saw a boom in monument construction around Italy as government at all levels sought to erect visible symbols of the new Italy. The institutionalization of hero worship, however, is more effective on a local level. Therein is the logic of Gennari's proposal to the town council of Ferrara. Putting Ariosto back together, literally reassembling the poet's objects around his tomb, is a gesture that imitates the melding of Italian territories into a single political entity. Gennari would have the Ferrarese do locally something similar to what has been done nationally, with the goal of the project to produce a more unified image of the poet: "per dare unità al concetto che ognuno può formarsi di quel sommo poeta alla presenza delle cose anche meno importanti che lo ricordano."[3] (to give unity to the conception of that grand poet that each person can imagine for himself in the presence of even relatively unimportant things that call him to mind.)

From Positivism to Intertextuality

The goal of unification, even the bringing together of the poet's mundane belongings, has nationalistic and chauvinistic overtones, to be sure. But unification is also one of the principles of positivistic philosophy, which dominated the intellectual climate in Gennari's day and affected Italian literary studies well into the twentieth century. Positivism evolved out of the empirical philosophy of Auguste Comte (1798–1857), who believed that knowledge is based on the methods and discoveries of the physical or positive (i.e., verifiable) sciences.[4] The Comtian program assumed that human thought had progressed through two stages, the theological and metaphysical, and had arrived at a third stage, the positive or scientific. The rationale for research, according to Comte, was to use the vantage point of science to verify the components of reality in order to predict subsequent developments in the real world as a whole. The empiricist position that scientific knowledge enables accurate foresight is not unlike Gennari's desire to assemble the parts of Ariosto in order to envision the Ferrarese poet, digit and all, as a unity. This is not to argue that Gennari is an important and undiscovered Comtian philosopher. He is not even, truth be known, a memorable interpreter of Ariosto. But Gennari's obscurity does not diminish the significance of his proposal. That this good citizen of Ferrara designs a monument respecting a basic tenet of positivism indicates the prevalence of that philosophical outlook in Italy in the 1880s. How had positivism become so widespread in Italy?

Comte's philosophy affected the way several influential French critics of the nineteenth century conceptualized literature. In particular, the Comtian thesis on the intelligibility of similarities became a topical issue that contributed to the foundation of comparative literature as a discipline. If one could recognize positively the essential similarities between two objects, one could then make a meaningful and scientific comparison of those objects. Charles-Augustin Saint-Beuve (1804–69), Hippolyte-Adolphe Taine (1828–93), and Ferdinand Brunetière (1849–1906) used Comte's ideas to lend rigor to their examinations of, especially, the interstices between the French and German literary traditions. These three critics, among others, transmitted the codification of Comtian philosophy to Italian critics writing in the second half of the nineteenth century.

Italian culture, for its part, was prepared to receive Comte's teaching. The intellectual tradition of the peninsula had been nourished by Giambattista Vico (1668–1774), who, like Comte, schematized a progression of the human mind that culminated in a scientific or rational age. And like the philosophy of an important predecessor of Comte, Henri de Saint-Simon (1760–1825), Vico's new science made the human being the focus of a brand of positivism that was concerned with the relationship between the individual and society. Like Saint-Simon and Comte in France, so Vico in Italy became associated with social positivism. The assimilation of Vico not only prepared Italian thinkers to receive the positivist teachings of Comte. There is also evidence of Vico's influence on the formulation of Comte's philosophy.[5] What Vico gave to the French Enlightenment on the eve of the Revolution, French culture gave back to the Italians during and after the Risorgimento as they struggled to found their own democratic republic.

The rise of nationalism throughout the Italian peninsula had a great impact on the dissemination of intellectual trends that had been developing in Europe since the Enlightenment. One of the more noticeable national institutions that contributed to the spread of European trends in the new Italy was the university system. Italian universities, many of which had been founded in the Middle Ages, were deservedly famous throughout the world. But as the country was unified politically in the 1860s, political leaders realized the need for the establishment of a national system of higher education. The new university system, established as positivism came into its own in Europe, made it part of its program to foster institutions of learning that valorized the physical sciences. This emphasis on science affected the faculties of humanities as well. During the 1870s and 1880s, for example, many humanistic journals of a scientific cast were first published, often under the auspices of the national universities. One of these journals, *Giornale Storico della Letteratura Italiana* (1883), was sponsored by the University of Turin, an institution founded in 1400 but revitalized by new programs in the sciences in the nineteenth century.[6] The *Giornale Storico,* which emphasized the historical method, came to symbolize the scientific scholarship that was to engage several generations of literary critics in Italy.

In the initial number of the *Giornale,* the editorial board outlined the kind of scholarly projects it would promote: biographical studies of authors, bibliographical research, editions of texts, collections of documents, and archival work on literary sources. The editorial board summarized its attitude toward scholarship in its claim that the journal would sponsor the "meticulous and painstaking work of the many" rather than the "expansive divinations of the few."[7] In other words, the slow and steady progress of the scientific method, not the inventive creativity of the aesthetically touched, should dictate the research of literary scholars. The language of the journal's editorial policy contained a not-so-veiled swipe at the critical principles of the Neapolitan professor and savant, Francesco De Sanctis (1817–83). De Sanctis and his many followers were practicing and promoting criticism of the Italian classics that was, at its worst, devoid of any understanding of the cultural setting in which those classics were created. The *Giornale Storico* came into being to confront this sort of ahistorical aesthetic response to literature associated with Italian romanticism.[8] This confrontational setting, then, produced the first positivistic studies of Boiardo, Ariosto, and Tasso.

I introduced Aldo Gennari's proposal for Ariosto's monument above because it reflects the positivistic tendencies of literary criticism in the 1880s. Had the monument been created (it was never completed exactly to Gennari's specifications), it would have actualized in tangible form qualities of many critical studies of Ariosto made during the second half of the nineteenth century. Rajna, Romizi, Zacchetti, and other critics under the influence of positivism attempted to reassemble many of the parts that comprise Ariosto's *Orlando Furioso.*[9] They dedicated their research to amassing and interpreting the sources that Ariosto brought together in the composition of his poem. These critics were part of a larger group, which included interpreters of Boiardo's and Tasso's poems,[10] and they practiced a criticism dedicated to the pursuit of sources, *Quellenforschung,* as it came to be known because of the many German scholars who practiced it. To uncover the sources behind these narrative poems became the main purpose, indeed the obsession, of many critical studies on Italian romance-epics in the 1880s and 1890s. Critics probed the medieval precedents of Italian vernacular literature, especially the entangled traditions of French and Franco-Italian romance, looking for thematic sources to which Renaissance authors alluded. At the same time, they scoured the poems of the classical tradition, especially but not exclusively Latin literature, to trace whatever origins of Italian romance-epics they might find there. The goal of such research into sources was to determine the details of influence, to answer questions such as, How could an earlier work have affected the shaping of a later one? What degree of influence might an earlier author have on a modern one? Such questions were posed under the aegis of scientific literary scholarship, much of which first saw the light in the *Giornale Storico.*

In the "Introduction," I alluded to Pio Rajna's disdain for what he considered to be the triviality of the scholarship of classical sources, which engaged the majority of his peers who published in journals like the *Giornale Storico.* It took Rajna, with his incomparable knowledge of medieval Franco-Italian literature and his disputatious style, to convince readers of the importance of the medieval narrative tradition underlying the *Furioso.* He argued for the utility of studies of Ariostan sources that one might designate "inventive" or thematic, as opposed to those that merely list (as most positivist studies did) numerous allusions to classical verbal art, that is, to examples of classical *elocutio.*[11] Subsequently, his position on sources was undermined by changing trends in the intellectual milieu that fostered literary criticism.

Universities in Turin, Bologna, and Pisa had become centers of positivistic research to the detriment of the university in Naples where De Sanctian criticism had originated. But this geographical shift in the cultural map was countered in the early decades of the twentieth century by Benedetto Croce (1866–1952), a Neapolitan intellectual who used his philosophy of aesthetics to take on the entire literary establishment of the north. He challenged the positivist platform (on which an increasing number of critics depended) for its failure to account for the essence of the literary work: the ideas that gave its aesthetic form coherence. He saw in positivism's obsession with the small detail of the literary source a remarkable inattention to the work of art as a larger whole.

In a section at the end of *Problemi di estetica* appropriately entitled "Skirmishes" ("Schermaglie"), Croce discusses the role of sources in literary criticism. He dismisses the intensive search for them as an "erudite hobby" (492) that is only useful when it serves to explicate the work: " . . . quando, cioè, [il richiamo e l'indicazione delle fonti] servono al comento dell'opera, spiegando il significato preciso di un'espressione o illuminando per virtù di contrasto la trasformazione che un pensiero, un'immagine, un'espressione hanno avuta nell'opera che si considera. Donde si vede che le ricerche delle fonti, delle imitazioni e reminiscenze non si giustificano se non come raccolta di materiali da servire, eventualmente, all'interpetre delle opere d'arte" (492–93). (. . . when, that is, [the recall and indication of sources] serve as a commentary on the work by explaining the precise meaning of an expression or by illuminating the transformation of a thought, an image, an expression in the work under consideration. Whence one sees that research concerning sources, imitations, and reminiscences is only justifiable if it collects material to serve future interpreters of the works of art.)[12] In Croce's view, the study of sources is merely the collection of data, assembled for the benefit of subsequent interpreters; it is never an end in itself. Moreover, the sources in question must be connected primarily with the ideas that give the work its meaningfulness.

Croce addresses the issue of the source more fully in his famous essay *Ariosto, Shakespeare e Corneille,* and he arrives at similar conclusions. The choice of Ariosto's poem as a point of departure for attacking the practice of source criticism was no accident. Rajna's magisterial study of the sources underlying the *Furioso* had established Ariosto's poem as the preferred text for this kind of positivistic criticism. Primarily for this reason, the *Furioso* became the most important site—the canonical locus—of the debate. In Croce's essay on the poem, he argues that sources are marginal or external to the poet's creative project; they are, he writes, "le cose esterne" (30). Sources are distinguished from the internal thoughts and emotions of the poet ("i sentimenti"), which constitute the poetic material from which he must draw. In Ariosto's case, that material is the stuff of his life, namely, according to Croce, love, politics, religion, and chivalric literary culture (31–39). Anticipating the reader's charge of strategic omissions from this select list of "sentimenti" underlying Ariosto's poetic material, Croce immediately claims: "[i sentimenti] le [le immagini] produssero anche quando sembra che quelle immagini l'Ariosto le prendesse da altri poemi e da altri libri, da Virgilio e da Ovidio, dai romanzi francesi o spagnuoli, perché, nel prenderle e col prenderle, le rese immagini dei suoi propri sentimenti, ossia, in quell'atto, vi soffiò dentro una nuova vita e, poeticamente, le creò" (40). (They [the emotional sentiments] produced them [the images] all the same, where he seems to have taken them from other poems or books, from Vergil or from Ovid, from French or Spanish romances, because in the taking and with the taking of them, he made them images of his own sentiment, that is to say, he breathed into them a new life and poetically created them in so doing.)[13] In Croce's qualification, the poet as Pygmalion turns the images he has borrowed from other works into "images of his own sentiment." Ariosto's reading of Vergil, for example, is affected by events in his own life, which lead him to internalize those aspects of the Vergilian model that he wants or needs to make his own. There is, of course, some accuracy in Croce's understanding of the artistic process. But the lack of specificity in his description of Ariosto's imitation suggests that he is not very interested in investigating that process with rigor.

One witnessses throughout the essay on Ariosto a spirited attack against the practitioners of positivist literary criticism. Rajna and many others are repeatedly called down by name for the shortcomings of their critical approach, but there is little attempt on Croce's part to articulate a reasoned position on the value of sources. The study of sources did not fit into his philosophical, aesthetic approach to the literary work of art. He went so far as to accuse Rajna of promoting his own contradictory philosophy—"filosofia materialistica e deterministica"—in *Le fonti dell'*Orlando Furioso. Croce won the fight against the promulgators of positivism; in fact, his skills in analytical philosophy and debate made his confrontation with them no contest. But the movement from aggressive source hunting to Croce's dismissal of the study of sources is a move from one extreme in literary critical habits to another. It remained for a later generation of critics to reassert the value of the literary source, to replace positivism's "influence" with a new way of talking about sources, with the discourse of "intertextuality." And this they did, with the *Furioso* continuing to be the primary site for the debate.

Many of the critics who began publishing their work after World War II took a position against Croce's interpretation of the *Furioso* as a timeless text of aesthetic harmony. For these readers the poem was best understood in its historical setting, thus they made a case for the renewed utility of source hunting in moderation, which enabled them to read the poem with an appreciation of its place in a literary-historical context. In an introductory essay on the *Furioso* written in 1945, Mario Santoro, for example, was already arguing for a more realistic interpretation of the poem.[14] In that essay and in others,[15] he traces sources of the poem to examine Ariosto's intellectual development, considering how the poet was transformed through his encounter with humanism into one of the great vernacular humanists.

Santoro was not alone in attempting to historicize his interpretation of the *Furioso*. Another critic who took the lead early on in proposing historical readings of the poem was Cesare Segre, whose criticism, however, focuses more on the historical-linguistic side of the *Furioso* than on the poem's cultural context. Consequently, Segre's interest in Ariosto's language has enabled him to move beyond the boundaries of Santoro's cultural criticism into the territory of more textual-based approaches to the poem, addressing the poem's intertextuality. Segre's article on Ariosto's debt to Dante's *Commedia* is a case in point.[16] It provides a schematized repertory of the Renaissance poet's allusions to the medieval poem, with some interpretive observations on Ariosto's reading of Dante. Such criticism is, one might conclude, merely a latter-day version of positivism. But this sort of essay is balanced in Segre's research by other, more provocative, pieces on the theoretical implications of source criticism. Indeed, no critic among current Italianists has devoted as much energy to the problem of sources as Segre.

A detail of Segre's brand of historicism that bespeaks its seriousness is its extension to an understanding of his own position in the development of Ariostan criticism. Like Rajna and Croce before him, Segre has continued to use Ariosto's work, especially the *Furioso,* as the primary text for discussing and redefining source criticism.[17] The most fundamental article of the last several decades in Italian on source criticism is arguably his "Appunti per una fenomenologia delle fonti," in which he develops Rajna's division of the critics of Ariosto's allusions into two camps: those who focus on linguistic or stylistic sources and those who focus on thematic sources.[18] Philologists have dedicated themselves to the former, comparatists to the latter. As Segre analyzes the critical reception of the poem, the majority of early commentators from the sixteenth century to Romizi in the nineteenth approached the poem as philologists. With Rajna, however, Segre marks the change to a more comparative reading of the *Furioso*. Rajna's response to the poem's narrative, in particular, catches Segre's attention, because it bears some similarities to modern responses to the poem and consequently to Segre's own concerns. In fact, in a revealing moment in his discussion of *Le fonti dell'*Orlando Furioso, Segre paraphrases the notion of thematic invention (which, as we have seen in the "Introduction," is central to Rajna's criticism) as "the elaboration of narrative materials."[19] To redefine the rhetorical category of invention in this way—to refer to it as the elaboration or the working out of the narrative—extends the traditional boundaries of the category by suggesting that it overlaps with that part of rhetoric a classical rhetorician would have called narrative arrangement or *dispositio*. Segre, however, does not go so far as to proclaim Rajna a precursor of narratologists.

Segre's redefinition of invention to highlight the disposition of the narrative suggests another way to think about sources: a poet may allude to the narrative arrangement or disposition of a source. A poet may allude to *the way in which* the narrative of his model is organized in addition to the matter of the story or the story's verbal artistry.[20] I specify "in addition to," for a poet does not imitate an isolated part of the rhetorical whole. Segre's term for this phenomenon is "vischiosità," which one could render, somewhat playfully, as "stickiness."[21] Sources introduced into a text inevitably bring with them more than themselves. Take, for example, the imitation of Petrarch in the Cinquecento. Pietro Bembo's program of imitation, codified in his *Prose della volgar lingua* (1525), focused on rhetorical issues in the context of the greater linguistic question of the Italian Renaissance. Bembo's promotion of Petrarch and Boccaccio as appropriate models of language led them to become stylistic models as well. In the process of writing, say, poems like Petrarch, an aspiring poet in the mid-sixteenth century could easily find himself (or herself, as was often the case) engaged in a full-blown imitation of Petrarchan poetry, drawing on Petrarchan themes and imagery, and even organizing the borrowed material to resemble the model. The imitating poet was on his way to becoming a bona fide Petrarchist. Under such circumstances, the imitation—to return to the initial moment of contact between the modern poet and model—is never merely a linguistic one. Themes, images, organizational patterns, and more are viscous inasmuch as they stick to the borrowed allusion, moving with it into the host text. In the subsequent chapters, we shall see examples of such "allusive stickiness" in the narratives of Boiardo, Ariosto, and Tasso.

"Vischiosità" also suggests the restrained flowing of a viscous, unclear liquid. As the poet brings sources together, as he "compromises" the different parts of rhetoric, different genres, and different literary traditions, he concocts a mixture that recalls Ariosto's image of the muddied source in *Furioso* 23. "Vischiosità," then, will prove a useful critical category for conceptualizing intertextual poetics, because its two meanings, stickiness and viscosity, focus, respectively, on the process and the product of intertextual allusiveness. "Vischiosità" is also useful because it implies the presence of the poet, without, however, requiring that presence. Thus it can be used to account for the influence of one author on another in positivist terms, while at the same time it can be used to describe the workings of intertextuality that depend much less, if at all, on the author per se. The poet introduces the viscous source into the narrative, to be sure, but that source can, as noted above, bring with it unintended elements that contribute to the total mixture of sources. To sum up, "vischiosità" is a concept that envisions the source not merely as an external influence on the poet's creative work, but also as an internal element incorporated into the work that contributes to its meaningfulness. The idea of viscosity, and the image of the muddied spring it calls to mind, suggests the fullness of poetic imitation.

Readers in the past did not address this aspect of imitation in Renaissance romance-epic adequately. Critics trained and inspired by the tenets of positivism tended to focus exclusively on dyadic relationships between authors. More recent readers, whose understanding of literary theory bears the imprint of semiotics and structuralism, have considered in greater detail the network of allusions to other texts in a poem like the *Furioso*. Modern readers have cultivated an enhanced understanding of the relationships among texts under the influence, as it were, of the pioneering work of theorists like Bahktin, Kristeva (who coined the term "intertext"), and Barthes.[22] Barthes, for his part, took the structuralist preoccupation with the text to an extreme in his claim that texts have no authors. His theoretical position made the development of intertextual studies more feasible, shifting the focus away from authors' personalities to the dynamics of textual interaction among "anonymous" texts. But we shall not go so far here. Nor shall we embrace an opposing model, that of psychoanalytic criticism, which posits agonistic relationships between new and old poets, best known through the work of Harold Bloom. I would not deny, however, that my own approach owes something to all of the above: positivists (philologists[23] and comparatists in Rajna's scheme), structuralists (especially as they are mediated through Italian critics like Segre), and psychoanalytic critics who follow in the wake of Bloom and company.

I have also learned much from the numerous recent readings of the *Furioso,* in which a recurrent concern is its network of allusions to other texts—its viscosity, if you will. Baldassarri, Wiggins, Marinelli, Beer, Ascoli, Javitch, Shapiro, Santoro, and Zatti, among others, confront the problem of the *Furioso*'s sources in trying to make sense of the poem and in trying to account for the way it works poetically. But in these various studies there is little attempt to treat what I have referred to above as the fullness of imitation from a theoretical perspective.[24] Specifically, there is no satisfactory treatment of the imitation of narrative arrangement, *dispositio,* in the context of the imitation of *inventio* and *elocutio.* Nor is there adequate consideration of the way genres and traditions overlap in Ariosto's intertextuality. This, then, is the tack I propose to follow.

A restatement of the problem of Ariosto's (and Boiardo's and Tasso's) poetic sources is in order. With witty elegance, Giovanni Pozzi suggests such a reformulation in regard to the study of sources in Marino's *Adone*, which, I think, may also suggest guidelines for a reassessment of the sources of Renaissance poets in general:

> Che i racconti mitologici del c. 19 derivino ora da Ovidio, ora da Nonno ora da Quinto Smirneo non ha importanza ora: ha importanza ora solo il modo con cui è strutturato lo scioglimento, per via di maleficio *ex machina*. Che le avventure di Malagorre o di Sidonio derivino da Eliodoro o da Stigliani non importa (ora!); ora importa dimostrare che un caso chiuso da un narratore possa essere riaperto da un altro cambiando solo la posizione di un personaggio, e che un caso aperto da un narratore debba essere chiuso da un altro esattamente nel modo previsto dal primo. In questi casi si viene benissimo a scoprire qual è la logica interna che muove il Marino nello sfruttamento delle fonti.[25]

> That the mythological stories of canto 19 derive now from Ovid, now from Nonnos, now from Quintus Smyrneus isn't really important now. Now only the way in which the resolution of the plot is structured, through a malevolent *ex machina*, is important. That the adventures of Malagorre or Sidonio derive from Heliodorus or Stigliani doesn't matter now! Now what matters is to show that a case closed by one narrator can be reopened by another changing only the position of a character, and that a case opened by one narrator may be closed by another in exactly the way anticipated by the first. In these situations one comes to discover clearly what is the internal logic that motivates Marino in his exploitation of sources.

Pozzi's point, to strip it of its adverbial wit, is that it should no longer matter to Marino's readers who took what from whom; what matters now is how things have been taken. The critic's focus shifts from tracking down subject matter, the *Stoff* of the literary imitation, to analyzing the arrangement of the subject matter.[26] In a less abstruse way of presenting Segre's notion of "vischiosità," Pozzi suggests, without stating it outright, that the poetic memory of an imitator recollects both the theme and/or the phrase it borrows, as well as the way the model text presents the theme and/or phrase. It is along such lines that I propose to analyze the narrative designs of the poems I have before me, in particular, their allusions to earlier poems, especially classical ones. I use the notion of compromise to analyze how certain sources link the classical and medieval traditions and how certain sources also bridge the rhetorical categories of invention, style, disposition.

The failure to treat adequately the imitation of narrative design may reflect a prejudice in the Italian critical tradition against the imitation of narrative structures. Torquato Tasso comments at the beginning of the *Discorsi dell'arte poetica* that the novelty of a poem lies not in its subject matter but in the organization of its narrative, in its crisis and resolution. He writes: "Fu l'argomento di Tieste, di Medea, di Edippo da vari antichi trattato, ma, variamente tessendolo, di commune proprio e di vecchio novo il facevano: sì che novo sarà la testura dei nodi, nove le soluzioni, novi gli episodi che per entro vi saranno traposti, ancora che la materia sia notissima e da altri prima trattata." ([D]ifferent ancients treated the stories of Thyestes and Medea and Oedipus; but, by arranging them differently, they successfully appropriated and renewed them. Therefore, that poem will be new whose complications and resolutions of plot are new and whose intermittent episodes are new, even though the subject is very well known and has been treated by others before.)[27] Tasso is promoting the combination of old and new, specifically, old stories in new designs. Such a premium on the originality of narrative structures would seem to preclude the imitation of a narrative precedent, but in the chapters that follow I shall present examples of how Boiardo, Ariosto, and even Tasso himself consciously imitated the designs of previous narratives. The poets do so as they invoke the same figurative language that Tasso uses here, "variamente tessendolo" (arranging [or weaving] them differently), to describe the act of composing their narratives. Throughout this study, I shall have occasion to return to "tessere," the verb of narrative construction, as I consider examples of imitation in their narratives. I shall also return to discuss the origins and implications of Tasso's term "traposti" (from "traporre"), used of "intermittent" or "interposed" episodes.

Tasso's position on narrative art must be understood in terms of the debates that characterized literary discourse in the Renaissance. The academization and institutionalization of literature in the sixteenth century led to a rigid definition of what constituted narrative art and, predictably, to a rejection by some literati of that definition. The generic boundaries between romance and epic were the site for the formulation and discussion of the problem, and then, as would happen later, in the age of positivism, the *Furioso* was the primary text for discussion. The debate, extensive and often acrimonious, grew out of an even more profoundly contested issue: literary imitation.

An important discussion of imitation that has implications for subsequent sixteenth-century theories of narrative mimesis is the exchange
between Angelo Poliziano and Paolo Cortese in the 1480s, in which the
metaphor of the path or way of imitation plays a predominant role in
defining the activity.[28] Poliziano, a curious blend of cultural conservative
and iconoclast, refused to accept the strictures of Ciceronianism with its
Neoplatonic overtones promoted by Cortese. In his rejection of what he
considered the servile imitation of Cicero's prose, Poliziano labeled his
disputant, Cortese, an ape. But these criticisms, as bitter as they sounded,
were tempered somewhat by his suggestions of other literary models
worthy of imitation. The subjects Poliziano taught at the Florentine *Studio*
from 1480 to the year he died, 1494, reveal his penchant for countering
the tendencies of the moment. While Cortese and practically all other
Latin stylists were promoting Cicero as the ultimate touchstone, Poliziano
was teaching Quintilian; instead of Ovid's *Metamorphoses,* he taught
the *Heroides, Fasti,* and Ovidian elegiac poetry; he devoted a course to
Statius's *Silvae,* acknowledging that it was not the best-known work of
the silver poet; and, surrounded by the Neoplatonic followers of Ficino,
he developed a series of courses on Aristotelian logic.[29]

The introductory lecture for his first course at the *Studio,* which
was on Quintilian and Statius (1480–81), is programmatic in tone. The
"Oratio super Fabio Quintiliano et Statii Sylvis" emphasizes that the two
silver Latin authors constitute new course material; it also outlines the
direction the course will take over the coming academic year. But the
programmatic tone at the beginning of the oration quickly modulates into
a polemical one. In fact, Poliziano admits from the start of the oration
that some critics will disapprove of his choices. He directly confronts
this criticism by arguing for the superiority of the new models he has
chosen, contrasting Quintilian and Cicero, on the one hand, and Statius
and Vergil, on the other. He argues that the models he proposes are in
some ways as good as, if not better than, the favored ones.

Poliziano's arguments for Quintilian in place of Cicero and for
Statius on a par with Vergil are not my concern here. Instead I am
interested in highlighting the metaphoric language he uses to describe
his imitative choices. Repeatedly in the oration he refers to literary
models as paths—new and different paths he will tread. In referring to
Statius as a literary model, he says: "Novas tamen quasique intactas vias
ingrediamur, veteres tritasque relinquamus" (870). (We enter new and,
you might say, untried paths; we leave the old and beaten ones behind.)[30]
In defending Quintilian as a model, he calls on the metaphor again: "Sed
neque inusitatas vias indagamus, cum veterum libros auctorum in manus

sumpserimus" (876). (But we do not go searching down unusual paths when we have taken in hand the books of the ancient authors.) Poliziano is careful to state that he is not rejecting Cicero for Quintilian, although he manages to develop his presentation with much veiled praise of the new model at the expense of the established one. Again, it is beyond the scope of my work here to recount how Poliziano achieves this muted adulation, but one detail deserves special note. For his comment on the paths offered by an author like Quintilian, Poliziano borrows "inusitatas vias indagamus" (we go searching down unusual paths) from Cicero's *Orator* (3.11).[31] What better way to antagonize the Ciceronians than to use a Ciceronian phrase to describe Quintilian as a model who in some ways surpasses Cicero himself! Having used Cicero's own words to make a case against heavy-handed Ciceronianism, Poliziano then invokes Cicero's decision to study not only Attic orators but also those from Rhodes and Asia Minor as an example of the need for multiple models (880).

The figurative *via* occurs elsewhere in Poliziano's oration,[32] but it is in these examples, in which the word describes imitative paths, that Poliziano's rhetoric is useful for my discussion of narrative art. Poliziano is considering the choice of a Latin model that is correct on the level of *elocutio,* linguistic style, for this was the context in which the Ciceronians against whom he was arguing proposed Cicero's prose as a model. But there is the suggestion in his defense of the *Silvae* and Quintilian's prose that *via* refers to more than merely style—that it bears other meanings associated with the structure of poetic narratives.

Another critic, writing in the generation after Poliziano and from a very different perspective, developed the metaphor along precisely these lines, to suggest the narrative arrangement of the literary model. In his *De arte poetica* (1517–27), Marco Girolamo Vida counters the positive appropriation of the *via* as it appears in Poliziano's oration. Vida criticizes the paths or narrative designs of poets who do not respect the standards of *dispositio* established by the *Aeneid.* Surely he is thinking of a romance poem, perhaps even the *Furioso,* which had recently been published, when he observes (2.166–75):

> Saepe vides, primis ut quidam longius orsis
> Disgrediuntur, et obliti quasi coepta priora
> Longe aliis haerent nulla sermonibus arte,
> Et longos peragrant tractus, aliena canentes.
> Ac velut in patriam peregrina siquis ab ora
> Ire cupit post exsilium, durosque labores,
> Ille tamen recto non qua via tramite ducit,

Carpit iter, sed nunc vagus hac, nunc errat et illac
Undique dum studio fontes invisit inani,
Fontesque, fluviosque, et amoenos frigore lucos.

You often see authors who depart far from the topics they started
with: as though they have forgotten what they began earlier, they
dwell at length and unartfully on something else, and wander
through long passages singing of matters quite irrelevant. It is as
though someone wished to return home from a foreign land after
exile and punishing labors, and chose not to travel by the direct
route, but rather wandered aimlessly here and there, and at every
point fruitlessly spent his time in visiting fountains—fountains and
rivers and cool lovely groves.[33]

Vida is describing the digressive art of the romance poet ("dis-
grediuntur," 167), but the image of wandering here and there could be
applied to the characters of a typical romance as well. The repeated
reference to "fontes" (174–75), where those characters often end up,
calls to mind the literary sources that a poet like Ariosto might use in
constructing digressions in a narrative.[34] Vida contrasts such a poet with
the sort who writes "so that the goal of his labors is not at all at variance
with his first steps through to the very end of the poem" (2.54–55, my
translation). Apply a rule like this to the narrative of a romance, even if it
is a classicizing one, and the resulting criticism is bound to be negative.

Vida is rather uncompromising, as it were, in his criticism of the
romance tendencies of some of his contemporary poets. By contrast,
his own neoclassical poems are consistent with the bias exhibited in his
critical theory. Although there are many possible responses to narrative
problems between the positions articulated by Poliziano and Vida, most
of the critics who follow in the Cinquecento continue to occupy one of the
two extremes established by these two critics: either pro-romance (and,
therefore, for narrative experimentation) or pro-epic/anti-romance (and,
therefore, against innovative narrative structures). That is, critics continue
to argue either for romance against epic or for epic against romance. But
this radical dichotomy in the critical reception of a poem like the *Furioso*
(and even, as I shall argue in chapter 2, of the *Innamorato*) contradicts
the dual nature of its narrative, which will eventually generate the critical
term "romance-epic."

Some critics, long before the twentieth century, were aware that the
Furioso is a successful amalgam of both romance and epic and that this is
precisely its genius as a poetic structure. The young Tasso, for example,
declares in the prefatory letter to the *Rinaldo* that his poem imitates

both ancient and modern models (134–36), only, however, after he has suggested that the *Furioso* and *Amadigi* (his father's poem) also blend old and new (83–92).[35] He, too, calls on the metaphor of the trodden path to describe his compositional options, first saying that he will distance himself somewhat from "the way of the moderns" (62), then claiming that he adheres to "the road of which Aristotle teaches" (106), and finally stating that he will follow both sets of models (134–36). The narrative implications of the metaphor and of Tasso's choices for models become clear in *Rinaldo* and *Gerusalemme Liberata,* for the issue is primarily one of how to structure a poem that might satisfy both sets of seemingly contradictory rules and conventions. He confronts this issue more fully at another juncture in his criticism, the final passage of his *Discorsi del Poema Eroico,* where the metaphor of the road leads him back to the beginning of what turns out to have been a kind of circular path. We shall consider that passage at the end of chapter 5, where it will have more resonance following our discussion below of the paths Bernardo Tasso, Torquato's father, took in his criticism of romance and epic. Bernardo may not have been as accomplished a poet, nor even as perceptive a critic, as his son, yet the elder Tasso negotiated—at least on a theoretical level—the critical problem of narrative structure with a finesse not fully developed in Torquato. In his criticism, Bernardo Tasso exhibits a disposition to compromise, we might say, and he thus offers the contemporary critic a way of examining Renaissance narrative art.

A Disposition for Compromise in the Renaissance

Narrative had become the topical issue for critics working in the 1540s and 1550s in Italy. Two reasons for the importance of narrative stand out: the reception of Ariosto's *Orlando Furioso,* published in its third and definitive edition in 1532; and the critical assimilation of Aristotle's *Poetics,* which began slowly with Pazzi's Latin translation (1536) and continued through the efforts of Lombardi, Maggi, and Robortello in the 1540s.[36] The reception of Aristotle contributed to the theoretical interest in narrative and to the sense that the conventions of narrative were in crisis.[37] The crisis derived from the perceived need to reconcile a vernacular model of romance (of which Ariosto's poem was the prime example) with an Aristotelian theory of epic narration.[38] In simplified terms, the crisis in the theory of narrative was attributable to the conflict between contradicting authorities, that is, between narrative models informed by the medieval chivalric tradition versus classical narratives promoted as exemplars of Aristotelian theory.

In the aftermath of humanism, one, perhaps predictable, reaction to this conflict was to depreciate the *Furioso* as a chivalric romance. Ariosto became, thereby, a modern Homer or Vergil as critics began to make a case for the classicism of the *Furioso*.[39] This kind of comparison in turn readily lent itself to the rhetoric of outdoing the classical model. Giovambattista Pigna concludes, after comparing the poetic careers of Ariosto and Vergil, that the modern poet's work is the more worthy because of its greater stylistic and imitative variety.[40] But canonizing Ariosto as the Ferrarese Homer or Vergil or even proclaiming him a better version of the classical poets did not resolve the narrative problems that confronted would-be romancers who used the *Furioso* as a model.

In an attempt to overcome the conflict in narrative models, some sixteenth-century romance poets tried to find compromises that would allow them to maintain their allegiances to both the medieval chivalric tradition (primarily a Franco-Italian phenomenon) and the classical one. This strategy manifested itself in several ways. Poets could draw from classical sources that themselves did not adhere to Aristotelian narrative rules. Ovid's *Metamorphoses* was arguably the privileged source in this regard, and, as we shall see in chapter 3, Ariosto's example gave poets plenty of reason to imitate the Ovidian model. But works of Herodotus, Xenophon, Lucian, Apuleius, and the Greek novelists, among others, were also recognized for their non- or even anti-Aristotelian narrative tendencies. These works were known for the way their narratives combined repetitions, juxtapositions, and transitions in defiance of the Aristotelian "unities" of action, time, and place. By drawing sources from works that nominally belonged to the classical tradition but whose narrative designs did not contradict the norms of chivalric romance, a genre with no semblance of unity in the Aristotelian sense, the romance poet could satisfy the cultural requirement of imitating a classical model without ruling out the possibility of following a medieval one. The romance poet's choice and treatment of a classical source affected his contemporary reader's perception of both classical and medieval traditions.

The search for narrative compromises also animates much of the literary criticism of the mid-Cinquecento. A case in point is the criticism of Bernardo Tasso.[41] Tasso develops a strategy of compromise in his analysis of the *Furioso*'s narrative as he attempts to define the narrative of his own romance poem, the *Amadigi,* which he is preparing for its eventual publication in 1560. In various passages of his correspondence (an extensive body of letters in which he works out his literary ideas), Tasso refers to the narrative pattern used by Ariosto and himself as "rhapsodic," by which he means an episodic narrative that lacks a single unifying character, plot, or theme.[42] He invokes the practice of the rhapsodes of antiquity, singers who recited and reworked the Homeric poems before audiences, as a precedent for Ariosto's narrative technique.

The category of the rhapsode enables Tasso to interpret the narratives of the *Furioso* and the *Amadigi* in classical, but non-Aristotelian, terms, while his inventive fiction on the origins of romance narrative techniques allows him to reconcile the modern work with his notion of chivalric romance.[43]

The term "rapsodo" first appears in a letter of 1556 addressed to Giovambattista Giraldi Cinzio (2: 71),[44] in a passage where Tasso refers to Ariosto's imitation of "the artifice of the rhapsodes":

> Ma se questi tali [those who criticize the *Furioso*] considereranno che questa sorte di Poesia potrebbe esser quella istessa ch'antica-mente presso de' Greci, e de' Latini fu usata da coloro ch'alle tavole de' gran Prencipi cantavano i magnanimi fatti degli Eroi; e che l'Ariosto nella disposizione dell'opera sua piuttosto l'artificio di questi Rapsodi, che quello d'Omero, nè di Virgilio, si propose d'imitare; sperando peravventura, più che per questo sentiero, che per lo loro, camminando, di poter il mondo dilettare; giudicheranno che non a caso, (come molti dicono) ma con molta prudenza, e molto giudicio abbia tessuta l'opera sua: la qual con ragione, e con verità Eroica si potrà nominare; poichè in essa e di fatti eroici, e di cavalieri illustri, e d'Eroi si tratta continuamente, e si ragiona.[45]

> But men such as these [who criticize the *Furioso*] should consider that this sort of poetry could be that same kind used by those who sang of the courageous deeds of heroes at the tables of the great princes among the ancient Greeks and Romans; and that in the disposition of his narrative Ariosto proposed to imitate the artifice of these rhapsodes rather than Homer's or Vergil's artifice. Ariosto did this, hoping by chance to be able to delight the world, keeping to this path more than Homer's and Vergil's. If such men consider the situation, they will judge that he has woven his work with much prudence and judgment and not haphazardly (as many say). One could observe that his work exhibits reason and heroic truth, because it deals continually with heroic deeds and famous knights.

There are problems with Tasso's approach to narrative in the letter, several of which are inherited. He begins with the literary-historical hypothesis that Ariosto's poem "could be that same kind" of poetry rhapsodes sang at the tables of their patrons in ancient Greece and Rome. He bases this assertion on thematic similarities: the rhapsodes sang about the courageous deeds of heroes ("i magnanimi fatti degli Eroi"), just as Ariosto's poem is about heroic deeds ("fatti eroici"), which contribute to the work's "verità Eroica." Tasso's reference to "disposizione" indicates that he also finds structural parallels between the rhapsodic art and Ariosto's narrative technique, parallels that he apparently believes support the generic connection he is making. Ariosto has woven ("abbia tessuta") his narrative in a way that recalls rhapsodic improvisation in performance. But the logical problems of contrasting a written text (the *Furioso*) with an oral performance,[46] whose essence is its unwritten nature, constrain Tasso to leave this aspect of the comparison undeveloped. He never states what the rhapsode's "artificio" (artifice) involves, forcing one to come to a conclusion about artifice based on his reference to the performance of the rhapsodes.

Another crucial point Tasso raises in this passage is the status of the established text upon which the rhapsode (and Ariosto by comparison) bases his improvisations. If the rhapsode weaves together passages from Homer's texts, what text is the source for Ariosto's "improvisations"? Rather than force an unwanted comparison to the extent of likening Boiardo, Ariosto's most apparent source, to Homer, Tasso leaves this point moot. Even with these silences, and perhaps also because of them, the letter to Giraldi reveals Tasso's attempt to situate the essentially un-classical compositional technique of the *Furioso*'s narrative in a classical context, albeit an unusual one.

Having received Tasso's letter, Giraldi responded almost immedi-ately on June 12, 1556.[47] He opens with a page-length statement outlining his recent problems with a former student, Giovambattista Pigna, whom he believed to have plagiarized his ideas about romance. The response proper to Tasso begins with a reference to his use of the term "rhapsode": "Ma lasciando questo da parte, e tornando alla gentil lettera di V. S. mi è molto piaciuto ch'ella si sia comfermata col mio parere intorno al cantare dei Rapsodi; però che da questo costume antico, credo io che sia tratto l'uso dei Canti dei nostri Romanzi."[48] (But setting this aside and returning to the courteous letter of your Lordship, it pleased me greatly to realize that it agreed with my opinion on the singing of the rhapsodes. I believe that the use of cantos in our romances derives from this ancient custom.)

Giraldi correctly attributes Tasso's reference to rhapsodes to his own discussion of the ancient singers in the *Discorso intorno al comporre dei romanzi* of 1554. The pertinent passage in the *Discorso* reads:

> . . . siccome era costume appresso i Greci ed appresso i Latini . . . di cantar colla lira ne' conviti e nelle mense dei gran maestri i gloriosi fatti e le grandi imprese degli uomini virtuosi e forti; cosí i nostri Italiani, seguendo quel costume antico (parlo dei migliori poeti) hanno sempre finto di cantare dinanzi ai principi ed a nobile brigata i lor poemi. E questo costume tanto oltre passò appresso i

Greci, che i cantori loro, i quali si chiamano Rapsodi, non altrimenti divisero le composizioni di Omero, secondo alcuni, per farle atte ad essere cantate, che facessero i poeti scenici le loro favole in atti, o forse i nostri poeti i loro romanzi in canti.[49]

. . . as it was a custom among the Greeks and Romans to sing to the lyre about the glorious deeds and the great undertakings of strong and virtuous men at the banquets and dinners of the great lords, so our Italians, following this ancient custom (I mean our best poets), have always pretended to sing their poems before our princes and their noble retinues. And this custom passed down from the Greeks of dividing Homer's compositions, according to some, to make them suitable for singing by singers called rhapsodes, is similar to what our dramatic poets do when they divide their plots into acts, or perhaps to our poets who divide their romances into cantos.

Tasso owes much to this discussion of the rhapsode, the opening sentence of which he studiously rewrites in his letter to Giraldi considered above (2: 71). Giraldi's phrasing "appresso i Greci ed appresso i Latini . . . di cantar colla lira ne' conviti e nelle mense dei gran maestri i gloriosi fatti e le grandi imprese degli uomini virtuosi e forti" is recast in Tasso's letter to read "presso de' Greci, e de' Latini fu usata da coloro ch'alle tavole de' gran Prencipi cantavano i magnanimi fatti degli Eroi." But Tasso's understanding of the problem is not entirely Giraldi's. Where the latter claims assuredly that the Italian poets "are following this ancient custom" of rhapsodic art, Tasso introduces a hypothesis in the conditional mood, observing that the Renaissance romance "could be (potrebbe essere) that same kind" of poetry that rhapsodes used to sing at the tables of their patrons in classical times.[50]

Yet both critics base their view of the rhapsode on a willfully anachronistic perception of literary history. They are determined to find a classical model for the narrative technique used in Italian romance. And this insistence causes them to distort the relation between the Renaissance poet and both his classical and his medieval sources.

Giraldi, moreover, not only denies the chivalric romance its intermediary spot between the past and present. He also criticizes contemporary minstrels, or "cantastorie," a group who made their living reciting and performing "cantari," vernacular compositions based on passages drawn from chivalric romances.[51] The excerpt from Giraldi's *Discorso* continues: "Da questa usanza dunque greca e latina hanno tratto i nostri Italiani questa loro divisione di canti, non dal cantar di questi plebei, che con le loro ciance tendono le reti alle borse di chi li ascolta."[52] (Therefore, our Italian poets have taken this division of their poems into cantos from this ancient Greek and Latin convention and not from the singing of these lowerclass minstrels who stretch out their purse-strings to whomever will listen to their banter.) Giraldi's disparaging criticism of the minstrels is not, despite his moralizing rhetoric, directed against the economics of their art. His problem with them is simply that they are not classical. This unstated difference leads him to argue incorrectly that the rhapsodic tradition handed down the term "canto" for the divisions of Renaissance romance poems. Futhermore, Giraldi's rhetoric of exclusion necessitates a complete and untenable rejection of minstrels from his discussion of the origins of the *Furioso* and its romance narrative techniques.[53]

In subsequent letters of the summer of 1556 addressed to Giraldi, Tasso begins to elaborate a theory of how his own practice is connected with rhapsodic art. While developing these ideas, he clarifies what that art involves and begins to distinguish his theory of rhapsodic art from Giraldi's. In a letter of July 3, 1556, Tasso explains that the *Amadigi* will be different from epic poetry in its narrative organization, its "disposizione" (2: 74).[54] He describes the poem's narrative in terms that recall his earlier remarks on the design of the *Furioso:* " . . . l'opera mia, l'ho tessuta con tre fila principali, le quali continuamente conducono sin'al fine l'opera cominciata" (2: 77).[55] (. . . my work, I have woven with three main threads, which lead the work from its beginning continuously through to its end.) He develops his dependence on the vocabulary of weaving in several ways: (1) Ariosto describes his composition in terms of woven art; (2) Ariosto imitates the artifice of the rhapsode in his narrative composition; (3) rhapsodes, therefore, can be said to weave their narratives.[56]

Could Tasso, who studied Greek as an adolescent, have known that the word "rapsodo" derives from the Greek verb *rapto,* "to sew together"?[57] According to this etymology, rhapsodes were responsible for stitching together the various episodes that make up the cycle of Homeric stories in the *Iliad* and the *Odyssey.*[58] As the texts of Homer's poems became canonized there was less room for the rhapsode to improvise; however, he could always exercise his creativity in constructing the narrative. A virtuoso was probably known for his ability to produce satisfying transitions from one episode to another just as the audience's patience and memory waned.

Giraldi and Tasso believed that the rhapsode singing before his patron would develop several plots or "threads" in the same narrative, much as did Ariosto in the *Furioso* and Tasso himself in the construction of the *Amadigi.* This accounted, the critics thought, for the artist's need to break into the narrative to organize its parts. Giraldi, again working backwards from Renaissance poetry, explains that the rhapsodes, as opposed to Homer and other heroic poets, established a precedent for this sort of authorial intervention: " . . . il qual uso [reciting before an audience], se ben non fu servato dai Poeti Eroici antichi nelle scritture loro, fu nondimeno introdutto da Rapsodi che cantavano alle mense dei gran Maestri i fatti degli antichi Eroi."[59] (. . . which custom, if it was not correctly observed by the ancient, heroic poets in their writings, was nevertheless introduced by rhapsodes who used to sing about the deeds of ancient heroes at the dinners of their great lords.)

Tasso also adopts this explanation for authorial intervention in a letter to Girolamo Molino of January 29, 1558. There is, however, an important qualification: " . . . e mi pareva che questa maniera di Canti, forse tolta delle Rapsodie antiche, fosse stata rinnovata con molto giudicio da' moderni poeti."[60] (. . . and it seemed to me that this convention of cantos, perhaps taken from ancient rhapsodies, had been made new with much judgment by modern poets.) He proposes that the modern technique of judiciously interrupting a lengthy narrative for the sake of the reader is *perhaps* modeled on the rapport that the rhapsodes of antiquity had with their audiences. Tasso is willing to entertain the analogical possibilities between the romance poet and the rhapsode as Giraldi had first developed them, but he is reluctant to dismiss completely the medieval heritage of interlaced poetry with its own conventions. Such reluctance is characteristic of his strategy of compromise.

The most striking reference to rhapsodes in Tasso's criticism occurs in a letter to Sperone Speroni of September 26, 1557, written about a year after the letters to Giraldi. Speroni was an unstinting critic of the theories that Ariosto and Boiardo could somehow be linked to an earlier oral tradition. It was Speroni who exclaimed, " . . . che la divisione in canti sia fatta, perché si cantassero, o si debbano cantare, è una pazzia."[61] (. . . that the poems are divided into cantos because they are sung or ought to be sung is a crazy idea.) In what becomes a formulaic statement, Tasso, for his part, claims not to follow Homer or Vergil in the narrative design of the *Amadigi;* rather, his classical model is the art of the rhapsode: "Dico adunque, Eccellente Sig. mio, ch'essendo questo mio Poema diverso da quello di Omero, e di Virgilio, e quasi simile alle Rapsodie antiche, e a quella sorte di Poesia che cantavano i citaredi alle tavole de' gran Prencipi (la quale era però Eroica, perchè trattava di persone, e di fatti Eroici) dee anco esser l'artificio."[62] (Therefore I say, my excellent lord, that this poem of mine is different from Homer's and Vergil's and almost like the ancient rhapsodies and like that sort of poetry that the lyre players used to sing at the tables of the great princes [which was heroic because it dealt with heroic individuals and their deeds]. So also is the artifice of my poem like that of the singers.) The reasoning is sound: a different sort of poem requires a different sort of narrative technique.

Tasso then elaborates his reference to the rhapsodes in terms of the lyrelike instrument they sometimes played, the cithara. In another attempt to reconceptualize literary history, he attributes to Lorenzo de' Medici the introduction into Italian literature of the rhapsodic convention that interrupts a first-person narrative in order to address the audience. Lorenzo, who wanted to introduce "in questa nostra lingua . . . tutte quelle maniere di Poesia ch'usavano gli antichi, introdusse anco questa: e Luigi Pulci tutti i Canti della sua Opera cantò alla tavola sua."[63] (into this language of ours . . . all those kinds of poetry that the ancients had, introduced this type too: and Luigi Pulci sang all of the cantos of his work at his table.) It was Lorenzo, then, who employed his court poet, Luigi Pulci, as the Quattrocento equivalent of a classical rhapsode.

Again Tasso's sense of literary history is incorrect, and it is significantly his own. Pulci probably recited his *Morgante* to the Medici audience, but if one assumes for the sake of argument that he sang it, he did so because the chivalric romance tradition in which he worked encouraged the poet to sing, or to feign singing, to the audience. Tasso's historical error bespeaks his desire to find a position of compromise by situating the classical phenomenon in a more contemporary setting. In claiming to have Pulci as a precedent for designing a narrative in which the poet sings to his patron, Tasso is not merely imitating a classical convention (or what he interprets as a classical convention); he is imitating what he perceives to be a medievalizing Italian imitation of a classical convention. Thus he invents a tradition that extends from the time of the rhapsode's distant past through the Medicean revival of vernacular poetry in the latter decades of the Quattrocento to his own day in the 1550s.

Tasso resolves his dilemma as a classicizing romance poet and a critic by recognizing in Pulci an intermediary between his poetry and the classical rhapsodic tradition. Tasso thus makes a gesture towards earlier Italian literature and strengthens the historical lineage he aims to reaffirm in his romance composition. The critical reassessment of Pulci distinguishes Tasso from Giraldi, who, not surprisingly, has no place for the Florentine romancer in his history of the genre.[64]

While Tasso uses Pulci to make sense of his own narrative practice in the *Amadigi,* his recourse to the Florentine is primarily a reflection of the cultural trend to assimilate the *Furioso.* Tasso's role in its critical reception challenged the traditional comparison of Ariosto to Homer or Vergil by likening the Ferrarese poet to a rhapsode. To view Ariosto as the Ferrarese rhapsode is to view the *Furioso* as a poem that represents a wide range of narrative possibilities inspired by both classical and medieval traditions. And it is to recognize the *Furioso* as the crowning vernacular achievement of the humanist movement. The notion of Ariosto as the Ferrarese rhapsode did not prevail,[65] however, and Tasso's strategy of critical compromise, with its focus on the description of literature (in his case, an inventive description of literature and literary history), soon gave way to the polarized academic disputes that focused on the normative prescription of how literature should be.

We will have occasion to consider some of the issues of these debates in the chapters that follow, especially chapters 4 and 5. But first let us turn to the example of Boiardo.

CHAPTER 2

*R*adical Neoclassicism in Orlando Innamorato

The face of the historian should not betray the storyteller's
animation; it should be a mask of dispassion.

SIMON SCHAMA, PARAPHRASING HIS CRITICS

Herodotus says: very few things happen at the right time, and
the rest do not happen at all; the conscientious historian will
correct these defects.

MARK TWAIN[1]

*I*n this chapter I discuss how Boiardo used his interpretation of Herodotean historical narrative and Vergilian epic to obfus-
cate the boundaries between chivalric romance and epic in his *Orlando
Innamorato*. I argue that Boiardo's familiarity with classical narrative
needs to be taken much more seriously in interpretations of his poem.
Before I consider how Boiardo read the classical works in question, I
examine Ferrarese cultural institutions of the Quattrocento that affected
a humanist-poet like himself.

At the Source: "Limpida e Larga Vena" or
"Torbidi Torrenti"?

The reader's assumption upon first looking into Boiardo's *Orlando
Innamorato* is that the poem conforms to various medieval literary traditions, oral and written. In many ways it recalls the oral poetry that developed in Italy from around the eleventh through the fifteenth centuries—
to which Giraldi referred so harshly in the passage from his *Discorso*
discussed in chapter 1. The wandering minstrels, or "cantastorie," of
medieval time composed poems, "cantari," which they recited at fairs
and festivals. They tended to use either the matter of France (the stories

surrounding Charlemagne's war against the Saracens) or the matter of Britain (the Arthurian legends) as the basis for their narratives.[2] Thence we can establish a literary-historical tie between these artists and Boiardo, who depended on the same two sequences of stories, the Carolingian and Arthurian cycles, as sources for several of the plots in his own poem.[3] The *Innamorato,* however, shares more than subject matter with the poems of the "cantastorie." Its ungainly bulk gives it the appearance of a medieval "cantare," or, rather, of several of them strung together. Boiardo's poem sounds like one, too, with its octave stanzas to be declaimed by the poet in his guise as minstrel. Moreover, from the opening of the poem the poet addresses his audience in propria persona, as if a group were gathered about him in the town's piazza on market day.[4]

The *Innamorato,* of course, is not technically an oral work. At times even the narrator himself drops his pose as "cantastorie" and refers to the act of reading the poem.[5] The poem's division into large books, "libri," composed of smaller songs, "canti," appropriately suggests its dual nature as a product of written and oral cultures. When we consider it as a written document, it appears, at first glance, noticeably medieval. The narrative construction has many of the characteristics associated with the chivalric romance, most importantly, the interlaced design of its multiple plots, which uses the narrative technique of "entrelacement," familiar to readers of French romance. Then, too, the principal plot of the lovesick Orlando, Charlemagne's nephew and the greatest Christian warrior, lends itself to many of the thematic motifs of romance: the damsel in distress, the hero determined to save her, the quest for the damsel amid trials and tribulations, and so on. One easily concludes that this is the stuff and shape of medieval or medievalizing writing, whether in imitation of Italian "cantari" or French romance. But my thesis in this chapter is that one's initial assumption about the shaping of the *Innamorato*—an assumption that has been encouraged by the critical tradition—is wrong: Boiardo's poem owes as much to classical sources as to medieval ones, even in respect to its narrative design.[6]

The criticism of the *Innamorato*—what little attention it has received—is discouraging in its persistent denial of the fullness of Boiardo's literary experience.[7] Boiardo brought to his re-creation and adaptation of medieval genres a keen understanding of classical narrative, in both poetry and prose. His knowledge of classical literature derived generally from his humanistic education, which was in many ways typical for his class and time. But it also derived from the specific experience of translating several classical works, one of which, the *Histories* of Herodotus, I shall examine below. While most critics are aware that Boiardo made these translations, few entertain the possibility that these nonvernacular literary experiences may have contributed to his development as a writer. Fewer still actually discuss how the composition (I choose this specific word for reasons that will become clear below) of Boiardo's translations may have affected his reception of popular culture. I shall engage many of these critics in the following pages and notes as the argument requires. For now I wish to focus upon one reader of the *Innamorato* whose interpretation allows me to suggest ways in which the criticism of the poem should be reoriented: Gianvincenzo Gravina.

Gravina (1664–1718) is best known as one of the founding members of the Arcadia, the Roman academy he helped to establish in 1690.[8] The immediate purpose of the Arcadia was to counter a new kind of poetry written during the seventeenth century by the epigones of Giambattista Marino. That poetry, characterized by a flamboyant luxuriance of rhetorical conceits, we now call baroque. In opposition to the overblown rhetoric of the Marinisti, the Arcadia promoted a return to the purity of classical art, hence its rules became part of the process that codified and legitimized the neoclassical aesthetic in Italy. This cultural program prejudices Gravina's remarks on the sources of the *Innamorato,* of which he comments: "Credono molti che il Boiardo avesse ordito il suo poema ad imitazion de' Provenzali perché l'ombre e i nomi di quegli Eroi per esso veggon trascorrere. Ma da molto più limpida e larga vena trasse egli l'invenzione e l'espression sua, cioè da' Greci e Latini, nel cui studio era versato, senza che a' torbidi torrenti Provenzali dovesse ricorrere."[9] (Many people believe that Boiardo arranged his poem in imitation of the Provençal authors because they see the figures and names of those heroes race through the poem. But he drew his subject matter and his manner of description from a much clearer and grander vein, from the Greeks and Latins whom he had studied for a long time, without having to turn to the muddy streams of Provence.)

One should note that Gravina's observation is inaccurate in two respects. First, in creating the *Innamorato* Boiardo borrowed not from Provençal literature, at least not primarily, but from the traditions of French literature associated with northern France. Furthermore, as mentioned above, his "source" of French traditions was closer to home. It was from the "cantastorie," who composed their poems in a mixed dialect of French and Venetian, the so-called Franco-Venetian, that Boiardo first heard the names and places of the French literary tradition. The second inaccuracy involves the critic's understanding of imitation. Gravina argues against the position that Boiardo was a medievalizing "cantastorie" in order to classify him as a Renaissance rather than a medieval author. He makes this move using the metaphor of the literary source, claiming that Boiardo drew from the "clear and extensive vein" of classical waters rather than the "muddy streams" of medieval French. Both cultural politics and the aesthetic program of the Arcadia determine Gravina's dismissal of Boiardo's medieval French sources. He argues elsewhere for the classics, claiming that they are more native to the Italian peninsula than, say, the romances of the north, and that they can thus contribute to the Arcadian plan of a culturally united Italy.[10] Regardless of Gravina's reasons for invoking the classics, it would behoove me to stress his emphasis on Boiardo's classical sources in arguing my case against the blinkered quality of much Boiardo criticism. But my reading of *Furioso* 23 in the "Introduction" should make it clear that there is a methodological problem with Gravina's formulation. Boiardo drew from classical sources, to be sure, but my contention is that there was nothing limpid in his allusiveness. Generally speaking, imitation is never a neat and discrete act, as Gravina's image suggests; it has much more in common with the muddied, viscous waters he dismisses. In appropriating and correcting Gravina's paradigm for my own purposes, I am reiterating a point made in the second half of the "Introduction," namely, that imitation is a con-fusing process that fuses different sources together into a new entity. It is precisely this aspect of imitation that I wish to focus upon as I read several passages from Boiardo's poem in conjunction with a variety of his sources.

Gravina's basic assumption—that Boiardo wrote like a Renaissance poet—is correct. But Boiardo is not of that period by virtue of merely having alluded to Greek and Latin authors. He draws much of his material (what Gravina, like Rajna later, calls "l'invenzione") and a paradigm for recasting those borrowings into language ("l'espressione") from classical models. In other words, the degree of Boiardo's imitation of Greek and Latin authors is profound and binding. To my knowledge, Gravina is the earliest critic to claim that Boiardo's study of the ancients informed his vernacular narrative. (Ariosto, I believe, learned from Boiardo's example, while Torquato Tasso, in his critical writings at least, does not seem to appreciate this aspect of Boiardo's art.) Thus, notwithstanding Gravina's errors in literary topography and the shortcomings of his theory of imitation, his observation on the sources of the *Innamorato* is in itself important for Boiardo criticism.

From this reformulation of Gravina's remarks, I shall explore some of the lesser-known sources for the *Innamorato*'s narrative design— Herodotus and Vergil—in an attempt to answer this question: In what ways was the poet's treatment of these classical sources similar to his treatment of vernacular ones? In focusing on Boiardo's obfuscation of the distinction between classical and vernacular, I shall move beyond the limits of Gravina's remarks. First, however, I need to establish the historical context of Boiardo's reading of these authors, indeed of his reading in general. What were the opportunities for a reader in Quattro-cento Ferrara? How might such opportunities have affected Boiardo's career? The cultural setting in which Boiardo read and wrote contributed to the circumstances that ultimately led to the decrease in popularity of his own work. Understanding the ironies of the process that led to the "sfortuna" of the *Innamorato* will give us a better understanding of the poem as a whole.

The Education of a Poet in Renaissance Ferrara

The House of Este ruled in Ferrara from the end of the twelfth century until the demise of the family in 1597, when Alfonso II died with no heir apparent. The following year Pope Clement VIII annexed the town and its surrounding territory to the Papal States, thus reducing, if not altogether quenching, the brilliance of Estense Ferrara.[11] The town had been a power for over four hundred years, politically and culturally, and its center was the Estense court. Trends of all sorts had their origin in the circles of knights, courtiers, and humanists who made the court their focus and the source of their livelihood. Courtly life determined their dress, food, behavior, the way they lived.[12] Trends emanating from the court also affected the way the Ferrarese studied and learned, for in 1429 the Estense family sponsored the founding of what was to become one of the most influential schools in Renaissance Europe: the school of Guarino Veronese. Boiardo, Ariosto, and Tasso participated varyingly in courtly life, and each poet benefited from the intellectual possibilities created by Guarino's school and those subsequently maintained by the Ferrarese *Studio* that grew out of it. The Estense family, its court, and its school influenced both Boiardo and Ariosto. Tasso, for his part, was not schooled in Ferrara, but he became an active member of the court under the patronage of Cardinal Luigi d'Este. The following sketch of Ferrarese courtly and intellectual life focuses primarily on the fifteenth century, the time of Boiardo, but there are occasional glimpses ahead to the times of Ariosto and Tasso.

The Este family, originally from the town of Este in the Euganean Hills south of Padua, extended its interests into the area around Ferrara in Emilia in the second half of the twelfth century, vying for power with other prominent landowners of north-central Italy.[13] During the 1230s, in the midst of the ongoing political struggle between the papacy and Emperor Frederick II, the family emerged victorious in the control of Ferrara. From the 1240s onward, succeeding generations of the family controlled the government with few interruptions. The Este were able to establish a medieval *signoria* in Ferrara, the duration of which rivaled any other feudal aristocracy during the Middle Ages in Italy.

Niccolò III, ruler from 1393 to 1441, is generally credited with beginning the process of modifying the medieval aristocracy into a Renaissance principality. He practiced a shrewd diplomacy, which his three sons, Leonello, Borso, and Ercole, who governed in peaceful succession until 1505, perfected.[14] Through the energies of these four men, Ferrara became a successful city-state despite its small size and relative lack of natural resources. Each ruler took advantage of the intermediate position of Ferrara among more powerful neighboring states to manipulate political expediencies. This continual maintenance of the family rule is arguably the greatest achievement of the Estensi, yet each man added his own particular accomplishment to the state's success. In 1438, for example, Niccolò graced Ferrara by sponsoring the church council that proposed a plan to unify the Greek and Roman churches.[15] Leonello (1441–50) fostered the burgeoning growth of intellectual institutions in the city. Borso (1450–71) had the territory surrounding Ferrara elevated to a dukedom. Ercole (1471–1505) personally oversaw the "Herculean addition," Biagio Rossetti's masterpiece of urban planning that doubled the size of the medieval town to create what Burckhardt called "the first really modern city in Europe."[16] In addition to Rossetti, Ercole supported a host of artists, including Boiardo.

Between 1505 and 1534, Ercole's eldest son, Alfonso, Ariosto's patron from 1517 until the poet's death in 1533, continued the family's domination of the duchy in the face of frequent threats of foreign (usually papal or Venetian) invasion. In supporting Ariosto and others, Alfonso continued his family's tradition of public munificence. Este patronage sponsored the famous school of Guarino, as well as the ducal library, theatrical productions, and, in one way or another, much of the poetry and art created during the Quattrocento and Cinquecento in Ferrara. Boiardo, for his part, was profoundly shaped by Ercole's court. His beneficial relationship with an Este patron had precedent. His grandfather, Feltrino, had been a close friend of Niccolò III, whom he accompanied on a pilgrimage to the Holy Land in 1414.[17] Much of the wealth of the Boiardo family derived from a lopsided redistribution in 1423 of feudal properties owned by various Boiardi that favored Feltrino, an arrangement sanctioned by Niccolò III.[18] By contrast, Ariosto, despite Estense patronage, remained respectfully aloof from the family and its large retinue. He claims in an autobiographical satire to prefer a turnip at home to all the hoopla of the court:

> Chi brama onor di sprone o di capello,
> serva re, duca, cardinale o papa;
> io no, che poco curo questo o quello.

In casa mia mi sa meglio una rapa
ch'io cuoca . . .   *Sat.* 3.40–44[19]

Let the man who hungers for the honor of the spur or of the [ecclesiastical] hat serve a king, a duke, a cardinal, a pope. I will not. Such trifles do not interest me. In my house a turnip tastes better to me that I cook myself . . .[20]

The Estense patronage, to be sure, extended to Torquato Tasso (1545–95). Known as a brilliant and precocious student at the universities of Padua and Bologna, Tasso was invited to the court to serve Cardinal Luigi D'Este in 1565. Luigi and his brother, Alfonso II, who ruled from 1559 to 1597, were legitimate sons of Ercole II (1534–59) and his wife of royal French descent, Renée. The European religious controversies in the sixteenth century affected the reigns of Ercole II and Alfonso II. Ercole in particular was forced to camouflage his wife's Protestant sympathies. Alfonso was also concerned with the possibility of doctrinal erring among his courtiers, a worry that may have led him to sequester Tasso in the Hospital of St. Anna to prevent the inquisitors from prying any court secrets from the poet. Generally speaking, however, Alfonso was a patient and liberal patron for Tasso. For over fifteen years the duke and other members of the court tolerated and excused Tasso's odd behavior in an attempt to foster his creative genius.

Although a certain deterioration overtook the Estense family, cultural life remained alive and well in the waning years of the Ferrarese duchy. Witness Tasso's friend, Giovanni Battista Guarini (1538–1612). Guarini is best known for his pastoral drama, *Il Pastor Fido,* a work that blends vernacular and classical conventions into the new genre of melodrama in accord with the Ferrarese tradition of experimental theater. He is also noteworthy as a direct descendant of the family of Guarino Veronese. After a brief stint as a professor of rhetoric and poetry at the University of Padua, he became an influential member of Alfonso's inner circle (ca. 1567–88). His position at the court provided the intellectual history of Ferrara during the fifteenth and sixteenth centuries a continuity that paralleled its political continuity. Guarini, Tasso, and the others who make up the last generation of Estense poets in Ferrara were the final bearers of an intellectual tradition, a revolution, that began with Guarino Veronese. What was the institution behind that revolution?

In 1429, Niccolò III invited Guarino Veronese (1374–1460) to Ferrara to establish a school for the young prince Leonello.[21] Guarino already had a reputation as an excellent teacher, especially of Greek, and he had taught extensively in Venice and Florence. His school in Ferrara rapidly gained prestige throughout Europe, rivaling even the University of Bologna.[22] In 1436 it served as the basis for the foundation of the *Studio,* precursor of the University of Ferrara. Guarino personally directed the school until his death, in 1460, when his son, Battista (followed in turn by his son, Alessandro), assumed its direction.

The school was deservedly famous, and the extent and duration of its fame were Guarino's own doing.[23] The teacher never ceased reminding former students that they owed their success to their training in the liberal arts. While the stated rhetorical goal of the program was to produce good citizens, its primary goal was more modest. Guarino designed the curriculum to underscore the general *educatio* of the student, his "upbringing," with the teacher very much, to borrow from Quintilian, in loco parentis. Since the majority of his students took room and board at the school, Guarino oversaw their progress day and night, for better and for worse. The schoolmaster laments in a letter that one of his boarders tried to sell a copy of an Ovidian text to a wandering scholar. But in this one instance, at least, the scholar got the better of the surrogate parent, for Guarino expressed much more concern about the potential loss of a text—it was a handsome copy of Ovid's *Metamorphoses*—than about the ethos of his young charge.[24] This is probably the exception that makes the case, for he usually managed to combine with equanimity the duties of the teacher-parent and the humanistic bibliophile.

Guarino's understanding of pedagogy derived from several sources. First, his own experience as a student predictably affected the kind of teacher he became. He was a product of medieval schooling, which introduced the student to the rudiments of Latin through jingles, rhyming ditties, and versified *artes.* Students then used their linguistic skills to work their way through the anthologies (*florilegia*) that served as the texts of the old curriculum. The subjects studied in the typical me-dieval classroom were grammar, rhetoric (i.e., advanced composition and reading), and dialectic (i.e., analytic philosophy). With this kind of education as a foundation, Guarino spent approximately five years, from 1405 to 1409, studying Greek literature in Venice and Constantinople with the great Hellenist, Manuel Chrysolaurus.[25] From his Byzantine teacher, Guarino learned the rudiments of Greek and was then led deep into the mysteries of classical literature. At the same time he was also introduced to the mundane and extremely useful practice of taking notes as he read, a mainstay of the Byzantine classroom. Once back in the West, Guarino perfected the Greek practice of note-taking. He had each student compile a notebook as he read, a handy collection of annotations to be used as a guide to other readings. These notes were of all sorts—lexical, grammatical, syntactical, morphological, and, to a lesser extent, literary critical. Compiling the notes was half the process; organizing them into some sort of rationally coherent whole to which the student could later make reference was the other.

The second source of Guarino's pedagogical program was a literary one: Quintilian's *Institutio Oratoria.* His school's threefold sequence of courses followed the outline recommended in the *Institutio* I–II, beginning with elementary courses that taught phonology and morphology through simple readings, progressing to the next level called the grammatical for its focus on points of grammar and syntax, and culminating in advanced courses in rhetoric that treated issues of literary style. The first sequence of courses emphasized oral work and memorization, much in keeping with Guarino's own experiences as a schoolboy. The middle sequence was divided into two segments called method and history. The course in method introduced the student to the grammar and syntax of classical Latin and Greek, while the course in history introduced him to classical authors whom he analyzed grammatically—this was always Guarino's starting place—and then read for historical and mythological knowledge. Among the authors used in the historical segment were Herodotus, Vergil, Ovid (the *Metamorphoses* and the *Fasti*), Statius, Justinian, and Valerius Maximus.[26] Guarino often required students to translate as part of the process of mastering the languages they studied.[27] This occurred at all levels of instruction but became a more useful part of the process at the higher levels, where the student could study the style of the author under investigation through translation. Guarino no doubt corrected these classroom versions and sometimes must have done so against translations of his own. The teacher completed, for example, a working copy of a Latin version of Herodotus's *Histories* 1.1–71, likely intended for classroom use.[28]

The final sequence of courses involved the study of rhetoric, and it is in this part of the curriculum that Quintilian's philosophy of education is most visible. The student worked his way through texts by Cicero, Quintilian's *Institutio,* and the *Rhetorica ad Herennium,* a text of the first century B.C. attributed to Cicero that Guarino later came to disavow as Ciceronian. In keeping with the program of Quintilian, the student concluded his education with the study of Greek oratory. The ideology espoused in this final segment of the curriculum derived from the Roman ideal that the man who speaks well is a good man. Quintilian defines oratory precisely in these terms as the science and art of speaking well (1.Pr.18, and throughout book 12, especially section 1) and defines the orator as the good man ("vir bonus," 1.Pr.9–10). But such a goal was not always possible. Guarino confesses in private letters that he cannot necessarily and automatically transform the student, even the able and willing learner, into a civic leader; the transformation occurs where and when it will outside the classroom. True, the student's education will have had an effect on his development, but it cannot guarantee a specific development.[29] In recognizing this fact, Guarino concedes that there are limitations to humanistic *educatio.*

Nevertheless, the impact of Guarino on the humanistic culture of the period was unquestionably great. Not only did he teach princes, humanists, courtiers, and poets; he also educated teachers, most notably Vittorino da Feltre, who headed the ducal school of Mantua.[30] Followers like Vittorino heralded Guarino's method and curriculum beyond the walls of his modest classrooms in the Estense castle. They voiced none of the inconsistencies the master at times sensed in his own program. The ideology of Guarino's school, that the learned citizen is a better citizen, became a commonplace in Renaissance discourse.

Even though neither Boiardo nor Ariosto attended Guarino's school, both benefited from its presence in Ferrara. From well-connected families, they were in close contact with students of the school,[31] and at least one of Ariosto's private tutors had connections with it.[32] It is impossible to determine the precise influence of Guarino's teaching on the work of the two poets and to present specific evidence that might show how Guarino's use of classical authors in the classroom affected them. But we can speak with less hesitation about the indirect influence Guarino's school had on Boiardo and Ariosto as well as on other writers and artists of Renaissance Ferrara.

The school and the Estense court attracted humanists from all over Europe. Rodolphus Agricola delivered a public oration after Guarino's death, in 1476, in which he emphasized the geographical diversity of the many scholars who had come to Ferrara to study with the master.[33] Many of the day's leading humanists sat at his feet to learn the language and literature of Greece. The council of the eastern and western branches of the Church in 1438 further heightened interest in Greek culture. Poets growing up in Ferrara during these decades were in a position to take advantage of its rich humanistic activity. Humanists discoursed and argued; the poets listened. They saw, read, and heard the works of artists inspired by these humanists. And (perhaps most important for Boiardo and Ariosto as poets who knew Latin and, in Boiardo's case, Greek) they used the manuscripts and printed editions that were lodged in the school of Guarino and the ducal library (or copies of those books in circulation). Boiardo and Ariosto responded by reading classical literature, and, because of Guarino's school, they had the means, linguistic and material, to do so on their own.[34]

But the focus upon Guarino's school must not obscure the full panorama of Ferrarese life, especially its extensive popular culture, which was not, needless to say, a part of Guarino's curriculum. Long before Guarino arrived in Ferrara, the city had become an important center for the production, dissemination, and enjoyment of medieval literature. Artistic artifacts, collections of nonhumanistic manuscripts, and specific Ferrarese artists from around 1150 well into the Quattrocento document the civic fascination with the cycles of chivalric romance and with the medieval "cantari," which were heard and read in French, Franco-Venetian, and northern dialects of Italian. The patron saint of the city, St. George, in whose name the cathedral was consecrated in 1135, bespeaks the Ferrarese passion for chivalric values and the popular literature of romance.

Nor did Ferrarese culture completely change its tenor after Guarino's arrival in 1429. Medieval romances continued to be enjoyed throughout the century; for example, even during the ultraclassical decade of Leonello's reign, a play, inspired by romance, of St. George slaying the dragon was performed in the central civic piazza. Indeed, Ferrarese literary culture under the direction of Borso took on a decidedly popular tone, with a vast increase in the number of vernacular works composed, copied, and illuminated at his behest.[35] An inventory from 1467 lists and briefly describes some of these vernacular works, including copies of the *Spagna in rima, Lancillotto, Aspromonte,* and *Fioravante.*[36] Of course, just as the cultivation of the romance continued during the decade of Leonello's rule, so during the reign of Borso did humanists continue to play an important part in the court. A good example of this work is the recently discovered Latin poem by Tito Strozzi, Boiardo's uncle, in honor of Borso, the *Borsias.*[37]

During the reigns of Ercole and his son Alfonso, however, the play between the new culture of the humanists and the popular culture, with its origins in the Middle Ages, became something new, uniquely Ferrarese. Boiardo and Ariosto, whose narrative poems are only two of dozens of romance-epics, are the best examples of this new art form.[38] Books, still mostly manuscripts, were on the increase in the court. Another inventory, believed by Antonia Tissoni Benvenuti to be dated after 1474, lists 86 sacred texts in Latin and the vernacular, 155 classical texts in Latin and Greek, 118 texts in the various literary dialects of Italy at the time, mainly Tuscan and "Padano illustre" (the literary "koiné" of the Po valley), and 35 French and 2 Spanish texts—in other words, a balanced fare of old and new, of classical, medieval, and contemporary literature.[39]

Herodotus: Accept This Greek

One literary development in particular contributed to the increase of books in the court and is further evidence of the ongoing cultural compromise that takes place under Ercole and Alfonso: the translation into Italian of Greek and Latin classical prose, especially histories. From an inventory of the property, including books, in Ercole's private apartment, we find that fully two-thirds of the vernacular works at his bedside were translations of histories—Greek, Roman, and medieval.[40] Ercole, an avid student of history, was an aggressive collector of historical works. He knew, however, no Greek and little Latin. With a pressing need for translations, he commissioned dozens.[41]

Ercole's Ferrara was hardly the only cultural polity to contribute to this new branch of vernacular literature. What distinguished the city was that Boiardo, one of its most prominent poets, rendered several important translations of Greek and Latin works. His version of Herodotus's *Histories* is the first in any vernacular. His translations (including versions of Xenophon's *Cyropaedia,* Cornelius Nepos's *Lives,* and Apuleius's *Golden Ass*) deserve more serious consideration—although they tend to differ radically from the original texts—for they reveal his exposure to various kinds of classical narrative and provide some sense of the Ferrarese cultural setting in which experimentation with narrative was encouraged. Furthermore, Boiardo's translations of classical narrative prose may have provided later poets with an example of a partially successful attempt to fuse elements of the classical and the vernacular, to bring together high and low culture in a narrative context. Boiardo's "translations" of the classics anticipate in several ways the fusion of classical and medieval narrative that characterizes Ariosto's *Orlando Furioso.*

The list of classical works that Boiardo translated is significant in and of itself. Whether it was his genius that led him to choose suitable projects or whether it was the shrewdness of his patron, Ercole, to whom Boiardo dedicated all his translations, is not certain. In any case, with the exception of Cornelius Nepos,[42] Boiardo translated works as interesting for their narrative design as for their content. The best example of this is arguably Apuleius's *Golden Ass,* the only Latin novel that has survived in its entirety.[43] Xenophon's *Cyropaedia,*[44] an idealized biography of Cyrus the Elder, is at certain moments no less fictitious than the *Golden Ass,* and this blend of fact and fiction in its narrative is one of the reasons given for its possible influence on the development of the Greek romance.[45] The narrative of Herodotus's *Histories,* written in the fifth century B.C. about the first great war between the Greeks and the Persians, is based on a plot structure consisting of numerous stories, digressions, and anecdotes, among other things. And although there is some discussion of Herodotus's qualifications as a historian, there is little doubt that he is a narrative artist.[46] It is inconceivable that Boiardo could have failed to learn about

the complexities of narrative in the process of translating the *Histories.*
And yet, few scholars have recognized the importance of this translation
in Boiardo's literary development.[47]

One indication of this general disregard is that a recent editor
of Boiardo's work does not even mention the Herodotus translation in
his otherwise good introduction to the poet.[48] Another, more serious,
indication of the problem is the lack of a modern critical edition of the
work.[49] The Herodotus translation was reprinted five times between 1533
and 1565,[50] but subsequently it was abandoned at about the time Boiardo's
Innamorato was also falling out of favor.

What does Boiardo's translation of Herodotus teach us about the
poet's sense of narrative? The title of the prologue is a good place to
start: "Prologo nella traduttione di Herodoto Halicarnaseo padre della
historia per M. Matheo M. Boiardo conte di Scandiano, all'illustriss.
et eccellentiss. principe d Hercule Duca di Ferrara [*sic*]" (724).[51] The
prologue, which runs to a little over two pages in Zottoli's edition, is filled
with humanistic commonplaces like the designation of Herodotus as the
"father of history," a phrase borrowed from Cicero. The prologue begins
with a veiled reference to translation as the noble revelation to the public
of what has been rediscovered. "Antiquissimo costume fu sempre e dura
anchora tra gli huomini eccellenti di porre a publica utilita' quelle cose che
ritrovate avessero, . . ." (724). (There was once of old an ancient custom
among excellent men [still in use today among the same], of setting forth
for the public good the things that those men had discovered, . . .) The
periodic sentence develops for nearly half a page, over the course of which
one realizes that Boiardo is referring to Herodotus's act of making public
all that he discovered in the investigations that underlie his history. But
it becomes equally clear that the act of making public a new discovery
also applies to Boiardo's own translation of the Greek original, a task, it
is implied, no less useful than Herodotus's original composition.

Boiardo's implicit comparison between the translator and the original author suggests much self-confidence as he approached the task of
translating. If he was fulfilling a ducal commission that he felt to be
onerous, such sentiment appears nowhere in the text. And if, as has been
suggested,[52] Boiardo's command of Greek was so shaky that he had to
use Lorenzo Valla's Latin version of Herodotus as a trot, he does not
admit to such dependence. Contrast this with references in the prologue
of his *Ciropedia* to the Latin versions of Xenophon by Poggio and Filelfo.
But Boiardo's confidence in his knowledge of Greek had some legitimate
basis, for although he did use Valla to a certain extent, his Greek was at
least good enough to risk making mistakes independent of Valla's Latin
version.[53]

In this initial comparison between Herodotus and himself, Boiardo remains within the parameters of Renaissance theories of imitation, the language of which Boiardo adduces when he refers to his desire to follow ("seguire"), to keep on following ("seguitare"), and to imitate ("immitare") his ancient text (724). Boiardo evokes the same spirit of competition that characterizes the way in which Renaissance poets often approach their classical models. But he resists the usual rhetoric of surpassing his model, which would be inappropriate to a translation. He wishes rather to suggest similarities between himself and Herodotus.

The central issue of the parallel technique of the two authors is found in what Boiardo dubs "compositione" (725), the conscious, artistic shaping of narrative.[54] The specific point lies in how the ancient historian splices varied parts of the narrative into one whole: "The variety of his history, with its presentation of strange and wondrous things, with its frequent proverbs and sound teachings that are set into the narrative by him in abundance, provide delight and should be of use to those who hear it." The observation that the work carries within it the potential for utility and delight is common in the humanistic reception of classical literature. But in the same sentence Boiardo makes an atypical comment about Herodotean narrative, one that may well have arisen here for the first time in the history of Herodotus's reception. By making use of "interporre" to describe how some passages of the *Histories* are "set into" other passages, he suggests that the Herodotean narrative is constructed in a way that his audience could appreciate and understand: "buoni ammaestramenti che da lui fioritamente sono interposti . . ." (725). (sound teachings that are set into the narrative by him in abundance . . .)

"Interporre" is a technical term that derives from the Latin rhetorical tradition, in which the parallel verb "interponere" signifies an interruption or digression in any continuous narrative.[55] In Latin and Italian the verb means literally "to place between," and it suggests the placing of one narrative within another in order to interrupt the continuous flow of the prior narrative. Boiardo's description of Herodotus's work as an "interposed" narrative recalls the interlaced shape of medieval romance. Indeed, *interpositio* is in some sense a classical equivalent of medieval interlacing. Torquato Tasso, as we shall see in chapter 4, made use of "interporre" in both his critical writings and his poetry to comment on the narrative structure of the typical romance. "Interporre," then, is a term that has currency throughout the Italian rhetorical tradition as a gloss on narrative art. I take Boiardo's use of it as a measure of the sophisticated understanding he has of Herodotus as a narrative artist and as an indication of yet another way in which he envisions the two of them to be engaged in a similar enterprise.

Boiardo, moreover, draws other comparisons between himself and Herodotus. His reference to the listeners of the narrative ("gli ascoltanti") adduces the proximity of the oral and written traditions both in fifth-century Athens and in the Ferrara of Boiardo's day (725).[56] A century later Torquato Tasso will go so far as to claim that Herodotus had his bards no less than Homer. Tasso names a certain Hegesias, who was said to have actually given performances based on the history of Herodotus: "e s'alcune volte sono stati recitati i poemi d'Omero, de' quali fu istrione Ermodoro, come racconta Ateneo, furono ancora rappresentate l'istorie d'Erodoto; e l'istrione fu Egesio comico" (*Discorsi del Poema Eroico,* in *Prose* 2: 381). (If Homer's poems were sometimes recited, as by the rhapsode Hermodotus, according to Athenaeus, so too the history of Herodotus was performed by the comic actor Hegesias [204]).[57] Commentators have proposed that Tasso misread his ancient source, Athenaeus, *Deipnosophists* 14. 620D, substituting "Erodoto" for "Esiodo," "Egesio" for "Egesia," and "Ermodoro" for "Ermofanto," the latter of each pair occurring in the established text we read today.[58] But the scholarly tradition here is incorrect, for the text from which Tasso worked, Natale Conti's Latin translation of Athenaeus, reports "Herodotus" and not "Hesiod."[59] Tasso's annotated copy of Conti's version of Athenaeus (British Library C.45.G8) demonstrates clearly that the poet registered this detail about the performance of Herodotus. In addition to underlining the passage, he also notes in the top margin: "Hegesiam comicu' reru' Herodoti Histrionem."[60] (Hegesias the comic actor, performer of Herodotus.) Tasso and his contemporaries, then, had an authority from antiquity suggest that the text of Herodotus was poetic material ripe for public recitation. But I digress from Boiardo.

There are other, less tenuous, ways in which Boiardo suggests that he and Herodotus have much in common. In several passages the translator comments on the lack of verisimilitude in the classical text, as when he notes: " . . . che niuna cosa si legge più maravigliosa . . ." (725). (. . . that one doesn't read anything more wondrous . . .) The text is credible, nevertheless, Boiardo goes on to argue tendentiously, because Herodotus, being from the borderlands of Asia Minor, is a reliable witness of both Greek and Persian culture. In his own poem, Boiardo (like Ariosto) takes refuge behind the false credibility of his alleged source, Bishop Turpin, especially at those moments when the narrative is at its most fantastic. He plays with the notion that he is writing history and even begins the *Innamorato* with the claim that he uses Turpin's "vera istoria" as a source (1.1.4.1). Turpin's "true history," however, often gives way to the "bella istoria" (1.1.1.4), a major inspiration for the poet. Thence arises a paradox between the credible and incredible. Boiardo writing fiction from sources claims that it is fact; Herodotus's obsession with sources is an attempt to rid his factual account of fiction.

The "Prologo" concludes with the invocation of a humanist topos on the flight of Greeks to the west, a commonplace that assumed greater urgency in the second half of the fifteenth century after the fall of Constantinople in 1454. The translator pleads with Ercole to accept Herodotus, an exiled Greek, into the court of the Este in Ferrara: "E come spesse volte molti principi forestieri ho veduti in quella ricettare, e di Inghilterra et di Spagna, et di Ungaria, et dalle altre estremità del mondo: così gli adirizzo questo vecchio Greco di sua patria cacciato raccomandolo con me insieme alla V. Ecc." (726). (And since I have often seen foreign rulers received in the court, from England, Spain, Hungary, from all over the known world, I am sending there this old Greek man who has been chased out of his own country; I do so commending him and myself to your Excellency.) The rhetoric once again suggests that the translator and Herodotus are equals to be invited into the court where they might enjoy and share Ercole's hospitality.

Although the metaphorical language in the prologue's conclusion is typical of Renaissance translations, there is often more than rhetoric to this sort of appeal. The translator must make the ancient author acceptable to the community of readers of which he is a part. This is a delicate process that requires philological finesse and cultural sensitivity. The translator runs the risk of overpowering the original, as was largely the case when Boiardo's own *Innamorato* was recast in a Tuscan "rifacimento" by Francesco Berni at the beginning of the Cinquecento.[61] Thus in order to avoid denaturing the ancient text, and at the same time to make Herodotus readable for his Ferrarese audience, Boiardo arrives at a clever solution.

Boiardo "romancifies" Herodotean narrative. He deliberately translates the historical work so that its narrative bears a telling resemblance to the narrative of a typical chivalric romance. The thematic material of the *Histories,* much of which reads like the notes of an inventive anthropologist, is predisposed to such a treatment, one that would appeal to an audience raised on romance. But Boiardo's romancification of the work goes far beyond the thematic connection, for it shares some of the conventions of his own romance tradition in its narrative design. I have already pointed to similarities between Boiardo's poem and Herodotus's history, and I have drawn attention to the rhetoric of similarity that the translator uses in the prologue as he introduces Herodotus to his Ferrarese readers. Now I want to examine more extensively the connection that the translator implies between himself and Herodotus on the grounds of narrative artistry.

Boiardo best displays his sense of narrative art in the organization of the translation. The Italian version is approximately three-fifths the length of the original; it is also noticeably shorter than Valla's version in Latin. For example, in book 1 there are 216 sections in the standard Oxford edition of the *Histories* and in Valla's version, each section generally a paragraph long. Boiardo recasts these paragraphs into eleven grand chapters. While respecting the sequence of Herodotus's narrative, Boiardo omits entire paragraphs, especially as he nears the end of book 1. This pattern is magnified in each successive book until books 8 and 9, where extensive passages of the original are ignored. One can often determine why Boiardo skipped a given section in the translation. For example, he tones down references to petty tyrants, probably out of deference to his patron, Ercole.[62] The motivating factor for omissions toward the end of the work was most likely fatigue.

It is within each book, at the junctures between chapters and stories of the history, that one sees Boiardo's hand most visibly. And here at the seams of the narrative his hand is consistently romancelike, even in passages where Herodotus's text does not exhibit what one might consider romance qualities. And although he does not romancify the translation at every possible turn, he does so frequently enough to indicate that he assumes his responsibilities as translator include such a revision of the original. Several examples will show him at work.

One sign of romancification lies in the creation of transitions between sections of the reorganized original. These transitions function like those in a romance poem and look (and sound) like such transitions because Boiardo makes use of several formulas sanctioned by the romance tradition itself. Most noticeable in this regard is his dependence on phrasing that encompasses either one of the paired verbs "lasciare-tornare" or "seguitare-narrare." For example, the translator concludes a section near the beginning of book 2 with the "lasciare-tornare" formula, a device used at numerous points in romance when the narrator brings one portion of the narrative to an end while simultaneously preparing the reader for what follows. In the original, Herodotus has just finished describing the upper reaches of the Nile and is on the verge of investigating the Egyptian practice of religious sacrifice. Here is Boiardo's version: "Ma lasciando tale narratione tornero à dire le altre cose della provincia di Egitto della quale piu lungamente ne ragiono perche piu che altra provincia ha in se cose maravigliose da ragionare" (B43v).[63] (But leaving such a story, I shall return to say other things concerning the region of Egypt about which I shall speak at greater length because more than any other region it contains wondrous things to recount.) The phrasing of the transition could be lifted verbatim from numerous passages in the *Innamorato*. An example of the convention is found at the beginning of Boiardo's poem: "Lassiam costor . . . E ritornamo in Francia a Carlo Mano . . ." (1.1.8.1+3). (For now, we leave them . . . Onward to France: there, Charles the Great . . .)

Herodotus by contrast uses the metaphorical language of leaving one story behind to return to another only once in his entire work. At 4.82 the narrator says "I shall go back to the story which I began to relate," and the narrative then resumes a story line left off at the beginning of the book. Herodotus employs the verb *anabēsomai,* a verb of motion, to express this idea.[64] Boiardo translates the verb at 4.82 correctly and appropriately: "Hora è tempo di ritornare alla accominciata historia" (B133r). (Now is the time to go back to the story already begun.) But this is the exception that makes the case in Herodotus's original, for there the narrator usually depends on various forms of the verb "to say." For the passage on the Nile and Egypt Herodotus writes simply, "It is sufficient to say thus much concerning the Nile. But concerning Egypt I will now speak at length, because nowhere are there so many marvelous things, nor in the whole world beside are there to be seen so many works of unspeakable greatness. Therefore I shall say more about Egypt" (H2.35). Boiardo's version of this passage not only enriches the nonmetaphorical language of the original; it also makes the original sound more familiar to the audience of the translation. The poet normalized the Herodotean original to make it more acceptable to the Ferrarese audience, who expected that a narrative full of incredible marvels be presented in a specific way. The *Histories,* romancelike in many of its tales, cried for the organization and conventions of romance. In short, it should be made to sound like Boiardo's own poem.

The formula "seguitare-narrare" functions similarly in the translation. In Boiardo's rendition of H1.94ff., for example, the narrator announces that he has finished discussing one topic, the subjugation of the Lydians, and he clears his throat to begin the next: " . . . nella fine furno soggiogati da Cyrro e da Persiani nel modo che di sopra narrato havemo. Hora seguitando narraremo chi fusse questo Cyrro e chi fusseno e Persiani che l'Asia soggiogarno" (B22v). (. . . in the end they were subjugated by Cyrus and the Persians in the way that we have narrated above. Now in following we shall narrate who this Cyrus was and who were the Persians who subjugated Asia.) Like the "lasciare-tornare" formula, the formula "seguitare-narrare" is a common feature of the *Innamorato*'s narrative. Boiardo's narrator may open a canto with the formula: "E la istoria passata seguitando, / Narrar vi voglio il fatto tutto intiero" (2.31.2.3–4). (My story is continuing. / I want to narrate everything.) And he may conclude a canto in much the same way (2.30.62–63). The Herodotean passage that Boiardo renders with the romance formula does not contain this same language: " . . . The Lydians, then, were enslaved by the Persians (1.94). But next I should inquire in my history who this Cyrus was who brought down the power of Croesus, and how the Persians came to be rulers of Asia."[65] Again, the formula serves to turn the translated version into a text that sounds and reads like a conventional chivalric romance with which the Ferrarese would be familiar.

To be sure, Boiardo is not totally dependent on romance formulas to move from one section of the translation to the next, although he usually incorporates some form of transition at these narrative junctures. But the attention to transitions distinguishes passages in the translation from Herodotus's original. Where the original moves abruptly from one section to the next without any guidance from the narrator, Boiardo, even without the romance formula, usually adds something to bridge the two parts of the narrative. He may add a single sentence (B46r=H2.45); he may summarize what has been described or anticipate what is to come (B150r=H4.167); he may even revert to a Herodotean-sounding transition, a simple "I have said and I shall speak" formula, introducing a transitional passage where the original has none (B120r=H4.15).

Perhaps the most interesting, albeit less typical, feature of the romancified translation is a passage in which the narrator intervenes to remind the reader of a passage encountered earlier in the narrative. In the Herodotean original the narrator only intervenes once in this way (4.82, mentioned above). Such intervention, however, is a common feature of the narrative disposition of the *Innamorato*. Indeed the romance poet regularly addresses his audience as he resumes a story line so that the reader/listener may reorient himself to the narrative. At B72v Boiardo renders the Greek text fairly accurately:

> Tenne Psamio sei anni solamente il regno e mori nella impresa di Ethiopia ove era passato con grande esercito et Aprio suo figliuolo hebbe il regno il principio del quale hebbe fortunatissimo impero che soggiogo il regno di Sidonia e vinse i Phenici in battaglia navale e prese la Citta di Tyro. Ma non dovendo la fortuna ne à esso ne ad altrui tenire ferma fidanza *gli intervenne quello che al presente narrero con poche parole reservando à mostrarlo piu difusamente quando sero giunto a dire delle cose d'Aphrica.*" (emphasis mine)

Psamio reigned for only six years and died during the Ethiopian adventure where he had passed with a large army, when Apries, his son, began to rule. At the beginning of his reign, Apries was most fortunate, for he subjugated the kingdom of Sidon and, conquering the Phoenicians in a naval battle, he took the city of Tyre. But since fortune did not have to be faithful to him or to his father, he suffered what I shall briefly narrate now, waiting to tell the story more fully when I arrive at the point where I shall speak of the things of Africa.

True to his word, after a brief description of a defeat at the hands of the Cyrenians the narrator abandons the discussion of Apries. He promises, however, to return to the discussion later, and he does approximately seventy pages below at B148r: " . . . et a spiegate bandere combaterno presso alla fonte di Thestino, e furno in tal modo sconfitti gli Egitti che pochi de essi ritornarno nella patria. Per la qual si rebellarno ad Aprio *come è detto di sopra nel secondo libro*" (emphasis mine). (. . . With flags unfurled they fought near the fountain of Thestinus and the Egyptians were defeated such that few returned to their country. For which reason they rebelled against Apries, as was said above in the second book.) The passage is an accurate translation of H4.159 except for the last clause, "come è detto di sopra nel secondo libro," which Boiardo has added to the text. This addition makes the text easier to follow, and at the same time it renders it more like a romance. Perhaps the reference to "libro" points Boiardo's audience toward the bookish world of the romance. At the beginning of this chapter, I distinguished the oral "cantari" from the written culture of the Italian romance artist. Despite the feigned postures of orality throughout the *Innamorato,* Boiardo's world is decidedly that of the book.

A detail regularly appears in the transitions, both in the original and in the translation, that broaches the issue of fiction versus history. Often at these self-reflexive moments in the narrative there is an emphasis on the method of the historian. The clearest example of this is Herodotus's habit of commenting on the quality of the sources of information he is about to relate. As he moves into a new section he often casts doubt on the veracity of his sources. His comments at times may even suggest that his sources are merely alleged. At one point early in the work, for example, he claims: "I mean then to be guided in what I write by some of the Persians who desire not to make a fine tale of the story of Cyrus but to tell the truth, though there are no less than three other accounts of Cyrus which I could give" (H1.95). He then rejects a story that Cyrus was nursed by a bitch in the wild, proposing instead, as a rationalization of the legend, that Cyrus was raised by a woman whose name means "dog" in the Median language (H1.110ff.). Since Herodotus is rejecting a story that is clearly the stuff of folklore, it is easy to assume that the story of which he approves is true—at least many readers have apparently done so.[66] And yet the story of the Median woman named "Dog" is as ridiculous as the rejected tale. Such manipulation (and invention) of sources raises legitimate doubts in the reader's mind about the veracity of the historical project as a whole. Thus, one wonders about Boiardo's program when, in one sentence of the prologue, he claims that Herodotus has brought Greek history out of the realm of fiction: "Sono per lui manifestate le Grece hystorie che tra le fabule nascose erano . . ." (724). (By him are made manifest stories of Greek history that were hidden among fables. . . .) Whereas, in another sentence, he observes "che niuna cosa si legge più maravigliosa" (725). (that one doesn't read anything more wondrous.) Herodotean history in Boiardo's rendering satisfies two seemingly different urges: the urge for true and verifiable history and the urge for the pleasures of marvelous, incredible romance. Boiardo's Herodotus will take us along the borders of fact and fiction, of history (or epic) and romance.

Boiardo carefully translates passages on sources and method, such as the one on Cyrus: " . . . [io] scrivendo non secondo coloro che hanno voluto abelire la cosa: ma secondo che e la verità sappendo molto bene la vita di Cyrro essere stata scritta in altre maniere" (B22v). (. . . writing not according to those who wanted to render the subject beautiful, but according to the truth about Cyrus's life, knowing full well that others have written about it in different ways.) To be sure, in his guise as translator he has an interest in rendering the passage accurately, but as a poet, whose *Innamorato* is grounded in the historical setting of Carolingian Europe, his interest lies in the topic itself. Boiardo may even overtranslate a Herodotean passage to contrast the functions of poets and historians more sharply: "E certamente questi duoi nomi Eridano e chasiteride che Greci sono dimostrano questa essare fittione de Poeti e non vera narratione di historici" (B106v=H3.115). (And these two names, Eridanus and Chasterix, which are Greek, demonstrate clearly that this is a fiction of poets and not a true narrative of historians.) Here the translator has added the final clause, "e non vera narratione di historici," to make his point unambiguous: historians tell the truth, while poets fabricate lies. It is as if Boiardo wanted to make the passage sound even more Herodotean, which he does by focusing the audience's attention on the boundaries between poetry and history.

The line between poetry and history dissolves, however, and the doubling hand of the poet/translator becomes visible in the poetry that Herodotus cites throughout his prose text.[67] Like most authors of classical prose, Herodotus quotes poets, mainly Homer, to support geographical, historical, and anthropological details in his work. He also frequently reports the prophecies dispensed by various oracles around Greece, which were uttered in the dactylic hexameters of Homeric poetry. The incorporation of Homeric verses into the history allows the translator to be even more overtly poetic in the midst of the historical essay. Boiardo's renderings inevitably veer far from the original. In the transitional passages Boiardo gives his prose a romance cast; here, however, the generic infiltration of another genre is not the primary issue. If it were he might have tried to render the hexameters and occasional elegiac couplets with octave stanzas. In these short poems, ranging from a single verse to a dozen or so lines, Boiardo employs the terza rima of Dante's *Commedia,* perhaps to imitate the somber tone of the divine utterance itself.

In conclusion, Boiardo achieved the romancification of Herodotean narrative through a program of compromise, decking the classical history in the trappings of romance. Taking the text of Herodotus, whether the Greek original or Valla's Latin version, and recasting it into a Romance tongue became an occasion for the romancification of the text's generic structure. Perhaps in this compromise between romance and history there was the possibility of a future influence on the relationship between romance and epic in Ferrarese literary history, where the legacy of humanistic teaching greatly complicated the reception of classical and medieval literature. Boiardo's translation of Herodotus constantly moves the reader between the classical work and the model of romance, much as Ariosto's *Furioso* will do for its readers of the next century. The result of Boiardo's deliberate obfuscation of the boundaries between romance and epic was a new kind of work, theretofore unseen and certainly unclassifiable in the traditional taxonomies of literary types as they were understood in the Quattrocento. *Storie* is an accurate rendition of the title the manuscript tradition had assigned to Herodotus's work, but the title in Italian also happily contains within its plural form the possibilities of the two kinds of stories that Boiardo announces as his subject matter in the *Innamorato:* the "vera" and "bella" stories of the past. Thus, "storie," the plurality of stories and/or history, suggests the boundaries between the historical truths associated with epic and the beautiful lies of romance.

Boiardo's exploration of the problematics between romance and epic is clearest in the *Innamorato.* In his poem, although there are very few actual thematic and lexical allusions to Herodotus, one can make a case—as I have tried to do here—for certain structural parallels between their narratives. Surprisingly, one can make a similar case for another classical work, which the Quattrocento considered the most epic of all the works from antiquity, Vergil's *Aeneid.* Even in it Boiardo found a model for the construction of his romance narrative. But just how did he read Vergil's poem?

The Phantom of Vergil's Narrative

Vergil, against whom Dante measured himself in composing the masterpiece of medieval literature, remained an important poetic model beyond the Middle Ages and into the Renaissance. Many critical studies, including several recent ones, document his permanence in European culture over, now, two millennia.[68] The Italian Quattrocento played a crucial role in this ongoing reception of the Roman poet. And within that century Boiardo did his part to accommodate the poet to the literary culture of his Ferrara. Despite Boiardo's entanglement in the medievalizing world of romance, his poetry in many ways is in tune with Vergilian classicism. To adapt Herodotus to the world of romance may not have been too difficult because of the affinities, thematic and structural, between the *Histories* and the *Innamorato;* to incorporate Vergil into the world of his narrative poem was another matter entirely and, as we shall see, the occasion of a poetic tour de force.

Like many Renaissance poets,[69] Boiardo alluded to the corpus of Vergilian works extensively in his poems and used the sequence of Vergil's poems—from pastoral through didactic to epic—as a guide for establishing a sequence of compositions with which to demarcate the progress of his poetic career.[70] Vergilian pastoral informs both his Italian and his Latin lyric poetry;[71] allusions in his lyrics and in the *Innamorato* attest to his familiarity with the *Georgics;*[72] and throughout the *Innamorato* he refers to the *Aeneid,* especially to book 4 and the battle scenes in the second half of Vergil's epic.[73]

In the remainder of this chapter I consider an allusion to the structural design of the *Aeneid* in the *Innamorato*'s narrative, which leads the reader circuitously to the thematic center of the Latin poem. In *Innamorato* 1.5, Boiardo imitates a scene from *Aeneid* 10, where a phantom Aeneas, fabricated by Juno, lures Turnus away from the battlefield; analogously, in his imitation the Renaissance poet uses romance narrative techniques to lure the reader away from the epic source of his scene in the *Innamorato.* We might call the source he draws from Vergilian epic, then, a phantom, for it flitters tenuously in the midst of his romance narrative, but it moves away when approached, seeming other than it is. This particular example is indicative of a general pattern, I believe, in Boiardo's imitation of the *Aeneid.* It is as if Boiardo imitates certain epic details, only subsequently to cloud their presence in his narrative, to rid his narrative of their traces. Alberto Limentani has characterized the tendency of some literary artists to cover their tracks in this way as the removal of the source from the imitation ("la rimozione della fonte").[74] To put it in my terms: I would say, rather, that Boiardo blends, fuses, compromises the classical source with the chivalric form in his imitation of Vergilian epic to the point of seeming to remove it from his romance narrative.

A commonplace of Vergilian criticism, extending back to the first readers of the *Aeneid,* is that its narrative combines both Homeric epics.[75] Although Vergil wrote approximately 250 years after the Alexandrian debates over the generic forms of the epic and the epyllion, the narrative of the *Aeneid* is a response to questions raised in the debate. Vergil's solution to the problem of the appropriate size of the epic narrative is to combine the polarized positions set forth in the dispute. His poem is an epic (following the example of Apollonius Rhodius), but it reduces the forty-eight books of Homeric epic poetry to twelve, as if to respect the dictum supposedly articulated by Callimachus, the archrival of Apollonius: "Big book, big evil." Vergil's epic is something of a contradiction in its structural design, for it combines the structure of Greek epic with elements of much shorter genres—lyric, drama, romance.

The *Aeneid,* then, is not merely a combination of the Homeric poems; it also condenses the dual Homeric precedent. Brooks Otis among other more recent critics has given currency to the description of the Vergilian epic as a poem of halves: the Odyssean books 1–6, which represent the wanderings of Aeneas from Troy to Latium; and the Iliadic books 7–12, which describe the fierce struggle between the Trojans and the indigenous peoples of Latium.[76] This schematization of the *Aeneid* is based, in part, on a thematic analysis. Its first half deals with themes associated with the *Odyssey:* Aeneas wanders through a landscape of marvels; at the same time, he is morally errant in his failure to press on to his Roman finale. The second half of the *Aeneid* is decidedly Iliadic in its representation of battlefield combat and in its scrutiny of the causes and consequences of war. But Vergil's imitation of Homer is not so slavish as to restrict specific material to one half of the poem or the other. There are significant allusions to the *Iliad* in the first half of his poem, as, for example, the funeral games for Anchises in *Aeneid* 5, which recall the games for Patroclus in *Iliad* 22. Similarly, the second half of the *Aeneid,* the Iliadic half, contains Odyssean marvels, as, for example, when the Trojan ships metamorphose into sea nymphs in *Aeneid* 9.77–122.

Themes enable a Homeric classification of each half of the *Aeneid,* as do the narrative structural patterns of the poem. From Donatus to Otis, critics have considered narrative design in their schematization of the *Aeneid* into distinct halves. One expects an open-ended, nonlinear narrative in an Odyssean tale of moral and literal wandering—the kind of narrative that depicts the endless actions of the knights-errant in the typical chivalric romance. By contrast, one expects the narrative of epic warfare to be closed and linear, to have a teleological orientation, to be designed around structural principles that move toward a definitive conclusion, toward the death of a warrior like Hector in Homer's *Iliad.* It is with this specific Homeric precedent in mind that Vergil positions the dramatic slaughter of Turnus at the very end of his epic—an abruptness that treats the generic convention so seriously as to trouble generations of readers to come.

Since the reader associates these narrative patterns with specific themes, a poet following Homer, if he is aware of the patterns, can play with the reader's expectations of these conventions. Vergil's earliest readers may have been surprised to find the description of Anchises's funeral before the end of the first half of the *Aeneid.* Indeed such a scene suggests the reduction of narrative possibilities: death and a grand funeral should come at the end of the poem. But, in a sense, the games of *Aeneid* 5 do signal an end, not to the narrative of the poem, of course, but to a moment in the life of Aeneas. With his father dead, Aeneas is now obliged to proceed to another stage in his career, to move from the private life of the son to the public realm of the father, and on to the sphere of the founding father. The intimation of an ending has thematic relevance even at this point in the narrative.

A similar confusion occurs for the reader in *Aeneid* 10, a book of battle in the Iliadic half of the poem, when Juno spirits Turnus away from the battlefield. The removal of Turnus interrupts the narrative of killing in book 10, postponing temporarily the poem's relentless race toward Turnus's own death. We follow Turnus as he chases a phantom Aeneas from the lines of battle to the seashore, where they board an empty ship that sails mysteriously out to sea. The phantom vanishes, and Turnus finds himself sailing on a boat that has much in common with what one critic has called, in a different context, the boat of romance.[77] The boat of romance carries "knights-errant to whatever adventure may be currently available to give them an opportunity to demonstrate their prowess. The enchanted boat, which travels without human guidance carrying the hero from episode to episode, is a common topos of chivalric romance."[78] For the character of epic, however, confinement to such a boat is the narrative equivalent of being caught in the doldrums. The place for the epic hero to demonstrate his prowess is on the battlefield, away from which the boat of romance inevitably transports him: "In epic narrative, which moves toward a predetermined end, the magic ship signals a digression from a central plot line. . . ."[79] Or so it would seem.

The episode of Turnus chasing the phantom Aeneas has several functions. The passage does indeed provide an interlude to the book's extended description of violence. But it does more. By introducing the characteristics of one generic mode into another, of romance into epic, it effectively (even if momentarily) obfuscates the generic boundaries between romance and epic. The passage thus becomes a site in the text for an investigation into the similarities and differences between the kinds of narrative associated with the two genres.[80] Themes, as well, are juxtaposed in the passage: epic battle and death versus the deviation and escape associated with romance. But the episode subverts the conventional expectations of the two genres, for a close reading of *Aeneid* 10 (as I believe Boiardo's was) leads to the conclusion that the space between the genres is not as clearly defined as one might expect. When Turnus enters into what appears to be a romance digression, he has a very un-romance-like glimpse of his death. His chase after the phantom and his subsequent ride on the boat re-create Aeneas's tracking and dispatching of him at the end of the entire narrative. From the perspective of romance, in other words, the reader has a vision of the end of the epic.[81] Boiardo's imitation of the episode suggests that he used Vergil's passage as an occasion for his own meditation on the generic implications of different narrative structures. After interpreting Vergil's poem as a work that compromises epic narrative on generic grounds, Boiardo then used the *Aeneid* as a source of compromise in his own poem.

To appreciate how Boiardo's imitation of the *Aeneid* focuses our attention on Vergil's narrative, we must first look at the sequence of events in the respective passages of the model and the imitation. Even a perfunctory comparison reveals how the modern poet modeled a section of his narrative on the ancient's. The outline of each passage is as follows:

Aeneid 10.606–88:

Juno asks Jupiter to withdraw Turnus permanently from the fighting (606–20); the king of the gods denies her request, but he does allow her to remove Turnus from the battlefield temporarily (621–32); Juno descends to earth (633–35); she fashions an image of Aeneas to entice Turnus away from the fighting (636–42); the false Aeneas briefly engages Turnus in battle, only to run away (643–46); Turnus calls after the phantom, reminding him of his bride (647–52); the phantom leaps aboard a ship moored nearby, Juno sends the ship out to sea, and the phantom Aeneas vanishes into thin air (653–64); the narrator reports that Aeneas is killing many men in Turnus's absence (661–62); Turnus prays to Jupiter in disgrace over having left the battlefield; he worries how his men are faring without him (665–81); three times

Turnus contemplates suicide by sword versus swimming back to the shore to rejoin the fight, but each time Juno intervenes to check any rash behavior (682–86); the ship carries Turnus to his hometown (687–88).

Innamorato 1.5.13–56:

In distant Cathay, Angelica yearns for Ranaldo (13–16); in order to win Ranaldo's heart, she seeks the services of her prisoner, Malagise, a magus and Ranaldo's cousin (17–22); Malagise agrees to act as go-between in exchange for his own liberty, and he flies off into the night on the back of a demon (23–24); having arrived in Barcelona, he finds Ranaldo before daybreak, who adamantly refuses to have anything to do with Angelica (25–30); Malagise conjures up demons who intentionally confuse the arrangements for a chivalrous duel between Ranaldo and Gradasso (31–35); Ranaldo goes to what he believes to be the appointed site for battle, and one of Malagise's demons comes in disguise as Gradasso (36–40); the two fight and the phantom Gradasso flees (40–43); Ranaldo calls after the phantom, reminding him of the horse, Baiardo (43–44); the phantom flies aboard a ship harbored nearby, Ranaldo follows, and as the ship goes out to sea the phantom vanishes into thin air (45–47); Ranaldo prays to God in disgrace; he worries how his men are faring without him (48–52); three times he contemplates suicide by sword versus suicide by drowning, but each time fear of hellfire checks his actions (53); the ship carries Ranaldo to a garden isle (54–56).

The structural parallels between the episodes in the *Innamorato* and the *Aeneid* are obvious. But buried as it is within the poem, at a point in the narrative that does not call attention to itself, Boiardo's imitation is not as noticeable as it might be were it elsewhere in the poem. Contrast this series of allusions to Vergil with, say, the allusions in the *Furioso* to the beginning and end of the *Aeneid,* and it becomes apparent that Boiardo's imitation is more subtle than might appear at first glance. There is also some discretion in Boiardo's recapitulation of the ancient model. Indeed, the imitator's divergence from the model reveals as much about his reading of it as do those sections that document his imitation more directly.

One notices immediately that Boiardo's amplification of the model increases it greatly, from 82 lines to 344. Such imitative prolixity is characteristic of Boiardo's relationship with prior texts, classical and medieval. In fact, in chivalric romance in general it is common for the romancer to increase the length of the previous version of his story.[82]

Boiardo amplifies the model in several ways, all of which are conventional in the romance tradition. At the most fundamental level, the poet may multiply a single word of the Latin model into several words: "[Q]uo fugis, Aenea?" (649) expands to "Aspetta un poco, re gagliardo" (43.7). (Where are you fleeing, Aeneas?) (Slow down, valiant king!) The *verba singula* of the original are doubled and tripled into new phrases in the translation-imitation.

Another way to amplify the original is to describe a borrowed character in more detail, as is the case with Boiardo's version of the phantom. Juno fabricates a phantom Aeneas to entice Turnus away; likewise Malagise makes a phantom Gradasso to lure Ranaldo away. But Boiardo (not to be outdone by his model) creates a second phantom from the hand of Malagise, a herald who first reports to one side and then, after a magical Dantesque transformation, to the other. Boiardo trundles out three phantoms to Vergil's one in a crude form of numerical amplification.

Asides to the audience—often as *sententia,* proverbs, maxims— also embellish the original, as when the poet says to his listeners, "Or non me domandate / Se meraviglia Ranaldo se dona" (47.1–2). (Don't ask me now if Ranaldo's shocked.) But the typical romance poet most often amplifies the model by digressing from its narrative, as Boiardo does throughout the *Innamorato.*

We observe a variation of amplification by digression in Boiardo's imitation of *Aeneid* 10, where he uses Vergil to digress from Vergil. The episode begins when Angelica sets out to assuage her pains of love. She plans to release her prisoner, Malagise, Ranaldo's cousin, in order to bring him into her employ. It is not surprising that the poet turns to a classical allusion to gloss the pain of Angelica, who suffers from her unrequited love for Ranaldo much as Dido suffers from Aeneas near the opening of *Aeneid* 4. Boiardo writes (1.5.14.3–8):

> Come cerva ferita di saetta,
> Che al lungo tempo cresce il suo dolore,
> E quanto il corso più veloce affretta,
> Più sangue perde et ha pena maggiore:
> Così ognor cresce alla donzella il caldo,
> Anci il foco nel cor, che ha per Ranaldo.

> And like an arrow-wounded deer
> Whose grief increases over time,
> Who loses blood and hurts the more
> The faster that it runs away,
> Each day the maid grows hotter for
> Ranaldo; that is, her heart flames.

82

Compare these lines with the Vergilian model (4.66–73):

> est mollis flamma medullas
> interea et tacitum vivit sub pectore vulnus.
> uritur infelix Dido totaque vagatur
> urbe furens, qualis coniecta cerva sagitta,
> quam procul incautam nemora inter Cresia fixit
> pastor agens telis liquitque volatile ferrum
> nescius: illa fuga silvas saltusque peragrat
> Dictaeos; haeret lateri letalis harundo.[83]

All the while the flame devours her tender heart-strings, and deep in her breast lives the silent wound. Unhappy Dido burns, and throughout the city wanders in frenzy—even as a hind, smitten by an arrow, which, all unwary, amid the Cretan woods, a shepherd hunting with darts has pierced from afar, leaving in her the winged steel, unknowing. She in flight ranges from the Dictaean woods and glades, but fast to her side clings the deadly shaft.[84]

Boiardo omits the entire portion of the simile dedicated to the *nescius pastor,* that part of the comparison that gives the Vergilian passage its poignancy. Aeneas as unknowing shepherd has wounded Dido so gravely that she is doomed to die like a wounded doe. By leaving this part of the model aside, and by alluding only to the lovesickness of Angelica, Boiardo diminishes the tragic impact of the allusion to Vergil. Indeed he shows little concern for the tragic ramifications of *Aeneid* 4.

Boiardo's character falls in and out of love with such regularity that it is difficult to take her seriously as Vergil's wounded doe. The reader of the *Innamorato* certainly does not expect the cause of the poem's "amore" to commit suicide at this point in the narrative, if at all. The princess of Cathay, much more than her putative model, is a witch, whose witchcraft repeatedly thwarts any tragic turns in the narrative. When she laments that Ranaldo does not love her, she reflects on how she has vainly endeavored to win his heart with herbs, enchantments, and gems (17.7–8). Her employment of Malagise is merely another in a long series of magical ploys. In Boiardo's ironic imitation, Vergil's Dido takes on some of the characteristics of Ovid's Medea.

Playing with an established Vergilian character like Dido to the point of ridicule indicates Boiardo's willingness to transgress his literary models. Ultimately, of course, transforming Angelica into Dido and Medea teases the reader. The reader is situated precariously between an image of Dido as the bleeding doe and Angelica, the very energetic mermaid, who jets off to an underwater prison so that she might take out a magical contract with Malagise. Angelica's Vergilian and anti-Vergilian characteristics suggest other responses to Vergilian narrative on the part of Boiardo.

Juno descends from heaven in her chariot to rescue Turnus in a miniature version of a constitutive motif of classical epic.[85] Similarly, Malagise's flight from Cathay to Barcelona on the back of a demon is one of the elements that contributes to the generic structure of Franco-Italian romance. To the point in the text shortly before the phantom jumps aboard ship, Boiardo follows the narrative organization of his model closely. But just before his phantom boards the ship, we begin to perceive differences. Consider the classical text.

In *Aeneid* 10.645–50, Turnus attacks the phantom as it moves along the battle line. The phantom then turns and runs toward the shore:

> instat cui [imago] Turnus stridentemque eminus hastam
> conicit; illa dato vertit vestigia tergo.
> tum vero Aenean aversum ut cedere Turnus
> credidit atque animo spem turbidus hausit inanem:
> "quo fugis, Aenea? thalamos ne desere pactos;
> hac dabitur dextra tellus quaesita per undas."

> Turnus went for it, and at long range he threw his whirring spear;
> the phantom turned tail and wheeled its steps about. Then it was that
> Turnus, since he believed that Aeneas had turned away in retreat
> and wildly drank in an empty hope in his mind, cried: "Where are
> you fleeing, Aeneas? Don't abandon your promised marriage! The
> land you have sought over the seas will be granted you by this right
> hand of mine."[86]

The taunting question "Where are you fleeing, Aeneas?" quickly yields to the more pointed remark: "Don't abandon your promised marriage." Turnus tries to arrest "Aeneas" with this veiled reference to his dynastic (and hence sexual) responsibilities. To leave the marriage bed empty is not the better part of valor. The subsequent claim is also a stinging critique of Aeneas's virility: "The land you have sought over the seas will be granted you by this right hand of mine." This is a macabre allusion to the earth that will, in his estimatation, make up Aeneas's burial mound.[87] For Turnus, Aeneas is neither a satisfactory dynast nor a competent fighter.

The note of sarcasm in Turnus's remarks can barely hide his growing frustration with the phantom. The verb to describe Turnus's speech, *vociferans* (shouting), suggests the limitations of what Turnus says. The narrator knows, Juno knows, the reader knows: the words are mean-ingless. Or are they? We learn in the next two verses that Turnus is brandishing a sword when he makes his sarcastic offer to the being that he thinks is Aeneas (10.651–52): "talia vociferans sequitur strictumque coruscat / mucronem, nec ferre videt sua gaudia ventos." (Shouting this he went in pursuit, flashing his drawn sword, and he did not see that the winds were carrying away his hopes of joy!) He is threatening "Aeneas," but the threat is an empty one, not because he is incapable of following it through, but because the threat falls on figmented air, a work of Juno's imagination that serves as part of her desperate attempt to save Turnus. Here she succeeds, for her charge does not realize that the wind is carrying away his triumph, literally, his "causes for joy" (10.652).

The image of Turnus screaming after a phantom warrior, indeed the scene as a whole, grimly foreshadows his own death at the end of the poem, when Aeneas comes screaming after him, before killing him and offering him up as a symbolic victim of the new Troy.[88] In a sense the conquest is complete when the Trojan invader kills the leader of the Rutulians. But Turnus's death is not merely evidence of a new political reality in Italy. Aeneas kills him in a fit of rage brought on by the sight of Pallas's baldric, which Turnus sports as a medal of conquest. In killing Pallas, son of Aeneas's ally, Evander, Turnus had driven Aeneas to swear revenge. Pallas dies, tellingly, just before the point in book 10 where Juno spirits Turnus away (10.439–509). The narrative concatenation suggests that the events are linked in some way. Turnus has no control over the subsequent events,[89] least of all his death, which in the poem's final lines transforms him, too, into a phantom fleeing to the underworld.

Jupiter dismisses Juno's desire to save Turnus before she is given an opportunity to make a case for her actions (625–27). But he does grant her the temporary reprieve that allows the goddess to set in motion the chain of events in book 10 (622–25). That Juno unwittingly provides her charge a glimpse of his death precisely while she is trying to save his life is ironic. Her intervention compromises the narrative by affecting its structure and, consequently, the reader's perception of the poem. The poet, in what might seem a strategy of illogical legerdemain, provides the reader with a glimpse of the end of the narrative in an episode that seems, at first glance, to detour from the path toward the poem's conclusion. What Juno (and many commentators) interpret as a digression is in fact a foreshadowing of death that takes us to the heart of narrative resolution. What seems merely the interposition of romance into epic is in actuality an exploration of the epic's most appropriate theme: death. Boiardo's appreciation of epic and romance, his ability to compromise the one with

the other, enabled him, I think, to see the scene in this way as he re-created
it in his poem.

The imitation at 1.5.43–44 depends on *Aeneid* 10.645–52. Here are
the Italian text and translation:

> Ben prese il tempo il demonio scaltrito:
> Volta le spalle, e comincia a fuggire.
> Crede Ranaldo averlo sbigotito,
> E de allegrezza sé non può soffrire.
> Quel maledetto al mar se n'è fuggito;
> Dietro Ranaldo se 'l mette a seguire,
> Dicendo:—Aspetta un poco, re gagliardo:
> Chi fugge, non cavalca il mio Baiardo.

> Or debbe far un re sì fatta prova?
> Non ti vergogni le spalle voltare?
> Torna nel campo e Baiardo ritrova:
> La meglior bestia non puoi cavalcare.
> Ben è guarnito et ha la sella nova,
> E pur ier sira lo feci ferrare.
> Vien, te lo piglia: a che mi tieni a bada?
> Eccolo quivi, in ponta a questa spada.—

> Ma quel demonio nïente l'aspetta,
> Anci pariva dal vento portato.
> Passa ne l'acqua, e pare una saetta,
> E sopra quel naviglio fo montato.
> Ranaldo incontinente in mar se getta,
> E poi che sopra al legno fo arivato,
> Vede il nemico, e un gran colpo gli mena:
> Quel per la poppa salta alla carena.

> Seizing his chance, the clever demon
> Turned on his heel and dashed away.
> Ranaldo's sure he's frightened him
> And can't conceal his ecstasy.
> That demon headed for the sea
> And close behind, Ranaldo charged,
> While yelling, "Slow down, valiant king!
> Run off, and you can't ride Baiardo!"

"Now, should a king act in this manner—
Running away? Aren't you ashamed?
Look, here's Baiardo, on the plain.
You'll never ride a better beast!
He's furnished well, his saddle's new,
and yesterday I had him shoed!
Come on! Take him! Why make me wait?
Here he is—on this point, this blade!"

That demon waits for nothing, but
Seems to be carried by the wind.
He crossed the water like an arrow
And climbed aboard the waiting ship.
Ranaldo waded through the waves,
And when he'd scaled the wooden hull
He saw his enemy and swung.
From poop to keel, that demon jumped.

Boiardo's version repeats the mechanics of fight and flight, as the phantom makes an abrupt about-face and flees (*Aen* 10.646 + *OI* 1.5.43.2). The vocabulary of such behavior occurs in both texts: *fugis* and words of flight (*Aen* 10.649, 656, 670) find parallels in the Italian (*OI* 1.5.43.2, 5, 8); *sequitur* finds its match in the verb "seguire" (*Aen* 10.651 + *OI* 1.43.6). There are, besides these linguistic similarities, other points in common. Just as Turnus believes he has overcome Aeneas (*Turnus credidit*, 647–48), so Ranaldo believes he has frightened Gradasso (43.3). Neither warrior contains his surprised delight at suddenly winning the battle by default—a delight that both poets express through circumlocutions. Vergil's phrase "confused in his mind [Turnus] drank up the empty hope" (648) becomes Boiardo's more simple description of a Ranaldo unable "to contain himself for his happiness" (43.4).

Each warrior addresses the respective phantom with an initial question that is not, in and of itself, noteworthy (649 + 43.7). But for each, the first question yields to a charge that the warrior in flight is forsaking something he desires and which he should return to acquire: in the case of Aeneas, his fiancée, Lavinia (649); in the case of Gradasso, the prized horse, Baiardo (43.8). Both speakers imply that flight is unseemly behavior for a groom-to-be, on the one hand, and for a king, on the other, but only Boiardo's text states this clearly (44.1).

Boiardo's imitation diverges from the model in details of propriety. Stanza 44 (with the exception of the verse concerning the sword, 44.8, for which cf. *Aen* 10.651–52) expands upon the reference at 43.8 to the horse, which, Ranaldo believes, Gradasso is honor-bound to win. Boiardo replaces Vergil's woman with a horse—a detail in keeping with his consistent rewriting of the chivalric tradition to create knights who venerate their ladies and horses with the same affection.[90] In other words, Boiardo's amplification (and alteration) of this Vergilian detail is tailored to the literary culture for which he is adapting the model.

Each character, once on board ship, realizes that he is deserting his companions and laments accordingly. As the outline of the passages above shows, there are several parallels in the laments of each man. Turnus presents himself with two options, however unrealistic the choice may be: he can kill himself, or he can jump overboard, swim back to shore, and return to the fight. Ranaldo, however, reduces the choice to a decision between modes of dying: he can kill himself by sword or by drowning. What for Turnus is a moral dilemma in the drama that momentarily reveals the poem's end becomes a short melodrama in the hands of Boiardo. Imitation yields to parody.

Vergil's episode concludes at lines 687–88, when Turnus is able to circle back to the theater of war in order to resume fighting against the Trojans. But even here, in a seemingly innocuous topographical detail, there is an ominous reference to the end of the poem, to Turnus's death. The warrior is led back to the city of his birth: "et patris antiquam Dauni defertur ad urbem" (688). The text is explicit: "he is carried back to the ancient town of his father, Daunus." This reference to Daunus anticipates the passage at the end of the poem where Turnus refers to his father as he pleads with Aeneas for his life (12.934). It is another example of a detail from 10 that illuminates the darkness of the poem's conclusion.

Boiardo's imitation diverges from the model at this crucial point in the narrative. Ranaldo's ship ferries him to yet another adventure, to a garden on an island far out at sea (1.5.55.6–8—56.1–2):

> se vede arivare
> Ad un giardin, dove è un palagio adorno;
> Il mare ha quel giardin d'intorno intorno.
>
> Or qui lasciar lo voglio nel giardino,
> Che sentirete poi mirabil cosa, . . .

> he sees he's reached
> a palace in a paradise,
> A garden guarded by the sea.

> I'll leave him in that garden now—
> I'll tell about its marvels later.

Just as Ranaldo is about to begin this next adventure, the narrator abruptly breaks off the tale in stanza 56. The episode of Ranaldo on the ship, we discover, is merely one in a sequence of stories, with little claim to uniqueness in the development of the narrative.

But how does Boiardo respond to the disguised centrality of the Turnus episode at *Aeneid* 10, 606–88? What we see in the episode of Ranaldo is the stuff of quintessential romance with not even the slightest intimation of death. How, then, does the modern author allude to the stunning revelation of Turnus's death-to-come in his imitation of the scene?

The allusion to the central moment of the Vergilian scene lies in the analogy between Turnus and Ranaldo and their respective relations to death and life. Turnus anticipates the end of his life and, at the same time, the end of the epic narrative; Ranaldo's actions, however, are a prefiguration of the non-ending quality of his life and the continuous narrative of romance. We learn in the scene from the *Innamorato* that Ranaldo is doomed to reenact one romance adventure after another, sailing off in the boat of romance time and time again. The literary tradition before Boiardo represents him in this way, and it continues to focus on the character as the embodiment of precisely those romance possibilities that frustrate epic: deviation, adventure, flirtation with everlasting life.

Ariosto, for his part, tempts tradition and teases his reader in the process by resuming the scene from *Innamorato* 1.5 deep in the middle of his poem, at *Furioso* 31.91ff., where Rinaldo and Gradasso arrange yet once more to duel.[91] To conclude their fight would bring at least temporary closure to one strand in the overarching narrative that connects the two poems. The Ariostan narrator suggests as much to the audience with his parenthetical aside: "credo ch'altrove voi l'abbiate letto" (31.91.2). (I think you will have read this elsewhere.) "Altrove," of course, refers to Boiardo's text, which the *Furioso* means to complete: Rinaldo now hopes to save face (31.109); Malagigi (his name has changed slightly from Malagise) dare not intervene again lest he further exacerbate Rinaldo (31.108); and Gradasso expects finally to win Baiardo, the prized horse (31.104). Adverbs emphasize the difference between Boiardo's then and Ariosto's now. In the end, however, there is no difference between then and now, for one interruption after another prevents the two warriors from finishing their duel in Ariosto's poem, too. Once Rinaldo, always Rinaldo. Indeed, in Ariosto's version Rinaldo not only fails to complete the private duel with Gradasso; he also misses the epic battle of Lampedusa in

Furioso 40–42, while he busies himself with his own adventures in 42–43, and thus in a renegade plot extends the narrative of the *Furioso* for the better part of two cantos before it returns to its epic conclusion. Tasso, too, has difficulty adapting his traditional character to the epic goal of the *Liberata*'s narrative, but he finally succeeds in harnessing his hero in the last quarter of the poem. In his earlier work, *Rinaldo,* the namesake of the poem plays his hearty romancing self. As late as the mid-nineteenth century, a "cantastorie" of the Veneto could refer to Rinaldo as a rascal who fathered over fifty bastards![92] The various fortunes of Rinaldo in later literature are consistent with the behavior of Ranaldo in *Innamorato* 1.5.[93]

The portrayal of Ranaldo in Boiardo's rewriting of *Aeneid* 10 suggests an appreciation of Vergil's poem as a repository of different generic possibilities. But in Boiardo's imitation of the Vergilian text these different generic modes are not delineated simply into Iliadic epic and Odyssean romance portions. The Renaissance poet's interpretation of the *Aeneid* as an epic with a romance interlude whose digression further emphasizes the poem's very epic-ness enables Boiardo to compromise the Vergilian source in his poem. That is, Boiardo's apparently slavish adaptation of the passage from *Aeneid* 10, which is followed by a predictable and anticipated romancelike diversion from the narrative (Ranaldo's adventure in the garden), in actuality masks the subtlety of his reading of the Vergilian epic's romance section as quintessential epic.

When Ariosto's Rinaldo accounts for having failed to show up to fight Gradasso in Boiardo's version of his life, he claims to be telling "la vera istoria" (*Furioso* 31.101.7). The phrase is lifted from Boiardo's prior claim to relate "the true story" of none other than Gradasso (1.1.4.1); consequently, the phrase demarcates the literary history and the allusive poetics we are examining as we move from Ariosto to Boiardo. Of course, that same "true story" leads us back further to Vergil's poem, which provides the source for Ranaldo's absence from the fight. Boiardo, *pace* Ariosto, had been reading, and reading carefully I might add, the *Aeneid.* In the following chapters we shall observe Ariosto engaged in a similar process with works the tradition hands down to him, including the *Aeneid* and the *Innamorato.* Indeed, for the methodology of fusing classical, medieval, and contemporary sources, of reading them, at times, completely in terms of each other, Ariosto would find in Boiardo a superb example very close to home.

CHAPTER 3

Narrative Choices in Orlando Furioso

"Nascono casi, e non saprei dir quanti."

ARIOSTO

"I casi sono tanti!"

PINOCCHIO[1]

Boiardo's interpretation of Vergil enabled him to use the classical author as a source of compromise in the *Innamorato* and, thus, to satisfy the cultural requirements of alluding to works in both the classical and medieval traditions. In this chapter, as well as in the following one, I examine how Ariosto developed the *Furioso* around the same principle of compromise. The focus remains primarily on narrative construction: Ariosto's choice of Ovidian poetry as a narrative model. What proved noteworthy about the Ovidian model was its suppleness in accommodating other models within the same narrative continuum. Ariosto's recourse to particular Ovidian works did not prevent him from simultaneously alluding to other narrative paradigms.

Ariosto's Narrative Opportunism

Ariosto has an extensive repertory of metaphors that shed light on his artistic creativity. Best known, perhaps, are those passages where he adduces the vocabulary of weaving to describe his narrative construction (2.30; 13.80–81; 22.3). He also likens his task as a narrative artist to that of a musician (7.19; 8.29; 30.16–17); a sculptor (3.3–4); a navigator (46.1); and a madman (1.1–3; 3.1; 29.50). While several of these metaphors figure in the discussion below, I begin with a passage from the *Furioso* that is telling for its move away from metaphorical language to a different kind of vocabulary. At 29.50 the narrator raises the possibility that he might be a lunatic, but then he abandons that image in the name of a kind of narrative rationality. This leads him to refer to the function of poetic choice in the construction of a scene.

> Pazzia sarà, se le pazzie d'Orlando
> prometto raccontarvi ad una ad una;
> che tante e tante fur, ch'io non so quando
> finir: ma ve n'andrò scegliendo alcuna
> *solenne* et *atta* da narrar cantando,
> e ch'all'istoria mi parrà *oportuna;*
> né quella tacerò *miraculosa,*
> che fu nei Pirenei sopra Tolosa. (emphasis mine)

> It will be a mad act to promise to recount to you one by one Orlando's mad acts, which were so very many that I do not know when I should finish, but I shall merely go on choosing from them some that are dignified and appropriate for telling in song and that seem to me fit for my story; nor shall I keep still about that marvelous one that happened in the Pyrenees near Toulouse.[2]

Orlando, gone thoroughly mad at this point in the poem, engages in a vast number of prodigious feats under the influence of lunacy. The paladin's seemingly endless acts of madness challenge the narrator's ability to carry his story line forward to an appropriate conclusion. To bring some order to the narrative before it is amplified to irreducible proportions, the narrator must privilege a selection of Orlando's accomplishments; he must anthologize the knight's deeds. The kinds of stories he chooses to tell bespeak Ariosto's art of compromise: one episode will be dignified ("solenne") and appropriate ("atta"), another will be full of wonders ("miraculosa"). This vocabulary suggests the dual nature of the *Furioso,* a romance-epic that depends on both the wonders of medieval romance and the grave solemnity of the classics. But there is more.

Ariosto's artistic choices, whether they derive from epic or romance sources or are of his own invention, must have one characteristic in common; they must be opportune: "e ch'all'istoria mi parrà oportuna" (50.6).[3] The narrator (read: Ariosto) will choose only those stories of Orlando's doings (read: sources) that appear advantageous to his story (read: poem). The distinction between epic and romance aside, the prime quality of a poetic source, then, is its capacity to provide opportunities for the narrator (or poet). Faced with a multitude of possibilities of a crazy Orlando, the narrator must resort to a creative opportunism to conclude his overarching story. Likewise the poet, Ariosto, faced with an abundance of sources, must resort to an opportunistic selection of material. He must choose those sources that work best, which are often, as we shall see, those that straddle the realms of the classical epic and the medieval romance—those sources that defy the neat generic categories of epic and romance.

Tasso's *Gerusalemme Liberata,* to be considered in chapter 5, contains many passages that are full of the sort of theoretical vocabulary we find in 29.50. In Tasso's narrative one has the impression that theory sometimes impinges on the poetic language, even against the author's desire. Although such passages in Ariosto's narrative are less burdened with the anxieties that Tasso brought to bear on the creation of his poem, they are present nevertheless. Inevitably such passages in the *Furioso* focus on issues of narrative design and construction, often suggesting the most opportune way to continue the narrative.

Narrative opportunism,[4] as much an attitude toward narrative construction as an actual technique, involves capitalizing on the possibilities at hand, or so it seems. There is an air of chance to much of what the narrator and the characters in the *Furioso* do and say. Orlando, especially, is under the rule of chance, while Dame Fortune, protector of madmen, watches over him during his lunatic rage (30.15.1–4). The poet invokes opportunity as a cornucopia of possibility, although it is he, not chance, who determines the exits and entrances of a character like Orlando. The feigned serendipity of the *Furioso*'s narrative anticipates the paradoxical aesthetics of nineteenth-century romanticism, summed up aptly in the observation, "He who wishes to write down his dream must himself be very wide awake."[5] The poem's feigned serendipity was grist for Croce's mill as he sought to transform the romantic aesthetics of De Sanctian criticism into something else, into an account of the *Furioso* as a harmonious cosmos with its poet as ironic creator. Ariosto, despite appearances and claims to the contrary, knows exactly why he presents and develops certain narrative opportunities.[6]

The stanza at 29.50 follows close behind another passage on narrative, which it aptly glosses. At 29.5–7 the narrator offers three contradictory versions of an episode's ending, implying that the reader should choose the one that best suits his own interpretation. Consider the example:

> Poi che l'empio pagan molto ha sofferto
> con lunga noia quel monaco audace,
> e che gli ha detto invan ch'al suo deserto

senza lei può tornar quando gli piace;
e che nuocer si vede a viso aperto,
e che seco non vuol triegua né pace;
la mano al mento con furor gli stese,
e tanto ne pelò, quanto ne prese.

E sì crebbe la furia, che nel collo
con man lo stringe a guisa di tanaglia;
e poi ch'una e due volte raggirollo,
da sé per l'aria e verso il mar lo scaglia.
Che n'avenisse, né dico né sollo:
varia fama è di lui, né si raguaglia.
Dice alcun che sì rotto a un sasso resta,
che 'l piè non si discerne da la testa;

et altri, ch'a cadere andò nel mare,
ch'era più di tre miglia indi lontano,
e che morì per non saper notare,
fatti assai prieghi e orazioni invano;
altri, ch'un santo lo venne aiutare,
lo trasse al lito con visibil mano.
Di queste, qual si vuol, la vera sia:
di lui non parla più l'istoria mia.

After enduring a great deal of tedious discourse from the valiant
monk and vainly inviting him to take himself off to his desert
without the damsel, and after seeing himself brazenly flouted by the
uncompromising fellow, the Saracen [Rodomonte] angrily grasped
him by the beard and pulled out a whole fistful of hair. / Then, his
rage redoubled, he closed his fingers round the other's neck like
pincers and, whirling him about a couple of times, tossed him up
into the sky, towards the sea. What became of the monk I cannot
tell—I do not know. Various and conflicting stories exist: one claims
that he was so shattered against a rock that there was no telling his
head from his foot; / another, that he landed in the sea, three miles
away, and died for not being able to swim, having vainly offered
up many a prayer and supplication; another, that a saint came to his
aid, carrying him ashore with visible hand. One of these may be
the truth—at any rate my story says no more about him.

The context for the scene is Isabella's encounter with Rodomonte.
A religious hermit, who seems to have rather un-Christian motives for ac-
companying Isabella through the woods, escorts her back to the Christian

camp. He tries—or so the narrator claims—to protect his charge from the aggressive Saracen, but the monk's efforts are to no avail: his life, together with his story, comes to an end. Or rather, to one of several "ends," for the narrator sketches three possible conclusions to the episode: the hermit may have died smashed on the rocks, he may have drowned, or he may have been saved by a saint.[7] Just as the poet must choose a "pazzia" (madness) at 29.50, so here the reader must select an ending to the story of the hermit. "Varia fama è di lui": the one character is the occasion of many stories (to paraphrase Carne-Ross, Nohrnberg, Zatti, and probably others). And it is up to the reader to recognize the multiplicity of the "various and conflicting" versions of potential endings to the single story.

An allusion to an Ovidian source underlying this passage at the beginning of canto 29 suggests ways of interpreting its open-endedness. In *Metamorphoses* 9, Hercules launches Lichas out to sea in much the same manner as Rodomonte throws the hermit: "terque quaterque rotatum / Mittit in Euboicas tormento fortius undas" (9.217–18).[8] ([W]hirling him thrice and again about his head, he hurled him far out into the Euboean sea, like a missile from a catapult.) Rodomonte has certain attributes in common with Hercules (strength, heroism, rage), while the hapless Lichas, an unwitting and innocent accomplice in Hercules' slow death, functions in Ovid's narrative analogously to Ariosto's hermit. Each minor character momentarily deflects attention from the major character's respective tragic circumstances: Rodomonte is about to kill Isabella; Hercules is dying. These thematic parallels encourage speculation on Ariosto's reasons for turning to the Ovidian model. But there are other similarities, formal ones, that determine Ariosto's choice of source at this moment in the narrative.

The very technique of providing different endings to a single story finds a precedent in Ovid's tale of Lichas. The narrator reports that Lichas could have either frozen to death in flight or been scared to death. A source from Epicurean science underlies the first version of Lichas's demise (Lucretius 6.495): like the atoms of precipitation when rain changes gradually into snow, so Lichas may have metamorphosed (220–22). It could be, however, that he died of fear, a possibility "old tradition" hands down to the present age ("prior aetas edidit," 225). It is for the reader to choose between the scientific and psychological explanations that account for Lichas's metamorphosis, or the reader may defer any such choice and simply enjoy the apparent contradiction in the narrative.

This lesson in how to construct a narrative with what we might call an inconclusive conclusion is repeated throughout the *Metamorphoses*.[9] It is also a feature of Ovid's *Fasti,* which is structured around a narrator who compiles and assimilates different versions of events celebrated in the Roman calendar. The passage on the festival of the Lupercalia, for instance, is typical in its proliferation of possible explanations for specific customs (2.243ff.). The narrator first notes the anthropological account of the event (281) and then acknowledges a pertinent Greek myth (303–04); he provides the Latin historical version of the festival's beginnings (359); and, finally, he adduces the etymological argument (381). At times, as in the section on Quirinus (2.475–80), even rival etymologies are given. We shall have occasion in chapter 4 to look more carefully at a specific Ariostan allusion to a passage from Ovid's sequence on the Lupercalia. For now suffice it to note that many of Ovid's stories in the *Metamorphoses* and *Fasti* feature an inconclusive ending or a multiplicity of possible ones. Ariosto's appreciation of narrative opportunism led him to the Ovidian model, where he discovered a technique that produced a kind of narrative radically different from one that is linear with a single, specific conclusion. We should now consider his reading of Ovidian poetry in more detail.

Interlaced Classics

Over the course of the Cinquecento, readers of the *Furioso* frequently used the *Metamorphoses* as a touchstone by which they assessed the degree of classicism in Ariosto's poem. Recently the "affiliations" that were seen to exist between the two poems have been examined.[10] Perceived similarities between the two works fostered interpretations of the *Furioso* as a new vernacular classic; translators and publishers produced versions of the *Metamorphoses* in Italian that made it look and sound like the *Furioso;* and in at least one case a classical scholar, Hercules Ciofanus, promoted a reappraisal of Ovid's *Metamorphoses* in the wake of the success of the Renaissance poem. By the end of the century, then, a strange literary-historical inversion had taken place: the vernacular work was influencing the reception of the classical author. But not all the attention given to the comparison of the two poems in the sixteenth century was positive. Readers of the *Furioso* who sought to discredit the modern poem for its narrative structure often reintroduced many of the same criticisms of Ovidian narrative that the classical tradition had handed down.[11]

The detailed examination of the external affiliations between the poems has made it possible to concentrate on other kinds of relationships between them. If, as Daniel Javitch suggests, Ariosto's poem may have "possessed particular features that enabled it to be deemed a classic" (*Proclaiming a Classic* 4), it follows that the poet may have derived those features from the direct imitation of specific classical texts. Internal affiliations, therefore, may exist between Ariosto and a given model. In the remainder of this chapter, I make a case for associating the *Furioso* and the *Metamorphoses* on the grounds of internal affiliations, specifically, for the similarities in the designs of their narratives. We have seen above a formal similarity between the episodes of Ovid's Lichas and Ariosto's hermit.

Like the *Furioso,* the *Metamorphoses* is an epic-sized poem that flouts Aristotelian and Horatian rules of epic poetry. Its multidimensional narrative illuminates multiple actions of multiple characters, rather than limiting its subject to one action of many, as does the *Iliad,* or to many actions of one, like the *Odyssey.* Its abundance of plots and themes required a structure, and Ovid's structural choices resemble to some extent the solutions of authors of romance-epic poems. But could the classical poet's choices have had a direct influence on Ariosto's own poetic decisions? I argue below that Ovid, a classical author sanctioned by medieval literary authorities, provided Ariosto with an acceptable narrative model as the Renaissance author reconfigured the chivalric romance into a new kind of poem. The novelty of Ariosto's engagement with Ovid—I shall stress—is his treatment of Ovidian poetry as a guide to narrative composition and not merely as a reference book on classical mythology. Other critics, long before me, have noted formal similarities between the narratives of the *Metamorphoses* and the *Furioso.*[12] But only recently have critics begun to argue that Ovid's long narrative was a model for, specifically, Ariosto's fusion of classical epic and romance.[13]

Historical evidence shows that Ariosto had plenty of opportunity to read Ovid. The reconstruction of his private library includes the classical poet's works,[14] and documents prove that as a young boy he had easy access to editions of Ovid's poems.[15] The Ovidian Latin verses he wrote as a youth and the numerous allusions to Ovid's work in his vernacular poetry testify that Ariosto made use of Ovid as a model from an early age.[16] In the sixth satire, addressed to Pietro Bembo and composed between 1524 and 1525, Ariosto refers directly to his engagement with Latin literary culture. The ostensible occasion of the poem is the author's request that his friend help him locate a tutor of Greek for his son, Virginio, who was around fifteen at the time (6.13–15). Ariosto explains that he has taught Virginio something of the Latin tradition (6.142–44):

> Già per me sa ciò che Virgilio scrive,
> Terenzio, Ovidio, Orazio, e le plautine
> scene ha vedute . . .

> He already knows from my instruction what Vergil and Ter-
> ence wrote, and Ovid and Horace, and he has seen the plays of
> Plautus . . .

But he goes on to confess that he does not know Greek well enough to teach it to his son. His priorities have always been with Latin (6.178–80):

> che 'l saper ne la lingua de li Achei
> non mi reputo onor, s'io non intendo
> prima il parlar de li latini miei.

> If first I do not understand the language of my native Latins, knowledge of the Achaean tongue can bring me no distinction.

The author then recounts in some detail the autobiographical circumstances that first fostered and eventually hindered his education in the classics. The remembrance of things past yields to what seems at first glance a typical humanistic encomium of classical culture, concluding with a plea that Bembo help Ariosto's son make his way to the top of Mount Parnassus.[17] While the satire does not single out the impact of a specific poet on Ariosto's own development, its suggestion that Ovid is one of Ariosto's foundational poets gives us leave to pursue the role of Ovidian poetry in the *Furioso*.

Giraldi Cinzio, one of the earliest and most influential critics to associate Ariosto's poem with Ovid's, uses weaving imagery to focus on the internal similarities between the poems. In his *Discorso intorno al comporre dei romanzi* (1554), Giraldi mentions the "fabric" of romance composition ("tutta la fabbrica della composizione") and then immediately refines the image: "per la quale fabbrica intendo ora la orditura e la testura di tutta l'opera" (53). (by which fabric I mean now the warping and weave of the whole work.) The words introduced to clarify "fabbrica"—"orditura" and "testura"—are technical terms from the vocabulary of weaving: "orditura" is the Italian for "warping," the act of stringing the ensemble of vertical threads that forms the basis of the weave, while "testura" (a literary form of "tessitura") is the act of weaving. By extension it can refer to the weave as a whole.[18] From the context it seems that Giraldi is imagining the process of interweaving the warp and the weft, the group of threads at right angles to the warp. He clarifies this imagery with a subsequent simile in which he likens the "orditura" to the subject matter of the poem and the "testura" to its arrangement. In other words, the "testura," or narrative *dispositio,* lends a meaningful shape to the "orditura."

This highly detailed imagery of weaving derives from the more general notion of a text as a weaving in words. Giraldi and other critics regularly use the verb "tessere," "to weave," to account metaphorically for narrative construction. The image is felicitous given the etymology of "text" ("testo" in Italian), which is derived from the past participle of the Latin verb *texere,* "to weave": a text, therefore, is a having-been-woven (*textus*) thing. The imagery is all the more appropriate given Ariosto's references in the *Furioso* to the poem as a woven creation.[19] He observes, for instance, as he shifts from one scene to another near the beginning of the poem, that he has "need of a number of warps and a variety of threads" (2.30.5–6). Giraldi himself develops the metaphor further when he refers to the way the typical romance proceeds in a "continuo filo" (59). He is envisioning the way a weaver passes the weft thread continuously back and forth through the warp. In this model of narrative construction, the movement of the weft thread over and then under the individual warp threads represents the process of arranging different stories (the warp threads) into a narrative (the completed weave) that has continuity (the weft thread).

Giraldi uses imagery derived from weaving throughout his section on the composition of romances in the *Discorso* (53–70). He emphasizes that the narrative is like a continuous thread, no matter how many different stories make it up and no matter how frequently these stories are interrupted by a narrator's voice, either within the story or at the beginning of the following story. In this model, continuity is perceived as the romance narrative's essential characteristic; stories that make up the narrative may be disrupted, suspended, or even forgotten, but the narrative itself, like the weft thread, proceeds. The very progress of the narrative's progression cements its disparate elements together.

Giraldi brings the *Metamorphoses* into the discussion of romance narrative by mentioning the manner in which Ovid organized the poem's material: "Ovidio . . . trattò con maravigliosa catena tanta varietà di cose" (56). (Ovid . . . treated in wondrous sequence so great a variety of things.) The phrase "con maravigliosa catena" (literally, "with a chain full of marvels") is a variation on the more precise description "con continua catena," which Giraldi uses interchangeably with "con continuo filo" to describe the ancient poet's narrative organization (59). "Maravigliosa" could call to mind the world of medieval romance, but since Giraldi makes general use of the word, it is perhaps best not to press this meaning upon it. "Catena," however, suggests a very specific image, an interdependence and continuity among narrative elements similar to that of the weaving imagery discussed above.[20] Although Giraldi does not refer to the *Metamorphoses* as a woven poem, the image of the wondrous chain suggests that he perceived its narrative in similar terms.

Subsequent readers employed the metaphor of weaving as a critical term in reference to romance narrative. In the twentieth century, critics of the *Furioso* have extended the image of the woven text to speak of the interwoven, or, as it is usually put, the "interlaced" text. Their discussions, however, do not begin with Giraldi, Tasso, or any of the sixteenth-century critics who discussed Ariosto's narrative art in these terms. Many of the recent analyses of the *Furioso*'s narrative depend on criticism of the French romance tradition, especially Ferdinand Lot's *Etude sur le* Lancelot en prose.

In his essay of 1918, Lot argues from a unitarian position that the prose *Lancelot* was the work of a single author and not the result of an artful ensemble of episodes by various romance poets. His conclusions on the authorship of the work have been disputed, but one of his arguments to prove that the poem is by a single author, namely, that such an elaborate narrative structure could only be the composition of one mind, has made its mark. Hence his analysis of the *Lancelot*'s narrative remains the starting place for criticism of the work and of romance narrative in general.

Lot focuses upon the narrative technique of interlacing, "entrelace-ment."[21] Although he never actually defines a technique per se, he describes interlacing in various ways that suggest a working definition. For him it is a "principe," "procédé," "système," and "enchevêtrement systematique" (17). Coupling these generalities with the ideas of "process" and "systematic entangling," Lot suggests that narrative art is akin to weaving, much as does Giraldi in his analysis of the *Furioso*'s narrative design. It is no surprise to discover the product of narrative interlacing described as a tapestry, "tapisserie," later in the essay (28).

The general argument of the piece provides many specific examples of interlacing in the narrative of the *Lancelot*. Of equal interest are his illustrations of how the technique works: "Au moment où le souvenir même du thème semble oblitéré, il reparaît soudain, puis replonge pour remonter à la surface. On ne saurait dire pourtant qu'il s'ensuive de la confusion, tant est prestigieuse la dextérité avec laquelle les fils se croisent, s'entrevoisent et se dénouent" (18). (At the moment when the memory itself of the theme seems obliterated, it suddenly reappears diving back in again to rise to the surface once more. One could say that this results in confusion, however, so noteworthy is the dexterity with which the threads are crossed, wound, unraveled.) The mixing of aquatic and weaving imagery is perhaps inelegant, but it makes the point that narrative threads (or fish) come in and out of the reader's view time and again as the narrative proceeds.

Lot writes directly and at length about the narrative technique of interlacing in a way that Giraldi does not, but there is little in the Frenchman's work that is not already implied in Giraldi's analysis of romance narrative. The sixteenth-century critic's conception of the ongoing thread of the narrative organization that weaves in and out of various stories anticipates much of the imagery of Lot's argument. What Lot adds to the discussion of interlacing is his emphasis on the technique as a process. He understands that narrative is a dynamic phenomenon. It is a phenomenon that "proceeds." But this metaphor ironically points to a shortcoming in the essayist's choice of "entrelacement" as the critical term to describe the technique.

Giraldi and Lot, like most of the critics who discuss how stories are composed in the typical romance narrative, employ the metaphor of weaving to elucidate the narrative as interdependent and continuous. That is to say, weaving stresses that a narrative is a dynamic and not static process. "Interlacing," however, evokes the knotted patterns of lacework and suggests, rather, a motionless or stalled process. The term "interlacing" derives from a perception of narrative as a completed thing and not a process under completion. The context of the earliest attestation of the word in English emphasizes this contrast between thing and process.

In 1374 Chaucer translates a pair of words from Boethius's *Consolation of Philosophy* (3.12.82), *inextricabilem labyrinthum,* with the phrase "the hous of Dedalus so entrelaced that it is unable to ben unlaced."[22] To render *labyrinthum* as "the house of Daedalus" is to gloss the word rather than to translate it. But "unable to be unlaced" is an accurate translation of *inextricabilem,* revealing as it does an awareness of the meaning of the word's suffix and prefixes. The translation highlights the notion of process contained in the compounded adjective. The notion contrasts with the static image of "the house of Daedalus," which is described in an additional gloss as "so entrelaced." The interlaced house is an entity; the problematic passage through it is a process. Narrative, described as interlaced, like the labyrinth, comes to be perceived as a thing, while a narrative described with the imagery of weaving is primarily a progressive entity. Since narrative is first and foremost a process, it is somewhat unfortunate that Lot established "entrelacement" as a critical term for much of the subsequent secondary literature. I too, however, shall follow suit, but with the qualification that I mean the term to evoke a narrative that is dynamic, not static. Ascoli provides a good working definition of "interlacing": it is a series of "systematic repetitions and juxtapositions of multiple plots and themes within a single work and among the texts of a given [romance] cycle."[23] One should add some mention of transitions, the positioning of which in an interlaced narrative is just as important as that of repetitions and juxtapositions. Transitions are in fact the cruxes of an interlaced narrative, for it is at these junctures that the poet brings together two distinct episodes and establishes the basis for interlacing. With the above expanded definition in mind, let us turn to a closer analysis of the *Furioso* and the *Metamorphoses*.

The *Furioso*'s narrative consists of three grand plots that develop around various repeated and juxtaposed themes: the conflict between Charlemagne's Christian forces and armies of the Arab world; Orlando's quest for Angelica and the effect of his failure to win her; and the love between Bradamante and Ruggiero. When Ariosto introduces these three plots in the opening stanzas of his poem, he hints at its narrative design by saying that he will recount them "in un medesmo tratto," "with the same stroke" (1.2.1).[24] In other words, he intends to develop the plots simultaneously. Later, in a moment of reflection, the poet comments on the nature of creating such a narrative: "Di molte fila esser bisogno parme / a condur la gran tela ch'io lavoro" (13.81.1–2). (To complete the great tapestry on which I am working I feel the need for a great variety of strands.) He needs different threads (plots) to develop the great web (narrative) on which he is working. The programmatic design of the *Furioso* entails the interlacing of these various multiple plots into one gigantic narrative. It is important to note that the narrator himself interrupts the narrative to discuss what he needs for its composition. His voice, prominent throughout the poem, contributes to the narrative interlacing.

The narrative of the *Metamorphoses,* for its part, does not consist of a series of sweeping plots that in themselves lend continuity to the poem, but the poet's description of his work as a *perpetuum carmen* (1.4) (my song in unbroken strains) indicates that he perceives it as unified. What Ovid means by the adjective *perpetuum* is problematic, and he, like Ariosto and many critics, turns to the imagery of weaving for partial clarification.[25] He calls on the gods "to lead down" the poem from the beginning of time to his own day, with the verb *deducere,* which he uses elsewhere for the spinning out of yarn and the process of weaving.[26] Ovid uses it in this latter sense to describe the tapestries in the contest between Arachne and Minerva: "illic et lentum filis inmittitur aurum / et vetus in tela deducitur argumentum" (6.68–69). (There, too, they weave in pliant threads of gold, and trace in the weft some ancient tale.) The adverbial phrase *illic et* encourages the reader to visualize the precise spot on the loom where the interweaving of warp and weft is about to occur, just as it does at lines 60–61: "illic et Tyrium quae purpura sensit aënum / texitur." (There are inwoven the purple threads dyed in Tyrian kettles.) The Arachne episode (and a few choice allusions to it in European art) thematizes the artist as weaver, an irreverent one at that, as Leonard Barkan has shown so brilliantly in *The Gods Made Flesh.*

Irreverence characterizes Arachne's frameless, iconoclastic, anticlassical tapestry, for which she is punished by the sternly classicizing Minerva. Barkan argues convincingly that Ovid associates himself with the figure of Arachne, whose perpetuity is guaranteed by her art (1–18). Ovid's choice of vocabulary for his poem's exordium and for subsequent episodes like that of Arachne suggests that the *perpetuitas* of the *Metamorphoses* can be attributed (on one level at least) to the interwoven nature of its narrative.

Although Ovid's language suggests that there is a degree of woven continuity in the poem, it does not confirm it. We should look at the narrative itself and momentarily ignore that the poet has asked the gods to help him weave a continuous poem.[27]

It is tempting to see the chronological arrangement of the poem's subject matter as lending some continuity to its diverse stories. The poem describes the relentless movement of time from its beginning to the narrator's present, "ad mea tempora" (1.4), from chaos to Caesar. But the occasional errors in chronology undermine time's effectiveness as a unifying principle.[28]

A greater sense of continuity is found in the episodes that are linked by the presence of repeated characters or by thematic similarity. The sequence of episodes involving Theseus from *Metamorphoses* 7 to 15 is an example of the reappearance of a character linking seemingly disparate episodes of the narrative. The sequence of episodes involving rapes and seductions of mortal women by Olympian gods establishes a thematic nexus in the first third of the poem, recapitulated and highlighted by Arachne's tapestry in 6.103–28.

One might expect the theme of metamorphosis to be a unifying element in the poem, but its treatment is often perfunctory and fails to give the narrative a thematic coherence. Many episodes lack metamorphoses, and many include a tagged-on transformation that does not bring the episode to a satisfactory closure. This rather casual approach to the poem's stated theme undermines its potential to unify the narrative.[29]

While metamorphosis per se does not hold the poem together, there is a noticeable consistency in the poet's treatment of the topic, as there is in his treatment of myth in general. G. Karl Galinsky observes that Ovid uses myth "to comment on his literary aims rather than to speculate on the great problems of human existence."[30] Myths involving metamorphoses in particular become a literary principle that informs the composition of Ovid's poem—this is also Barkan's point. One can extend the analyses of Galinsky and Barkan to include the construction of the poem's narrative. Ovid may not describe a character's metamorphosis in every episode, but the poet inevitably engages in a literary process that is based on metamorphosing traditional material into his new poem. In addition to the immense range and variety of his sources, his poem itself attests to the different ways Ovid assimilates the traditional material he receives.

One constant in the midst of this variety is the primary voice of Ovid's narrator, which is itself the result of a literary metamorphosis. Aristotle states that epic poets should refrain from speaking in propria persona (*Poetics* 1460a7–8), and by and large poets in the tradition respect his injunction. Vergil, for example, seldom interrupts the action of the *Aeneid* in order to address characters in the poem, doing so only at moments of heightened interest, for example, after the deaths of Nisus and Euryalus (9.446–49) and before the death of Lausus (10.791–93). But Ovid repeatedly breaks this rule of epic convention. Among the many instances when he speaks in his own voice are his remarks to the gods (1.2; 4.661; and 15.861); Augustus (1.204); Narcissus (3.432–36); Bacchus (4.17–30); Medea (7.144–46); and Polyxena and Hecuba (13.483–85).

It has been argued that this omnipresence of the primary narrator unifies the *Metamorphoses*.[31] While that position is debatable, there is no question that the act of narration is a focus in the *Metamorphoses*. This focus is the basis of the thematic nexus that develops around the sequences of episodes told by secondary narrators, that is, by narrators who are characters in the poem.[32] The Minyeides, the Muses, Achelous, Orpheus, and Nestor all tell stories at great length. The art of narrating fiction becomes an important element of unity in the poem because of these major secondary narrators and because of the numerous minor ones, like Lelex, the Sibyl, and the occasional anonymous voice, who tell just one story or two rather than an entire sequence. Secondary narrators enable the poet to reflect openly on his art, and their inclusion in the narrative invites the reader to do the same. Their great number in the *Metamorphoses* constitutes a thematic development throughout the poem, climaxing in the narration of Pythagoras in book 15. This extended meditation on the art of storytelling, combined with the primary narrator's own intrusions into the narrative, arguably form the thematic sequence that exerts the strongest unifying force on the poem.

An example of how the reader learns to expect the primary narrator's voice and how much he or she might depend on it in moving from one episode to the next arises at the end of the Cadmus and Harmonia sequence (3.604ff.). The narrator ends the sequence by noting Cadmus's and Harmonia's pride in their grandson, Bacchus. In contrast to the Theban couple, Acrisius of Argos did not respect the new god on the grounds of Bacchus's questionable divine paternity. The reader might expect this remark to introduce a tale in which Bacchus visits Argos and punishes Acrisius, but instead the phrase serves as a transition to the story of Perseus, the grandson of Acrisius and son of Zeus. Acrisius predictably refused to believe the story of Danaë, his daughter, when she claimed that Zeus came to her in a shower of gold (4.610–14):

> non putat esse deum: neque enim Iovis esse putabat
> Persea, quem pluvio Danae conceperat auro.
> mox tamen Acrisium (tanta est praesentia veri)
> tam violasse deum quam non agnosse nepotem
> paenitet . . .

> Nor did he admit that Perseus was son of Jove, whom Danaë had conceived of a golden shower. And yet, such is the power of truth, Acrisius in the end was sorry that he had repulsed the god and had not acknowledged his grandson . . .

Before the narrative launches into the adventures of Perseus (he reappears in midflight with Medusa's severed head in his hand at line 615), Ovid reintroduces his name in the transitional passage. The parenthetical aside "tanta est praesentia veri" (612) draws attention to the narrator, who is responsible for connecting Bacchus and Perseus. The tone of the aside is also typically Ovidian: it purports a seriousness that can easily be interpreted as jocular. "So great is the power of truth," indeed: the narrator never tells the reader how Acrisius repented for his errors. Ovid neatly omits any reference to the legend of Perseus's accidental killing of Acrisius later in life. If the reader overlooks this omission, he might consider the aside a statement that expresses Ovid's sincere appraisal of the myth and his sources. But if the reader considers the omission, he must conclude that when truth, *verum,* is reported in a narrative fiction, it is often in an incomplete, imperfect form.

Ovid uses such asides to communicate with the reader in the *Metamorphoses.* And although this technique contrasts with Ariosto's direct addresses to the reader, the effect of each approach is similar: the narrator's voice gives each poem coherence as it articulates and effects the movement from one episode to another. In the *Furioso,* the method of moving among episodes usually draws on the conventions of chivalric romance. The fiction behind the poem's creation has it that the poet, like the "cantastorie" of the wandering minstrel tradition, recites his poem to an audience that includes his patron. Thus the poet can announce changes in the narrative's development and even beg his lord at the end of canto 14, a rather long canto, for permission to rest because he is hoarse! Much like Boiardo in the *Innamorato* and even, as we saw in chapter 2, in his translation of Herodotus, Ariosto frequently uses the formula "lasciare-tornare" to leave one character in the middle of an adventure while he explains to the reader or listener that he is returning to another whom he had forsaken earlier in the narrative. Rinaldo, on his way to Britain in search of reinforcements for Charlemagne's besieged troops in Paris, is caught in a violent storm at sea. Our hero is tossed around for several stanzas when suddenly the narrator's voice breaks in: "lascio Rinaldo e l'agitata prua, / e torno a dir di Bradamante sua" (2.30.7–8). (I shall leave Rinaldo and his pitching prow and return to the tale of his sister Bradamant.) Bradamante was last seen riding at full gallop through the forest at 1.64; the reader will return to Rinaldo (who in the meantime has landed in Scotland) at 4.50ff., as the formula is used once again: "Lasciànlo andar [Ruggiero], che farà buon camino, / e torniamo a Rinaldo paladino" (50.7–8). (Let us leave him on his way, for he will make a good journey, and let us return to Rinaldo the paladin.) We leave Ruggiero this time to return to Rinaldo as the weave continues.[33]

Criticism of this kind of transition disapproves of its apparent accidental nature. Why do we leave Ruggiero for Rinaldo at exactly this point in the narrative, instead of sooner or a little later? While some critics argue that the accidental nature of the narrative's transitions reflects Ariosto's worldview,[34] and others ingeniously argue that the accidental nature is only apparent,[35] it is best to argue simply for a deliberate narrative design. The quest theme around which the poem is built lends itself to this treatment. Characters riding through the forests of the *Furioso* in search of one another are constantly happening upon someone or something that occasions another story or at least a twist in the development of the one at hand. The first of many examples occurs at the very beginning of the poem, upon Angelica's encounter with Rinaldo (1.10.7–8). But a similar lack of logical transition is found in the *Metamorphoses.*

Transitions in the *Metamorphoses,* of course, do not depend on romance conventions, but they, too, often seem accidental. Ovid's characters occasionally encounter one another, as when Aeneas and Achaemenides meet Macareus near Cumae (14.154ff.), and subsequently such a random meeting may prompt a tale. But more often the accidental nature of narrative development in the *Metamorphoses* is due to the tenuous connections the Ovidian narrator (primary or secondary) makes in the grouping of episodes. A familial connection among characters can provide the link, as in the sequence that bridges books 2 and 3 involving Europa and her brother, Cadmus, and his offspring. Or the accident of geography can provide the basis for a sequence of episodes, as does Sicily in 5.346–641 and Anatolia in 6.1–411. A transition can also occur simply for its own sake, as in the description of Medea's flight in 7.350–90, which leads the reader eventually to Athens (398ff.) and a new set of stories.

But the Athenian segment does not begin until after a sequence of fifteen metamorphoses that are connected with the landscape Medea views from above in her chariot.

To what extent, however, are the tales that comprise each respective narrative logical and necessary in their order? What negative effect, if any, occurs if one deletes a tale from the middle of the narrative as a whole?

In the *Furioso,* Ariosto himself advises the reader on one occasion to skip a canto-length episode that contains a rather indelicate depiction of women: "Lasciate questo canto, che senza esso / può star l'istoria, e non sarà men chiara" (28.2.1–2). (Skip this canto: it is not essential—my story is no less clear without it.) He repeats the command more explicitly several lines later: "Passi, chi vuol, tre carte o quattro, senza / Leggerne verso . . ." (3.1–2). (Those who wish, then, may skip three or four pages without reading a line of them. . . .) Ariosto pretends that his narrative can tolerate this kind of reading. Following this same line of reasoning, John Harington, Ariosto's first great translator into English, appends to his version of the poem "The Principal Tales in *Orlando Furioso* that may be read by themselves."[36] He lists twenty-four episodes, including the misogynous story of canto 28, which he calls "Tale of mine host with Rodomonts invective against women." The early editions of his translation alert the reader to the possibility of skipping over stories through marginal notes that locate the place later in the narrative where an interrupted story continues. This allows the reader to take seriously Ariosto's facetious advice to skip several "carte" and be guided by the text to the point where he or she might resume reading.[37]

The *Metamorphoses* has also been read by those who approach it as a collection of independent stories. Ferrarese poets were especially fond of imitating several specific Ovidian stories copied from the *Metamorphoses:* Meleager, Phaethon, and Pyramus and Thisbe, to name a few of the most popular. Even Ariosto himself is said to have written a youthful dramatic work, now lost, on Pyramus and Thisbe, the *Tragedia di Tisbe.*[38] Renaissance poets, with no authorial sanction, lifted Ovidian stories out of context and used them with little concern for their narrative setting.

But as Ferdinand Lot knew well, "On ne peut découper dans le Lancelot de vraies tranches d'histoire, on ne peut supprimer une 'aventure' sans que cette suppression ait des retentissements proches ou lointains" (27). (One cannot cut actual pieces of the plot out of the *Lancelot,* one cannot suppress a tale of adventure without that act of suppression having extensive repercussions.) Lot is clear that one cannot remove an episode without affecting the narrative. He goes on to say that one also cannot add new episodes to the interlaced narrative of a poem without adversely affecting its structure (27). A subsequent critic who develops this idea, Rosemond Tuve, justifies the position by explaining that in an interlaced narrative what we read of one character often affects our interpretation of another character. Is our perception of a heroic knight or mortal woman victimized by the gods not altered by what an intervening character might portray? Interlacing develops in such a way that a character to whom we have returned is in a "condition of meaningfulness to which he has been pulled by the events occurring in following episodes written about someone else."[39]

Tuve focuses on medieval romance, but examples of the phenomenon abound in the *Furioso* and *Metamorphoses* as well. In the *Furioso,* when the narrator leaves Rinaldo to take up the threads involving his sister, Bradamante, and his rival, Ruggiero, in 2.30ff., he places that character in a condition that gleans its meaning from what transpires in subsequent episodes before Rinaldo returns at 4.50ff. The reader learns in canto 3, for example, that the union of Bradamante and Ruggiero, which produces the Este dynasty, will bring honor to Rinaldo himself as well as to the rest of Bradamante's family (3.38). In this way the characters' destinies are meaningfully interlaced (to paraphrase Tuve). By sailing north for reinforcements, Rinaldo sets in motion a sequence that will eventually make it possible for Bradamante and Ruggiero to marry (44.14). His mission involves the narrative in far different and greater matters than merely the immediate military needs of Charlemagne.

In *Metamorphoses* 12, when Theseus returns after an interlude of several books, his condition has been made significantly more complex by the actions of others in the intervening books. The satirical depiction of Herculean heroism in *Metamorphoses* 9, not to mention the ridiculous antics of a host of heroes including Theseus himself at the Calydonian boar hunt in *Metamorphoses* 8, effects a similarly comic interpretation of Theseus's actions in *Metamorphoses* 12 during the battle of the Lapiths and the Centaurs. Nestor aims to recount the heroism of the Lapiths and Centaurs in his tale, but this is the same Nestor whom the reader saw vault cowardly into a tree during the boar hunt (8.365–68). The narrator set a rather curious example of heroic behavior. When Theseus leaps up to confront a centaur (12.227), the reader is allowed to recall that he exclaimed in an earlier test of bravery, "licet eminus esse / fortibus" (8.406–07). (It is no shame for brave men to fight at long distance.) Theseus's heroic mettle, like Nestor's, is largely untested, thus the reader responds with a certain ironic distrust to his portrayal in the battle of the Lapiths and the Centaurs. If we were to read this passage without the context of the Calydonian boar hunt, we would view the narrator and his main character very differently. We would lose any sense of mock epic.

The ironic playfulness in *Metamorphoses* 12 would disappear. Ariosto's reading of this passage, which we should now consider, rings changes on the mock epic but ultimately keeps the Ovidian morphology very much apparent.

Choosing Ovid

Ariosto turned to the culmination of the Theseus sequence, the battle between the Lapiths and the Centaurs (12.210–535), as a model for the episode of Isabella and Orlando in *Furioso* 13.[40] The episode contains thematic allusions to *Metamorphoses* 12 that attest to Ariosto's use of the text. It also contains structural parallels between the passages, which include the organization of their interlaced narratives. In order to consider these parallels, it will be easiest first to present the Ovidian passage and then to discuss how the Ariostan passage is modeled on it.[41]

The setting for most of *Metamorphoses* 12 is the battleground stretching out before the walls of Troy, familiar to readers of the *Iliad*. During an interlude in the fighting between the Greeks and Trojans, the venerable Nestor of Homeric legend narrates a series of tales about heroes of the past, including Theseus. Nestor begins speaking at *Metamorphoses* 12.168 and finishes several hundred lines later, at 12.576. His speech is one of the longest in the *Metamorphoses,* its length in keeping with the Homeric depiction of Nestor as a garrulous orator. At the beginning of the speech, Achilles urges the old man to tell the story of Caeneus, an invincible warrior who was once a woman, with these remarks: "dic age! nam cunctis eadem est audire voluntas, / o facunde senex, aevi prudentia nostri" (177–78). (Tell on, old man, eloquent wisdom of our age, for all of us alike desire to hear.) Nestor first describes how a woman, Caenis, became a man, Caeneus (189–209), and then continues on to the battle of the Lapiths and the Centaurs (210–535). He concludes with the *aristeia* of Caeneus and his metamorphosis into a bird (459–535). In the midst of the battle description, the old storyteller digresses to include an idyllic tale on the romance of two young centaurs, Cyllarus and Hylonome (393–428). He completes his narrative of past heroes with a story about Hercules and Periclymenus (536–76).

At the conclusion of Nestor's lengthy speech, the primary Ovidian narrator once again adduces the speaker's Homeric associations with a phrase that is the equivalent of an epic epithet: "haec postquam dulci Neleius edidit ore . . ." (577). (When Nestor with sweet speech had told this tale . . .) "Dulci ore" recalls passages like *Iliad* 1.247ff., where sweet-voiced Nestor addresses his men with a "voice sweeter than honey." But the sweet voice of the Ovidian Nestor has little in common with the Homeric model, a discrepancy intended to cause problems for the informed reader. The old man's story is the report of an eyewitness, but, as has been observed, Nestor's credentials as a reporter are dubious at best.[42] Nestor himself admits that his age may prevent the accurate recollection of detail: "quamvis obstet mihi tarda vetustas" (182). (Though [old age] has blurred my memory.) And his dependence on the thoroughly disreputable figure of Fama vitiates much of what he says.[43] Nevertheless, he describes in detail the fighting that arose when a drunken centaur endeavored to rape the bride of Theseus's friend, Pirithous. There may be some poetic or mythic justice in Ovid's tale, because the friendship of Pirithous and Theseus is founded on escapades more centauran than human. They, too, attempt to rape a bride, none less than Persephone, but fail.

The narrative quickly becomes a ferocious parody of Homer and an indictment of Nestor as a storyteller. The fanciful framing episodes of Caenis-Caeneus set the battle of the Lapiths and the Centaurs in an unheroic context. The centerpiece of Nestor's narrative, the battle itself, is a catalog of senseless slaughter, with humorous splashes of realism that exceed anything in the *Iliad*.[44] Nestor introduces the goriest details imaginable in his recounting of the fight: a disemboweled centaur, for instance, trips over his entrails and falls to the ground with an empty belly (390–92). Epic heroism vanishes in the vulgarly comic hyperrealism of such a description. Proceeding seemingly ad infinitum, Nestor's tale exemplifies Homeric battle narrative gone awry.

As if to check the numerous variations on dying in battle, Nestor disrupts the narrative from 393–428 with an episode that traces the love between two young centaurs. The digression focuses on each centaur's natural beauty and stresses their reciprocal feelings: "pars amor est illis" (416). (They both felt equal love.) There is a certain symmetry, one notes, in their appearance at a wedding feast, but, as Nestor narrates, Cyllarus is suddenly killed and Hylonome nobly commits suicide soon thereafter. Or rather she tries to do so in the best noble fashion with a memorable last phrase that our narrator, alas, did not catch (12.426–28):

> ut videt extinctum, dictis, quae clamor ad aures
> arcuit ire meas, telo, quod inhaeserat illi,
> incubuit moriensque suum conplexa maritum est.

> But when she saw that he was dead, with some words which the surrounding uproar prevented me from hearing, she threw herself upon the spear which had pierced Cyllarus and fell in a dying embrace upon her lover.

Up to line 426 in the Cyllarus episode, the primary narrator has not raised questions in the reader's mind about the purpose of the digression, as he does in other episodes of the Theseus sequence. The digression provides background information that accounts for the presence of the young couple and which simultaneously prepares the reader for a tragic conclusion to their brief story. But Nestor's remark, "quae clamor ad aures arcuit ire meas," is a jarring reminder that the old man, despite his Homeric reputation, cannot tell a story well. The remark, spoken by an Ovidian Nestor, completely undermines the tragic quality of the scene.

Ovid's centerpiece, however, is a good story. It offers a clear beginning and middle and the pleasure of narrative closure. But the pleasure is subverted by Nestor's remark, which draws attention to him as a secondary narrator and leads into the resumption of his battle narrative. The reader's satisfaction is momentary and frustrated because it is not quite complete.

The other examples of Nestor's inability to bring a narrative to an acceptable conclusion occur within the interlacing of stories in the narrative: at the end of the Caeneus story (459–535), and in the Periclymenus episode that is tagged on to the battle narrative (536–76). Caeneus's death and resurrection are as probable as many transformations in the *Metamorphoses;* however, Nestor himself casts doubt on its closure with his remark, "credita res auctore suo est" (532). (This story was believed because of him who told it.) Mopsus legitimizes the story of Caeneus's metamorphosis into a bird, but Nestor's remark, in spite of its intentions, does not lend the story greater credibility. Once again Nestor's qualifications as a teller of tales come under suspicion. The stories Nestor relates should not be believed, precisely because he is their *auctor.* The Caeneus episode, ostensibly meant to form the second half of a neat frame to Nestor's battle narrative, instead causes the reader to doubt and then reconsider the entire narrative as a falsified account of what really happened. When the reader returns to Caeneus it is not so much the character's condition but the secondary narrator's that has been cultivated in the interim. This interlaced episode confirms the reader's doubts about Nestor as a narrator and supports the interpretation of the narrative as a parody of Homeric epic.

When Nestor finally concludes the battle narrative, a question submitted by a certain Tlepolemus prompts him to tag on an additional episode to the sequence. The Periclymenus episode represents one more example of Nestor's inability to stop talking. Tlepolemus, the son of Hercules, asks Nestor why he ignores his father's success in battle against the centaurs. Nestor's response is simple: he passes over the hero's deeds in order to avenge the deaths of his eleven brothers, including

Periclymenus, whom Hercules killed: "nec tamen ulterius, quam fortia facta silendo / ulciscor fratres" (575–76). (Yet for my brothers I seek no other vengeance than to ignore his mighty deeds.) Thus Nestor's avowed silence raises a final question about his accuracy as a reporter and storyteller. What else remains untold? Is his next tale to be that of Hercules' adventures against the centaurs? This garrulous old man with no sense of narrative closure could babble on forever.

In *Furioso* 13.32–44, Ariosto alludes to parts of Nestor's narrative in ways that reveal the extent to which he depends on the structure of Ovid's poem. No portion of Ovid's text is translated verbatim, as is the passage from *Heroides* 10 in the Olimpia episode of *Furioso* 10. Rather, Ariosto's allusions to the narrative structure of Nestor's speech are subtle inversions of the Ovidian original. Where Nestor's open-ended narrative seems to continue indefinitely, Ariosto's is structured very tightly around the collapse of the Ovidian model. The allusions suggest that Ariosto perceived the parodistic rationale behind Nestor's lengthy narrative and that he chose to compose his narrative in imitation of Ovid's so as to comment on it. In the spirit of Renaissance poiesis, he sought to outdo the classical model.

The narrative in *Furioso* 13.32–44 is interrupted five times in a short span: Isabella, whom Orlando has found held hostage in a cave, recounts her tale of woe to the hero (32.1–4); her captors, the robbers, return to their subterranean hideout (32.5–35.4); a fight ensues between Orlando and the robbers, with a quick victory for the hero (35.5–41.8); Gabrina, the old woman guarding Isabella for the robbers, escapes and meets an unidentified warrior (42.1–8); Isabella and Orlando leave the cave and travel for several days until they encounter an unidentified knight (43.1–44.5); the primary narrator leaves the pair and returns to Bradamante (44.6–8). This entangled welter of events is animated by Ariosto's brand of narrative opportunism discussed above. There is no lack of feigned serendipity in the development of the sequence of episodes. We shall consider this aspect of the narrative construction in further detail below. For now, let us return to the text.

It is against the backdrop of the sympathetic Isabella's story that Orlando overcomes the robbers. The narrator emphasizes this in several ways (13.32):

Così parlava la gentil donzella;
e spesso con signozzi e con sospiri
interrompea l'angelica favella,

da muovere a pietade aspidi e tiri.
Mentre sua doglia così rinovella,
o forse disacerba i suoi martiri,
da venti uomini entrar ne la spelonca,
armati chi di spiedo e chi di ronca.

The gentle maiden spoke like an angel, her words punctuated with many a sob and sigh, enough to move asps and vipers to compassion. While she was thus reopening her wounds, or perhaps allaying her grief in the telling of it, some twenty men entered the cave, armed with sickles and spits.

The adverb "così" in line 1 of the stanza refers to the previous stanzas in which Isabella has been speaking. The verbs in the imperfect tense, "parlava" (1) and "interrompea" (3), emphasize the progressive aspect of the action: her speech is continuous, or, more precisely, she is continuously at center stage, whether she is speaking or interrupting herself with fits of weeping. The adverbs "spesso" (2), "mentre" (5), and, for the second time, "così" (5), are additional indicators of her continuous actions. The fight between Orlando and the robbers interrupts the narrative of her story more effectively than she does herself. In fact, Isabella momentarily recedes into the background. The fight functions, then, as a kind of diversion. In its relationship to the ongoing story of the maiden, the scene, with its clearly defined beginning and end, recalls the Cyllarus episode in the midst of Nestor's battle narrative. But in contrast to the Ovidian passage, in which the interminable battle description is interrupted with an idyllic, pastoral interlude, here Ariosto interrupts the ongoing narrative of Isabella's love story with a fight. Ariosto has turned the structure of his Ovidian model around for the first, but not the last, time.

We left Isabella above, just as the troop of robbers entered the cave. The passage continues (13.33–36):

Il primo d'essi, uom di spietato viso,
ha solo un occhio, e sguardo scuro e bieco;
l'altro, d'un colpo che gli avea reciso
il naso e la mascella, è fatto cieco.
Costui vedendo il cavalliero assiso
con la vergine bella entro allo speco,
volto a' compagni, disse: —Ecco augel nuovo,
a cui non tesi, e ne la rete il truovo.—

Poi disse al conte: —Uomo non vidi mai
più commodo di te, né più opportuno.
Non so se ti se' apposto, o se lo sai
perché te l'abbia forse detto alcuno,
che sì bell'arme io desiava assai,
e questo tuo leggiadro abito bruno.
Venuto a tempo veramente sei,
per riparare agli bisogni miei.—

Sorrise amaramente, in piè salito,
Orlando, e fe' risposta al mascalzone:
—Io ti venderò l'arme ad un partito
che non ha mercadante in sua ragione.—
Del fuoco, ch'avea appresso, indi rapito
pien di fuoco e di fumo uno stizzone,
trasse, e percosse il malandrino a caso,
dove confina con le ciglia il naso.

Lo stizzone ambe le palpebre colse,
ma maggior danno fe' ne la sinistra;
che quella parte misera gli tolse,
che de la luce, sola, era ministra.
Né d'acciecarlo[45] contentar si volse
il colpo fier, s'ancor non lo registra
tra quelli spirti che con suoi compagni
fa star Chiron dentro ai bollenti stagni.

Their leader, a mean-faced man, had only one eye, and a surly, mischievous look; his other eye had been blinded by a blow which had sliced his nose and chin. Seeing the knight sitting in the cave with the lovely damsel, he turned to his companions and cried: "Here's a new bird landed in the net, though I never snared him!" / Then to the count he said: "Never did I see the right man turn up at a more convenient moment. I don't know whether you guessed, or whether you know from what someone has told you, but I have been longing for armor as fine as yours, and that fetching dark cloak you're wearing. You have come at just the right time to fit me out with the very things I need!" / Orlando had stood up. "I shall sell you my armor," he observed with a sardonic smile, "at a price that merchants don't normally reckon to pay." From the fire next to him he snatched a flaming, smoky brand, flung it, and struck the brigand, as it happened, on the bridge of the nose. / Neither eye escaped the brand, but it did more damage to the left one: it deprived him of his last source of light, and, not content with blinding him, the savage blow dispatched him to join the spirits whom Chiron and his crew guard in the fiery swamps.

The most basic thematic parallels with the scene in *Metamorphoses* 12 are between the characters: Orlando is to Theseus as Isabella is to Hippodame. Each hero endeavors to rescue a young virgin from bestial characters loose in a cave. Orlando is *cortese* (12.92.5) and *valoroso* (13.39.8), while Theseus is *magnanimus* (12.230) and *generosus* (12.234). But at the same time, Orlando is also described in terms that recall one of the centaurs who fought so viciously against Theseus. Lines 5–8 in stanza 35 allude to the passage in *Metamorphoses* 12 in which Rhoetus smashes a Lapith's head with a brand from the fire (12.271–73):[46]

> Ecce rapit mediis flagrantem Rhoetus ab aris
> pruniceum torrem dextraque a parte Charaxi
> tempora perfringit fulvo protecta capillo.

> Then Rhoetus caught up a blazing brand of plum-wood from the altar and, whirling it on the right, smashed through Charaxus's temples covered with yellow hair.

When Orlando, in the role of Theseus, is described in terms reserved for one of Theseus's enemies, the reader is invited to consider the implied comparison. Ariosto's hero is the embodiment of both the good and bad characters in the Ovidian model, or, to put it another way, Ariosto interprets the two sides at war in *Metamorphoses* 12 as indistinguishable and therefore as equally suitable analogues for Orlando.[47] The Renaissance poet thereby makes an implicit comment on the nature of Theseus in Ovid's narrative: the hero and the Lapiths are just as bestial as the centaurs. Such a view will come as no surprise to the reader acquainted with the escapades of Theseus and Pirithous, nor will it seem strange to any student of mythology who knows that Ixion, former king of the Lapiths and father of Pirithous, also sired the centaurs. In Ovid's scene we are witnessing a familial version of civil war. Ariosto seals the comparison between the robbers and the centaurs by referring to the centaur Chiron as he registers Orlando's killing of the robber (36.5–8). Orlando dispatches the dead robber to that part of Dante's hell guarded by the centaurs. With the centaur imagery coming full circle, the poet suggests that Orlando, the robbers, the Lapiths, and the centaurs are all of the same type. And indeed it is not long in the *Furioso*'s narrative before Orlando's own bestiality explodes (*Furioso* 23.111ff.).

The narrator's comment—that Orlando strikes the robber by chance where his brow meets his nose: "percosse il malandrino a caso / dove confina con le ciglia il naso" (35.7)—once again foregrounds, albeit subtly, Ariosto's narrative opportunism. In the Ovidian model, Rhoetus smashes Charaxus in his temples rather than at the bridge of his nose. The text may claim that Orlando swings haphazardly, "a caso," but the poet deliberately develops the imitation in this way to avoid too obvious a parallel with the Ovidian passage. In other words, chance does not govern Orlando's swing; rather, the poet's concern to check his imitation of the Ovidian model determines that Orlando hit the robber's nose so as to differ slightly but noticeably from Rhoetus's attack on Charaxus. Such a bald statement may be belaboring the obvious: any poetic text, of course, conforms in some way to its author's intentions, although, as modern readers have repeatedly pointed out since the New Critics, it is difficult, if not impossible, to determine what those intentions are.[48] Without addressing the complex issues raised by the notion of authorial intention, one can conclude that Ariosto's imitation of Ovid is intentional. In fact, in his treatment of Ovid one detects a pattern of Ariosto's imitative poiesis, which can be reduced to a simple axiom: the more the poet draws the reader's attention to the category of "chance," the less likely chance is to be operative in the design of the passage. Here in canto 13, as happens at other points in the poem, we catch sight of the poet's glimmering hand, with the ring of chance on his finger.

This same robber—he of the bashed head—had seen in Orlando, let us recall, the very opportunity that he himself turns out to be for the narrative. At 34.7, the robber exclaims—to paraphrase—that Orlando has come just in the nick of time to supply him with a new suit of armor. The robber's sarcasm is even sharper just above, in the same stanza where Ariosto has his doomed character invoke the vocabulary of chance: "Uomo non vidi mai / più commodo di te, né più opportuno" (34.1–2). Orlando will fit right in to the story's development as the robber envisions it; indeed, inasmuch as he is "commodo" and "opportuno," he provides the robber with the opportunity to rewrite the narrative to suit, as it were, himself. These key terms, whose meanings we weighed at the beginning of this chapter and in the "Introduction," are now seen to be synonyms in Ariosto's lexicon. Here Orlando presents an opportunity for the robber; later the poet must focus on one opportune example of Orlando's madness (29.50); and, as I argued in the "Introduction," Angelica as commodity (23.108) saves Medoro in a timely fashion, which enables the poet to remove them both from the narrative. As we saw in the earlier discussion of Angelica and Medoro, the semantic field surrounding *commoditas* is characteristic of Roman comedy and is respected in Ariosto's Italian versions of that genre. Here in canto 13 we are dealing once again with a poetic structure that straddles several generic borders. The denouement of this would-be tragedy turns into a mock epic by way of several comic twists, such as the robber's missed opportunity; or, perhaps it would be more accurate to say, by way of the robber's misunderstanding of the nature of *opportunitas*. The rule of narrative opportunism dictates that the narrative develop in ways that seem inexplicable but that are, upon investigation, wholly understandable. The robber, of course, could not have ended up any other way.

We saw above how Ariosto fuses Theseus and Rhoetus into a single source for Orlando; in so doing the poet effectively collapses the narrative structure of his source. Ariosto makes his description of the fight as brief and condensed as Nestor's narrative is long and distended. The poet furthers this collapse of the narrative with another allusion to the way Orlando fights. In Ovid's depiction there is some humor in the adaptation of the table setting as ballistic missiles: " . . . res epulis quondam tum bello et caedibus aptae" (244). (. . . utensils once meant for use of feasting, but now for war and slaughter.) The Lapiths and Centaurs hurl pots and pans at one another from behind tables turned up on their sides: "protinus eversae turbant convivia mensae" (222). (Straightaway the tables were overturned and the banquet in an uproar.) Ariosto in his condensed allusion narrates how Orlando simply uses the dinner table itself as a weapon (37–38). The hero casts it on the group of robbers and kills a dozen in a single blow. This rewriting of the *Metamorphoses* enables the poet to omit detailed descriptions of each robber's death enunciated by a Nestorian narrator. It also allows him to invoke once more the theme of "caso": "nascono casi, e non saprei dir quanti" (39.1). (The strangest things can happen, and I couldn't say how many.)[49]

The invocation of "caso," which calls to mind fortune, opportunity, and the family of words around "commodità," attunes us to a passage of heightened interest. At the beginning of this chapter I introduced the octave where Ariosto asks his reader to choose from the various possible endings to the life of the hermit whom Rodomonte tosses out to sea (29.7). Something similar happens here in 13.39, but the varied endings are acted out before the reader's eyes: some robbers die in one way, some in another, some even have "more propitious saints" and escape, anticipating the version of the hermit's story that reports that "a saint came to his aid." The representation of this multiplicity of actual deaths is achieved through a simile (38–39):

A chi 'l petto, a chi 'l ventre, a chi la testa,
a chi rompe le gambe, a chi le braccia;
di ch'altri muore, altri storpiato resta:
chi meno è offeso, di fuggir procaccia.
Così talvolta un grave sasso pesta
e fianchi e lombi, e spezza capi e schiaccia,
gittato sopra un gran drapel di biscie,
che dopo il verno al sol si goda e liscie.

Nascono casi, e non saprei dir quanti:
una muore, una parte senza coda,
un'altra non si può muover davanti,
e 'l deretano indarno aggira e snoda;
un'altra, ch'ebbe più propizii i santi,
striscia fra l'erbe, e va serpendo a proda.
Il colpo orribil fu, ma non mirando,
poi che lo fece il valoroso Orlando.

One had his chest stove in, another his belly or his skull; others had fractured legs or arms; some were slain outright, others maimed; those with least injuries tried to escape. It was like when a heavy stone falls upon a knot of serpents sunning themselves in the late spring, and some have their backs crushed, others their heads shattered. / The strangest things can happen and I couldn't say how many: one snake dies, another slips off without its tail, a third is paralysed all except for its tail, which vainly coils and uncoils, while the next, with more propitious saints, slithers off through the grass to safety. All in all a spectacular blow, but not to be wondered at, seeing that it was the work of mighty Orlando. (adapted from Waldman)

Through the workings of the simile, the robbers are transformed into snakes. We expect caves to be filled with beasts, and in this Ovidian cave we are not surprised to see men likened to animals. But there is another source lurking here that effects this transformation, or, to return to the guiding metaphor of this study, there is another source muddying these textual waters. When Orlando dispatches his first victim to the realm of the violent, guarded over by the centaurs in Dante's *Inferno,* the reader's attention is drawn momentarily to Ariosto's great vernacular predecessor (36.8). That allusion, however, is fleeting. But the comparison of the robbers to snakes marks a decisive link with *Inferno* 24–25, in which Dante the pilgrim encounters robbers being metamorphosed into serpents of all sorts. (These same cantos will be grist for Tasso's mill, as we shall see shortly below in chapter 4.) Ariosto confirms the connection between his snake-robbers and Dante's by borrowing rhymes from the climactic transformation in *Inferno* 25. At 25.128–35, Dante calls on the following words to end each line of verse: faccia, convenne, caccia, testa, lumaccia, presta, forcuta, resta. In recycling the Dantesque terza rima into the metrical pattern of his poem, Ariosto uses the sequence "-esta, -accia" in octave 38. It is not so much the repetition of words (in both poets we find "testa" and "resta") as it is the repetition of the rhyming pattern that leads us to conclude that Ariosto had the Dantesque model in mind as he composed his simile. But why?

Dante's passage to which Ariosto alludes by rhyme comes at the conclusion of the final metamorphosis in *Inferno* 25. This is the famous transformation that the poet introduces with a challenge to Ovid and Lucan: "Taccia di Cadmo e d'Aretusa Ovidio, / ché se quello in serpente e quella in fonte / converte poetando, . . ." (25.97–99). (Concerning Cadmus and Arethusa let Ovid be silent, for if he, poetizing, converts the one into a serpent and the other into a fountain, . . .) Dante's point is that he will surpass Ovid's poetic feat of describing one entity turning into another, for example, of Cadmus becoming a serpent. Instead, the Italian poet will describe two natures simultaneously transmogrifying into each other, which he proceeds to do. As Barkan has shown, much of the language of cantos 24 and 25 is drawn from Ovidian descriptions of metamorphosis, thus the entire episode and not just the final passage is in agonistic rapport with Ovid (153ff.).

Enter Ariosto. Why does he allude to Dante's allusion to Ovid? To surpass them both, which he does numerically and humorously. If Ovid can change one entity, and Dante two, Ariosto, it turns out, can change a dozen or so (to be exact would be pedantic of the Renaissance poet!). Dante's "Taccia Ovidio" has been transformed into Ariosto's "Touché, Dante," with the transformation of robbers into snakes keeping its Ovidian origins in sight as well as maintaining the fiction that Orlando, the heroic chivalric knight, can throw gigantic tables around at will. Here we are dealing with an imitation (Ariosto) of an imitation (Dante) of an original (Ovid), an Ovidian "original" that is also notorious for its rewriting of prior texts.

I have already suggested that Ariosto simplifies the Ovidian narrative by parodying Nestor's style. Just as Ovid's narrative with its comic hyperrealistic descriptions of hand-to-hand combat to the death parodies Homeric battle narrative, so Ariosto's abbreviated tale parodies Ovid's overblown version of Homeric epic. It is possible that Ariosto read some Homer in Latin translation and, therefore, may have perceived Ovid's conscious attempt at satirizing various conventions of the epic text. If so, he may have been conscious of establishing a similar relationship to Ovid's text, which he refracted at various points through his reading of other texts, like the *Inferno*. It is the ultimate form of flattery the imitator can pay the model.

But then, too, Ariosto treats other classical authors in a similar parodic way. For example, his allusion in *Furioso* 18–19 to the Nisus and Euryalus episode of *Aeneid* 9 is similar in narrative structure to Ovid's version of the *Aeneid* in *Metamorphoses* 13–14. Ariosto subjects Vergil's narrative in that episode to the romance technique of interlacing at the points where the narrative is intensifying. This creates a disruptive juncture that diminishes the pathos of the original model and frustrates the expectations of readers familiar with the classical text. Ovid's version of the *Aeneid* is similarly interlaced beyond recognition. At any point where the narrative begins to remind the reader of the Vergilian original, the narrator in *Metamorphoses* 13–14 quickly sets in motion a diversion that frustrates the reader's expectations.[50]

Parody as a means of commenting on a model is a conscious literary process. Ovid is always in firm control of his narrative, especially at those moments when he confronts the problems inherent in the narrative situation by reminding the reader of the varying degrees of credibility his authorities possess. At 12.360, in the description of the battle of the Lapiths and the Centaurs, Ovid calls on a telling parenthetical half-line, "credi sic ipse volebat." (At least that is what he himself would have us believe.) Theseus ducks when a centaur tosses a tree trunk at him because, as he told Nestor, Athena directed him to do so. Nestor's editorializing comment mocks those scenes in the *Iliad* in which the gods maneuver their favorite mortals in and out of danger. The remark also casts another shadow over the enterprise of storytelling. The line is an outright challenge to the nature of fiction and its interpretation.

Ariosto also frequently reminds the reader of the process in which he is engaged. He accomplishes this in *Furioso* 13 by referring to the number of robbers left alive when Orlando hurled the table on them all: "Quei che la mensa o nulla o poco offese / (e Turpin scrive a punto che fur sette), . . ." (40.1–2). (Those who escaped with little or no damage from the table [and Turpin specifically mentions seven survivors, . . .]) Bishop Turpin allegedly accompanied Charlemagne's army and kept a record of its battles against the Moors, but his authority here is highly suspect and points to the impossibility of Orlando tossing a table big enough to seat at least twenty men across the room of a cave.[51] The pseudoscientific reference to Turpin merely raises questions about the validity of the source.

The episode of the robbers ends in stanza 41, and in the following three stanzas new episodes begin, only to be immediately interrupted, and in each the narrator speaks openly in the first person as he reorganizes the narrative. He follows Gabrina for a stanza to note that she encounters a warrior: "ma diferisco a ricontar chi fosse / e torno all'altra [Isabella]" (42.8–43.1). ([W]ho he was, I shall tell you later, / and go back now to the damsel.) The narrator then follows Isabella and Orlando for several lines until they meet a knight: "Chi fosse, dirò poi; ch'or me ne svia / tal, di chi udir non vi sarà men caro" (44.5–6). ([W]ho he was I shall tell you by and by: just now I am being distracted by one whom you will be glad to hear about.) Eventually he resumes the tale of Bradamante, the poem's heroine, which had been shunted aside since *Furioso* 7. The narrator, not Turpin, takes responsibility for the narrative's structure and the organization of its material. He "defers" the story of Gabrina ("diferisco"); he "will tell later" whom Isabella and Orlando have met ("dirò poi"); and he "strays" off track somewhat by returning to Bradamante ("me ne svia"). As the sequence's focus turns from Isabella, the interlaced narrative draws attention to the narrator himself and his poetic designs. The situation parallels Ovid's Theseus sequence, in which the hero plays an ever diminishing role in scenes that are purportedly about him. And like the Theseus sequence, which tells the reader much more about Ovidian narrative in general than about Theseus as a specific character, stanzas 42–44 reveal much more about Ariostan narrative structure than about any specific character.

In adapting the scene in *Metamorphoses* 12 as the primary model for the scene in *Furioso* 13, Ariosto alludes to specific characteristics of the passage that are both thematic and structural. He resumes the interlaced structure of Nestor's narrative, but he refuses to imitate the Ovidian model in a slavish fashion. Instead he parodies its structure in much the same way that Ovid parodies Homeric narrative in *Metamorphoses* 12. And he does this to the same effect: one learns much about Ovidian poetry and Ovidian poetics in studying Ariosto's imitation. Whether or not the passage from the *Furioso* succeeds in outdoing the *Metamorphoses* is one question, but there is no denying that Ariosto's creative response to the narrative design of *Metamorphoses* 12 is an example of insightful literary criticism.[52]

I conclude with a remark by Bernardo Tasso, whose opinion of Ariosto's narrative I examined in some detail in chapter 1. Tasso dismisses the element of chance that underlies the narrative of the *Furioso:* "che non a caso (come molti dicono) ma con molta prudenzia, e molto giudicio

[Ariosto] habbia tessuta l'opera sua."[53] (Not by chance as many claim but with much prudence and judgment Ariosto weaved his work.) My reading of Ariosto's imitation of Ovid is in accord with Tasso's observation. But I would supplement the critic's comment by repeating a point made above. True, Ariosto did not weave his work haphazardly, yet he wanted his reader to experience the narrative of the *Furioso* as essentially accidental. That is, he wanted to make the choices underlying his narrative appear fortuitous. The logic governing the choice of the Ovidian narrative model is, however, not random at all. The degree to which Ariosto's choice seems arbitrary is a measure of his success in creating a credible vision of a random world. And the Ovidian source, perhaps more than any other classical source, encourages the poet's feigned inability to dictate what will happen in his own poem—a work in which, as Pinocchio might put it, "So many things can happen!"

CHAPTER 4

The Misshapen Beast:
The Furioso*'s Serpentine Narrative*

denique sit quod vis, simplex dumtaxat et unum.

HORACE, *ARS POETICA* 23

Così il Trissino E qui ha peccato quel grandissimo poeta che io non nomino per veneratione, ma il suo peccato gli sarà perdonato dal giudice il più severo se fosse ancora un Dracone perchè ha partorito tante maravigliose e divine bellezze.

TORQUATO TASSO'S GLOSS ON HORACE[1]

*I*n the previous chapter I made a case for Ovid's *Metamorphoses* as a classical example of an interlaced narrative that served Ariosto as a source of compromise. I considered how Ariosto imitated the formal narrative structures of the Ovidian model. In this chapter I shall continue the investigation of Ariosto's imitation of classical models, but my approach is slightly different. I begin by looking at Ariosto's poetics of compromise through the criticism of his sometime follower, Torquato Tasso. Historicizing my reading in this way—understanding Ariosto through a sixteenth-century reader's interpretation—enables me to come to some different conclusions about the narrative organization and design of the *Furioso*. It also prepares us for the book's final chapter, in which I discuss Torquato's reaction to the poetics of compromise he inherited from Ariosto.

Tasso: Dante: Ariosto

To criticize Ariosto's *Orlando Furioso* for its multiple plots, Torquato Tasso evokes an image from canto 25 of Dante's *Inferno,* the canto that depicts robbers being metamorphosed unendingly into snakes. In the second of the *Discorsi dell'arte poetica,* Tasso criticizes romance poems in general, although the context of his remarks makes clear that he specifically has in mind the *Furioso:* " . . . the interposing and mingling of their parts, one with another, is monstrous, resembling that beast Dante describes in this tercet (and in the passage that follows):

> Ellera abbarbicata mai non fue
> ad arbor sì, come l'orribil fera
> per l'altrui membra avviticchiò le sue;"

> Ivy was never so rooted
> to a tree as the horrid beast
> entwined its own limbs round the other's;[2]

Tasso adduces the snakelike creature wrapped around a man in the second half of the tercet as an example of radical unnaturalness. It is analogous to the *Furioso,* a gargantuan fusion of multiple plots worthy of an unnatural beast.[3] Since Tasso is a resourceful critic, one should not be surprised at an occasional allusion to the *Inferno* in the service of his criticism. This particular borrowing from Dante, however, is telling, for this same image of the snake-man monster that threatens Tasso's critical sensibilities plays a prominent part in Ariosto's poem.[4] In fact, a sequence of snake similes that partially derives its significance from allusions to *Inferno* 25 organizes the *Furioso*'s narrative.[5]

The same can be said of the ivy simile in the first half of the Dantesque tercet. Ivy on a tree as a symbol of fastness is a familiar, even trite, image in the classical repertory behind *Inferno* 25,[6] although Dante does invigorate his vernacular version with the words "abbarbicata" and "avviticchiò." Tasso surely appreciated this moment of innovative imitation in which Dante did his models one better. But what was the critic in him thinking when he trotted out this tercet to gloss the *Furioso*'s lack of narrative continuity? Like the sequence of snake similes important to the perception of the *Furioso*'s internal unity, there is a sequence of ivy ones, again linked to the passage in *Inferno* 25, which unifies the poem's narrative. In other words, the Dantesque tercet that bears Tasso's emblem of the misshapen narrative is twice contradicted by the actual text of Ariosto's poem. Two images, then, through which Tasso criticizes the *Furioso* for its lack of unity had been used by Ariosto to unify his poem.

What led Tasso to ignore these unifying textual details in the *Furioso* but at the same time prompted him to reclaim them subversively as symbols of the poem's narrative disproportion? Why the ivylike snake-man as a figure for Ariosto's multistoried narrative? Does this suggest that Tasso did not or could not read the *Furioso* very well? Did institutional pressures impinge on his interpretation of the poem, blinding him to inherent unities in Ariosto's narrative? Or—a final possibility—did Tasso understand exactly his resort to paradox when in a single stroke he simultaneously criticized and praised Ariosto's organization of multiple plots into a single narrative?

I reserve a final opinion until the conclusion of this chapter. I need first to set Tasso's reaction to the *Furioso* (with its Dantesque and Ovidian entanglements) in the context of his narrative theory and his own long poem, the *Gerusalemme Liberata.* Here Tasso's problematic position toward the ivy and the snake becomes acute. I shall then focus on the object of Tasso's criticism, the *Furioso* itself, especially on the simile of the snake, which provides a running commentary on the madness of the poem's titular hero, Orlando. It shapes the *Furioso* into anything but the misshapen beast to which Tasso objects.

Tasso's comparison of Ariosto's *Furioso* to an infernal creature bespeaks a complex relationship to the poem and to the poet, who was his major predecessor at the Este court in Ferrara. Ariosto had been dead for three decades when, in the 1560s, Tasso worked out the critical positions expressed in the *Discorsi,* but the *Furioso,* already published in over thirty different editions, was very much alive. No one was more aware of the *Furioso*'s extraordinary popularity, of its success as a sixteenth-century best-seller, than the young Tasso, who used the composition of his *Discorsi* to chart ever so tentatively a critical course that would negotiate the shoals of neoclassicism and post-Tridentine Christianity without forfeiting the fame and profit Ariosto's poem was accruing. At the theoretical level, Tasso's *Discorsi* reflect an uneasiness in the young poet's dismissal of Ariostan romance in favor of a dogmatically classicizing poetic propriety. This uneasiness is perhaps nowhere more present than in the passage on the relationship between plot and narrative construction. Here Tasso formulates his ideas on plot and narrative into a theory that he puts into practice in the *Liberata.*[7] The poem, for its part, constantly challenges and frequently undermines many of the theoretical positions that are articulated in the *Discorsi* against the typical romance narrative, for example, Ariosto's "misshapen beast." Much is at stake in Tasso's critical negotiations with the literary precedents set by the *Furioso.*

This becomes apparent when one sees how Tasso works out the *Discorsi*'s criticism of romance narrative in the *Liberata,* where various episodes composed of romancelike narrative threaten the poem's epic plot. In the passage from the *Discorsi* cited above, the aspect of romance narrative that specifically elicits the comparison to Dante's beast is "the interposing and mingling of their parts"—"il traporre e mescolare le membra." The verb "traporre" (here used substantivally) is a translation of a technical term that derives from the Latin rhetorical tradition: "interponere" in a narrative context means to interrupt a continuous narrative with a digression.[8] In Latin and Italian the verb means literally "to place between," and it suggests the placing of one narrative within another in order to interrupt the continuous flow of the prior narrative.

Tasso sets this theoretical verb in a dramatic context in the *Liberata*'s opening canto when he describes God's vexation with the Christian crusaders for delaying their attack on Jerusalem. Gabriel, the angelic interpreter, addresses Godfrey, the leader of the Christians, paraphrasing God's message (1.16):

> Goffredo, ecco opportuna
> già la stagion ch'al guerreggiar s'aspetta;
> perché dunque *trapor* dimora alcuna
> a liberar Gierusalem soggetta?
> Tu i principi a consiglio omai raguna,
> tu al fin de l'opra i neghittosi affretta.
> Dio per lor duce già t'elegge, ed essi
> *sopporran* volontari a te se stessi.[9]

Godfrey, behold the season now is ripe that is waiting for you to go to war. Why then *interpose* any delay in liberating captive Jerusalem? Assemble the princes at once in council, hurry the slothful on to the end of the task. Now God elects you as their leader, and *they will* willingly *subject* themselves to you. (emphasis mine)[10]

Military strategy is not the only information transmitted in the divine message to Godfrey. God, the cosmic artificer, suddenly becomes very much like a poet, an Italian one no less. But here the similarity does not depend on the usual humanistic commonplaces about poetic creativity, which often derive from Neoplatonic teachings on the mysteries of inspiration.[11] Rather, the view of God conflates in this passage with the perspective of the poet and highlights two contradictory methods of constructing the poem's narrative. The verbs "trapor" (16.3) and "sopporran" (16.8) suggest modes of narrative construction associated with romance, on the one hand, and epic, on the other. God is concerned lest his Renaissance Christian epic degenerate into a medieval romance.

The form "trapor" is a syncopated infinitive from "traporre," the key verb in the passage of the *Discorsi*. To build a narrative around this verb would be to write a romance made up of narratives within a narrative, a poem full of delays and delights, which would never achieve the goal of liberating the holy sepulcher of Christ, announced in the poem's programmatic opening stanza. In sharp contrast to the meaning of "trapor" is the syncopated form "sopporran," an irregular future from "sottoporre," which suggests not only an appropriate tactical strategy for taking Jerusalem but also the necessary compositional formula for a successful epic plot. Only when Godfrey's peers willingly "put themselves under" his leadership can the teleological machinery of the epic bring the plot to its close. Only when the divided Christian camp is reconstituted as a single fighting unit can Jerusalem be taken and subsequently defended.[12]

Readers of the *Liberata* know that this concession to Godfrey's authority is long in coming. Finally, in canto 18, Rinaldo, the last prince to submit to Godfrey's leadership, dutifully chops down a tree in the enchanted wood and thus rids the forest and the poem of its romance magic. Of course this cannot happen without one last example of narrative deferral (the poem after all manages to postpone its inevitable conclusion for twenty cantos). As Rinaldo prepares to chop down the enchanted tree, Armida, the magical pagan temptress, suddenly reappears, her actions marked by the verb of narrative interposition (18.34.1–4):

> Vassene al mirto; allor colei s'abbraccia
> al caro tronco, e *s'interpone* e grida
> "Ah non sarà mai ver che tu mi faccia
> oltraggio tal, che l'arbor mio recida!"

> He approaches the myrtle; whereupon she embraces the trunk and *interposes herself* and cries: "Oh it will never be that you do me such outrage that you cut down my tree." (emphasis mine)

The image of Armida in front of Rinaldo hugging the tree parodies an earlier moment in their romance when the young couple lay entwined in each other's arms shaded by entangled vines (16.11). But now things are different. Rinaldo, who has "put himself under" the authority of Godfrey, does not succumb to Armida, although she has interposed herself ivylike between the hero and his goal. Her transformation into a figure of ivy (and two stanzas below into that image of romance par excellence, a monstrous giant with enlarged parts, 16.36) is one of the final non-epic touches in the *Liberata*'s narrative and as such alludes nostalgically not only to earlier passages in the poem but also to several passages in the *Furioso* in which the narrator uses the image of entwined ivy to describe the amorous configurations of lovers.

There are, however, some noticeable differences in Ariosto's version of the ivy simile, despite its importance as a model for Tasso's Armida in 18.34 and its function as a mediating text between Tasso and the Dantesque tercet of the infernal snake-man. In Ariosto's rewriting of Dante's simile the configuration of lovers does not produce a monster. The embrace of Ruggiero and Alcina, the wayward hero and the pagan temptress in Ariosto's poem, is described with a reflexive verb (7.29.1–3):

> Non così strettamente edera preme
> pianta ove intorno abbarbicata s'abbia,
> come si stringon li dui amanti insieme.

> Ivy never clung so tightly to the stem round which it was entwined as did the two lovers cling to each other.

With a similar emphasis on amorous reciprocity, the Ariostan narrator describes the ivylike embraces of Angelica and Medoro in the grotto of ivy where the lovers appropriately leave an entanglement of inscriptions, in Arabic and Italian, as a graphic imitation of how they passed the time (19.36 and 23.103–6). When Ricciardetto, a minor character in the poem, recounts how he and Fiordispina embraced, he predictably calls on the by-now-familiar image of the clinging plant (25.69.5–8):

> Non con più nodi i flessuosi acanti
> le colonne circondano e le travi,
> di quelli con che noi legammo stretti
> e colli e fianchi e braccia e gambe e petti.

> Never did twisting acanthus entwine pillars and beams with more knots than those which bound us together, our necks and sides, our arms, legs, and breasts in a close embrace.

The figure of ivy in the *Furioso* is not directly associated with the misshapen beast as it is in Tasso's scene of Armida, but for Ariosto the image is nevertheless problematic. The erotic embrace deters the Ariostan characters from fulfilling their various duties, much as it does in the *Aeneid,* interposing itself and as a result creating new narrative possibilities. In *Furioso* 25, Ricciardetto tries to make up for his inadequacies on the battlefield by insinuating himself into Fiordispina's bed; his sexual prowess, not to mention his way with words, proves greater than his military skills.[13] Ruggiero escapes Alcina's clutches in canto 7 only to fall back into the deferred episodic narrative of romance at the end of canto 10, where he attempts to rape Angelica. This is in contrast to Rinaldo in the *Liberata,* who, once set right, dispatches his duty without further delay: "Ma pur mai colpo il cavalier non erra, / né per tanto furor punto s'arresta" (18.37.5). (But yet the knight never misses a stroke, nor stays a moment for all that madness.)[14] It is as if Tasso's character were finally able to free himself from Ariostan "furor," from a literary model cast in the mold of romance. Like the character in his poem, Tasso is finally able to resist the temptations of episodic romance by canto 18 of the *Liberata,* whence the poem hastens to a suitable epic ending. But then, too, overcoming the threat of romance in Rinaldo's decisive meeting with Armida hardly discounts the ongoing dalliance with romance narrative in the better part of the *Liberata.*

The inclusion of romance elements in Tasso's poem depends in part on the poet's ambiguous relationship to the *Furioso*'s narrative. But his recourse to ivy as a sign for the narrative interposition of romance is contradicted by the same symbol in Ariosto's poem. The three examples of the ivy simile in the *Furioso* do not threaten to disrupt the narrative; on the contrary, they contribute to its unity by establishing a network of anticipated allusions within the text and beyond it to Dante's *Inferno.* The contradiction between Tasso's theory and Ariosto's praxis is greater and even more apparent in the *Furioso*'s sequence of snake similes in which the snake-man rears his misshapen head.

Similes of the Snake and Metaphors of Narrative Poiesis

The similes of the snake in cantos 1, 23, 39, and 42 are textual markers that signal Orlando's move in and out of madness and point to Angelica as the prime cause for the hero's fall.[15] By alluding to one another within the text, the four similes establish an *intra*textual continuity that helps the reader negotiate the vast distance from the beginning of the poem to canto 42, near its end. At the same time, the similes' allusions to other texts beyond the *Furioso*—classical, biblical, and vernacular—provide a sort of commentary on Ariosto's treatment of literary models that also contributes to the poem's unity. The simile in canto 1, for example, alludes to *Inferno* 15 and, through Dante's poem, to the New Testament, Vergil's *Aeneid,* and Ovid's *Fasti.* These various allusions (and others) are repeated in different ways each time the simile returns over the course of the narrative, with Ovid's *Fasti* in particular serving as a base for Ariosto's *inter*textual poetics. The snake simile becomes a kind of crux in the *Furioso,* an intertextual crossing point where many and differing texts are brought together through the poet's imitation.

Consider the first example of the simile, in which Angelica, the Oriental princess, object of many knights' desires, flees the snake (1.10.7–11.8):

entrò in un bosco, e ne la stretta via
rincontrò un cavallier ch'a piè venia.

Indosso la corazza, l'elmo in testa,
la spada al fianco, e in braccio avea lo scudo;
e più leggier correa per la foresta,
ch'al pallio rosso il villan mezzo ignudo.
Timida pastorella mai sì presta
non volse piede inanzi a serpe crudo,
come Angelica tosto il freno torse,
che del guerrier, ch'a piè venia, s'accorse.

Entering a wood and following a narrow path, she came upon a knight who was approaching on foot. / He wore a breastplate, and on his head a helmet; his sword hung by his side, and on his arm he bore his shield; and he came running through the forest more fleet of foot than the lightly-clad farmer sprinting for the red mantle at the village games. Never did a timid shepherd-girl start back more violently from a horrid snake than did Angelica, jerking on the reins the moment she saw the armed man approach on foot. (adapted from Waldman)

Ariosto departs from the tradition of chivalric romance in Boiardo's *Orlando Innamorato* and Niccolò degli Agostini's continuation of Boiardo precisely where Angelica flees the Christian camp. She manages to escape on horseback just as the Saracens overcome the Christian army encamped in the shadow of the Pyrenees. No sooner has Angelica entered a wood—Is this perhaps a figure for the narrative of Ariosto's poem itself?—than she encounters a knight, whom we eventually discover is Rinaldo. The repetition of the qualifying phrase, "ch'a piè venia" (10.8 and 11.8), calls the reader's attention to something unusual about this knight: he has no horse.[16] The poem will frequently fix on the paradox of the horseless equestrian, indeed, the theme of the "cavalliere" without his "cavallo" that is introduced in these lines will contribute to the resolution of its multiple plots as the poem works toward its end.[17]

In stanzas 10 and 11 of the opening canto, the knight who approaches Angelica wears a full suit of armor, as if to make up for the lack of a horse. Here the text signals another paradox, this time not through repetition but through a playfully serious pun, the first of many in the *Furioso*. The knight's armor does not impede him; quite the contrary: "e più leggier correa per la foresta, / ch'al pallio rosso il villan mezzo ignudo" (11.3–4). He is like a country runner in speed and agility (indeed he is faster than a racer). The pun on "più leggiero," which here has the sense of "more gracefully" but literally means "more lightly," suggests that Rinaldo runs fast despite his armor. The pun works in that his armor actually makes him heavier (not lighter) than the comparison implies. This emphasis on the dress of the knight makes the subsequent focus on the vehicle of comparison, the "villan" as "mezzo ignudo," rather curious, for this knight is, if anything, overdressed. In fact, the reader sees him (through the eyes of Angelica) as a horseless suit of armor, emphasized piece by piece: first the cuirass, then the helmet, then the sword dangling at his side, and finally the shield in hand (1–2).

Why then does the poet compare the knight to the country racer? Surely not merely to focus on speed and dress. The allusion is to a passage from the end of *Inferno* 15, which describes Ser Brunetto racing back to join his particular group of sinners: "e parve di coloro / Che corrono a Verona il drappo verde / Per la campagna" (121–23) (and [he] seemed like one of those who run for the green cloth in the field at Verona [Singleton 161]). The Dantesque source in turn alludes to a passage from the Second Letter to Timotheus (4:7–8), where Paul describes the Christian's experience of life as a race to the end, with God as the ultimate judge. The Dantesque allusion, with its sexual overtones (Ser Brunetto is a condemned homosexual) and with its foregrounding of the issue of winners and losers, calls to mind as well a contemporary event of Ariosto's Ferrara, the palio of San Giorgio, a public contest full of sexual coding.[18] Whether or not the poet alludes directly to this contemporary race, this depiction of the "villan" prepares the reader for later scenes of knights racing like naked "villani" in and out of the narrative picture.

The second half of stanza 11 portrays Angelica's reaction to Rinaldo in its juxtaposition of the knight as sprinter to Angelica as shepherdess.[19] The two similes overlap in Rinaldo, who metamorphoses from the "villan" into the frightening snake. The snake simile focuses not only on Angelica's fear but also on the speed with which she turns away and thereby generates the centrifugal movement for which the *Furioso*'s first canto is so famous.[20]

Angelica's deft retreat before the figurative snake alludes to a passage in the *Aeneid* that describes how a Greek, Androgeos, on the rampage inside Troy, mistakes a band of Trojans in the dark for his compatriots: "improvisum aspris veluti qui sentibus anguem / pressit humi nitens trepidusque repente refugit" (2.379–80). (Just as he who has squashed an unseen snake along some path of briars, when stepping on the ground, and suddenly frightened pulls back [my translation].) Although Ariosto does not follow the model rigorously (his character manages to escape the snake, whereas Androgeos is killed), an early commentator, Lodovico Dolce, made much of this allusion to the *Aeneid* in the poem's opening simile.[21] Dolce's agenda was to align the *Furioso* with the Roman epic so that the Venetian publisher, Gabriele Giolito, might capitalize on the public's association of Ariosto with Vergil—a successful marketing strategy that led to twenty-seven printings of the Giolito edition with Dolce's commentary between 1542 and 1560.

A late-sixteenth-century commentator on the *Furioso*, Alberto Lavezuola, was the first to suggest another source for the simile of the snake, proposing Ovid's *Fasti* as the more likely model for the shepherdess and snake: "ut saepe viator / turbatus viso rettulit angue pedem" (2.341–42). (As often a traveler / startled at the sight of a snake pulls his foot back in fear.)[22] Lavezuola's response to the *Furioso* is conditioned by an agonistic reading of Dolce's commentary, which he hardly disguises in his account of the relation between Ariosto's text and the Ovidian simile.[23] Yet, having aggressively distinguished himself from Dolce (and from Girolamo Ruscelli, who in 1556 published a plagiarized version of Dolce's commentary), Lavezuola then borrows an observation from the commentaries of his predecessors.[24] He notes, as do Dolce and Ruscelli, that the passage from *Aeneid* 2 is actually an important subtext for a later version of the snake simile in *Furioso* 39.31–32. This observation constrains him to develop Ariosto's use of the simile from its first example to its later version and to read horizontally, as it were, from cantos 1 to 39 as he accounts for the classical models that underlie vertically various passages of the modern text. Such a reading from cantos 1 to 39 reflects the essential nature of Ariosto's art of imitation, indeed of his poetics in general: namely, how an intratextual interpretation must combine with an intertextual reading of the poem.

Yet why did Ariosto draw on Ovid's *Fasti* at such a prominent moment in the *Furioso*'s narrative? And how might he have come to know it? Like the *Metamorphoses,* the *Fasti* was part of Ariosto's humanist education. I mentioned in chapter 2 that both Ovidian works were central texts in the curriculum of the school founded by Guarino Veronese in the 1430s and run by his family during Ariosto's lifetime. Ariosto never attended the school, but he was in close contact with students who did, and at least one of his private tutors taught there. Once Ariosto began to read the *Fasti,* he found in the work a repository of themes dealing with madness and desire that he would use for the literal and figurative center of the *Furioso*'s narrative. I do not mean to propose that Ariosto encountered these various themes only in the *Fasti,* but rather to suggest that the numerous allusions in the *Furioso* to the Ovidian work document the Italian poet's dependence on that model and attest to its influence on several central episodes in the poem.

The *Fasti* purports to be a commentary on the days of the Roman calendar. It is, however, much more than a work of anthropological interest.[25] The poem reflects no lack of literary artifice, and its narrator is as subversive as his counterpart in the *Metamorphoses.* The passage Ariosto alludes to in his poem's opening simile is linked to the passage in *Fasti* 2 that deals with the festivals of February. Ovid proposes an etymology of the month's name that connects it with the theme of purification and the Luperci (an order of Roman priests), who purify the ground with strips of hide (*Fasti* 2.19 and 31–32). The stories that the narrator then recounts (and there are many) consistently set the issue of purification in the context of the problematics of desire. One particular narrative is that of Faunus, to which the snake sequence in the *Furioso* alludes in structure and theme.

The story of Faunus is offered as a possible explanation for the curious custom of purification, one which, we shall see momentarily, may be a model for Orlando's behavior after he has gone mad. The gist of the Faunus narrative is as follows: once the woodland god saw Hercules returning to a cave with a beautiful woman, Omphale, whom he immediately began to desire. Later that night Faunus crept into the cave, intending to have her while Hercules slept. He didn't know that Hercules and Omphale were purifying themselves for a feast of Dionysus the following day, that they were enduring a night of chastity (their beds pushed apart accordingly), and that, oddly enough, they had exchanged clothes. The outcome of the escapade is predictable: Faunus tiptoes past the guards; he reaches up to the first bed, feels the cloak of the Nemean lion, and recoils (*Fasti* 2.341–42): "ut saepe viator / turbatus viso rettulit angue pedem." (As often a traveler / startled at the sight of a snake pulls his foot back in fear.) The narrative continues (343–50): "Next he touched the soft drapery of the neighboring couch, and its deceptive touch beguiled him. He mounted and lay down on the nearer side. His groins were swollen harder than horn. Then he reached up under the tunics at the lowest hem. There he encountered legs that bristled with a thick rough hair. When he would have proceeded further, the Tirynthian hero suddenly thrust him away. . . . ." Everyone laughs, especially Omphale, who sees Hercules through the dark with her tunics, one can imagine, pulled up over his head, a caricature of a hero. From that day on, betrayed by garments, Faunus urges all followers to come to his rites undressed.

Faunus's solution to his problem is not to check his desire but to let it run rampant. When such a solution is applied to the world of the *Furioso,* however, it inevitably leads the typical heroic knight to abandon his proper station and go astray. It can produce an effeminate hero who resembles the Hercules of *Fasti* 2 (e.g., Ruggiero on the island of Alcina in canto 7).[26] Or it can produce a madman like Orlando, whose identity, sexual and otherwise, is totally confused. Indeed, before Orlando can be identified with the wisdom of Silenus in *Furioso* 39, he must pass through the bleak and (for him) very unhumorous experience of a Faunus.[27]

Later in the narrative, in the vicinity of the snake simile's second version, Orlando initiates the travesty that will transform him into a wild version of the woodland god. In the lair of the snake, as it were, Ariosto foregrounds the issues of sex and sexuality (23.123):

In tanto aspro travaglio gli soccorre
che nel medesmo letto in che giaceva,
l'ingrata donna venutasi a porre
col suo drudo più volte esser doveva.
Non altrimenti or quella piuma abborre,
né con minor prestezza se ne leva,
che de l'erba il villan che s'era messo
per chiuder gli occhi, e vegga il serpe appresso.

Amid such bitter anguish the thought occurred to him that on this very bed in which he was lying the thankless damsel must have lain down many a time with her lover. The downy bed sent a shudder through him and he leapt off it with all the alacrity of a yokel who has lain down in the grass for a nap and spies a snake close by.

The interlacing of episodes from cantos 12 to 23 allows the paladin to arrive at the nuptial bed of Angelica and Medoro. In canto 19 the narrator recounts how the two fall in love, consummate their relationship, marry, and depart for Cathay on an extended honeymoon (19.17–36). The narrative immediately thereafter provides a proleptic glimpse of Orlando gone mad when he encounters the couple as they travel to Cathay (19.37–42). In any case, by the time Orlando arrives at the grotto the text has already provided the reader with an extensive tour of the ivied love nest. And should the reader have forgotten, the narrator reminds him that he has already seen this place (23.102.5).

As Orlando enters the grotto, the narrative recalls the first instance of the snake simile in canto 1 (23.101.1–6):

Il merigge facea grato l'orezzo
al duro armento et al pastore ignudo,
sì che né Orlando sentia alcun ribrezzo,
che la corazza avea, l'elmo e lo scudo.
Quivi egli entrò per riposarvi in mezzo;
e v'ebbe travaglioso albergo e crudo.

A welcome breeze tempered the noontide for the rugged flock and
naked shepherd, and Orlando felt no discomfort, for all that he was
wearing breastplate, helmet, and shield. Here he stopped, then, to
rest—but his welcome proved to be harsh and painful.

The breeze makes the setting pleasant for the flock, even at noon, and for
the shepherd, who is described, curiously, as "ignudo" (2). This seemingly
gratuitous adjective works in two ways: it foreshadows Orlando's discovery that nature made this a comfortable place in which to undress, and it
recalls the "villan mezzo ignudo" who earlier flashed into Angelica's view
before quickly turning into a snake. The allusion to 1.11 is signaled by
the repetition of two of the rhyming words from the stanza, "ignudo" and
"scudo." Orlando's armor, whose enumerated parts recall the formulaic
language of 1.11.1–2, keeps him from feeling the breeze.

What is of interest in 23.101 is the poem's backward glance, its
intratextual meditation on itself. This moment suggests that a troubled
confusion of the sexes underlies the juxtaposition of the two similes in
1.11. The reference to "pastore ignudo" combines the two vehicles of the
double simile in 1.11, the "villan ignudo" and the "timida pastorella." It
turns the shepherdess, who sees the half-naked snake-man, into the naked
shepherd. And this new metaphorical configuration stands as an indirect
comparison to Orlando, who is, for the moment at least, fully dressed.

The issue here involves gender and simile. In *Furioso* 1.11 Ariosto
matches the gender of the vehicle to that of the tenor in each comparison:
Rinaldo is compared to a racer and Angelica to a shepherdess.[28] The
neatness of this division, this fastidiousness to gender, loses its superficial schematization in canto 23, where a retrospective reworking of the
problem of gender takes place.

In 23, as Orlando is haunted by a nightmarish image of his lady
repeatedly giving herself to Medoro, the simile's vehicle is another
"villan" (123.7), who, like the "pastorella" of canto 1, reacts quickly to the
image of the serpent: "né con minor prestezza" (nor with any less speed)
(123.5). The ramifications of the figurative language increase as it works
backward and forward in the narrative. At stanza 133 Orlando becomes
the "ignudo villan" once he has ripped off his armor (again described piece

by piece).[29] This phrasing recalls Rinaldo, to be sure, but it also prefigures later scenes in which Orlando, thoroughly mad, is repeatedly associated with the sphere of the "villan." In 24 he invades the Arcadian world of the shepherds, who try to fend him off with a "villanesco assalto" (attack of peasants) (8.8). When he arrives at Rodomonte's jousting bridge, he fails to abide by the proper chivalric codes, and the offended Saracen calls him an "indiscreto villan" (reckless peasant) (29.41.7) and a "bestia balorda" (impudent beast) (42.2). By canto 39, just before Orlando retrieves his wits, the "villan" has regressed further along the rural chain of being into a bull, a horse, an ox, and a generic beast (45–54). Ironically, a snake of sorts comes to the rescue.

In canto 39, just before Orlando bursts back onto the scene, the narrator describes how Rodomonte commissions a helmsman to ferry his prisoners across the Mediterranean, from France to Algiers (39.31–32):

> Quivi il nocchier, ch'ancor non s'era accorto
> degli inimici, entrò con la galea,
> lasciando molte miglia a dietro il porto
> d'Algieri, ove calar prima volea,
> per un vento gagliardo ch'era sorto,
> e spinto oltre il dover la poppa avea.
> Venir tra i suoi credette e in loco fido,
> come vien Progne al suo loquace nido.
>
> Ma come poi l'imperiale augello,
> i gigli d'oro e i pardi vide appresso,
> restò pallido in faccia, come quello
> che 'l piede incauto d'improviso ha messo
> sopra il serpente venenoso e fello,
> dal pigro sonno in mezzo l'erbe oppresso;
> che spaventato e smorto si ritira,
> fuggendo quel, ch'è pien di tosco e d'ira.

Here the helmsman, unaware of the enemy's presence, brought in his galley, leaving the port of Algiers, his intended goal, many miles astern, for a strong wind had got up and driven him beyond it. Now he imagined he was putting into a safe refuge, like Procne returning to her twittering nest. / But when he noticed the Imperial Eagle, the Golden Lilies, and the Leopards close by, he blanched like a man suddenly aware that his incautious foot has trodden upon a horrid poisonous snake which has been slumbering torpidly in the grass: he recoils in a fright and flees from the angry, venomous reptile. (adapted from Waldman)

The mission fails, however, when the helmsman, blown off course, lands in the midst of the Christian fleet in its preparation to attack Biserta. From the shore the soldiers recognize their companions on board the prison galley, many of whom are important fighters for the Christian cause. Their reunification enables the narrative to continue with the naval battle between Dudone and Agramante, the sack of Biserta, and, most importantly, the revival of Orlando, who appears just after the prison galley comes to harbor. It takes the combined force of the warriors on shore and those on the ship to restrain the mad Orlando while Astolfo prepares to purify him for the ritual of reawakening.

The snake simile comes into play in canto 39 to describe the helmsman's realization that he has sailed into enemy hands. Ariosto establishes the simile in this overtly political context by an allusion in stanza 31 to the myth of Procne, which he knew from another Ovidian source, *Metamorphoses* 6.[30] The Ovidian passage contains several parallels that contribute to the snake's third occurrence. In Ovid's version of the myth, a tale of betrayal and revenge, Tereus rapes his sister-in-law, Philomela, once he ferries her from Athens to Thrace. His actions betray his marriage vows to Procne as well as the trust of his father-in-law, Pandion. Once the plot is uncovered, Tereus, Procne, and Philomela are punished by being transformed into birds. The passage in the *Furioso* alludes to the plot of the myth in Ovid but then immediately subverts it: the helmsman coming to shore with his prisoners is like the bird returning to the nest, or, in the terms of the myth, the helmsman is like Tereus bringing Philomela to shore. In stanza 32 we discover that the helmsman in the end is more like Philomela than Tereus; the helmsman becomes a prisoner himself. The key terms in this equation are "fido" and "credere" (31.7). Philomela trusts in Tereus, just as the helmsman trusts in the place where he is about to land. But both are betrayed by faith.

Stanza 32 opens with an adversative conjunction "ma" that signals the helmsman's reinterpretation of what lies before him. Procne has flown into the claws of the Imperial Bird—one more allusion to the Ovidian Tereus compared to an eagle, "the bird of Jupiter" (*Met.* 6.517). The helmsman sees the banners of the eagle, the lilies, and the leopard and suddenly knows that he is in the midst of the joint armies of the Holy Roman Empire, France, and England. But with a chivalric wind at his back, "vento gagliardo" (31.5), there is no retreat. So the familiar simile recurs as the helmsman is now likened to an indeterminate man ("quello") who carelessly steps on a sleeping snake. The snake simile takes precedence over the formulaic reference to the helmsman as "pallido" (32.3), a topos usually associated with a ship on a stormy sea and the shipwrecked sailor.[31] Here, in the comparison between the helmsman and the man stepping on the snake, the knights awaiting the ship become that very creature. The figurative metamorphosis of Christian knights into a single serpent, into *the* serpent, registered by the linguistic shift from the "serpe" of cantos 1 and 23 to the "serpente" of 39, is significant.[32] On the one hand, it is the first time in the sequence of the simile that the snake itself is asleep. This provides an appropriate gloss on the Christian forces finally on the verge of awakening to despatch the infidels. On the other hand, the image of the Christians as a serpent is ironic, especially because they have been such ineffective defenders of the faith heretofore in the poem. To compare them to the symbolic and archetypal enemy of Christian good exactly at the moment of positive Christian action reminds the reader of all that the narrative has postponed and left undone. The deviation of narrative plots one traditionally associates with the genre of romance is about to yield to a more purely epic movement that is signaled by the Christians' attack on Biserta. And yet at this moment one encounters the archetypal image of deviation. Clearly Ariosto posits some difficulty in the poem's concluding "epic" cantos, and a hint of what is to come can be garnered from the full comparison proposed by the simile: the man who squashes the snake manages to escape while the Christians capture the helmsman whom they mercifully sentence to rowing duty on a prison galley. The snake, for its part, also escapes, only to resurface later in the poem's figurative language.

The snake returns when Brandimarte dies. One could say, in fact, that the snake kills him. The snake simile is directly involved with Orlando's shift from madness to sanity in 23 and 39.[33] Its final appearance in the narrative, however, marks a fall back into madness (42.7):

> Qual nomade pastor che vedut'abbia
> fuggir strisciando l'orrido serpente
> che il figliuol che giocava ne la sabbia
> ucciso gli ha col venenoso dente,
> stringe il baston con colera e con rabbia;
> tal la spada, d'ogni altra più tagliente,
> stringe con ira il cavallier d'Anglante:
> il primo che trovò, fu 'l re Agramante.

> As the Numidian shepherd will grasp his stick with frantic rage, seeing the horrible snake slither away once its poisonous fangs have slain his child playing in the sand: so did Orlando rabidly grasp his sword which was unmatched for sharpness. The first man he came upon was King Agramant.

This octave contains a crucial variation in the simile's development: for the first time, the serpent actually bites the unsuspecting human. At last Ariosto resolves the implications of *Aeneid* 2, where the Greek, Androgeos, is killed by the Trojan snake. Ariosto's imitation, however, is more pointed in its phrasing than the Vergilian model. In canto 42 a father sees a serpent bite his son, who immediately dies: its "poisonous fangs have slain his child" (7.4). The poet underscores the father's pathetic plight by calling the serpent "orrido" and the child a "figliuolo." There is no contest.

The simile glosses Orlando's anger at his realization that Gradasso has killed his boon companion, Brandimarte, in the battle of Lipadusa. It alludes not only to Vergil but also to a somber passage near the end of Pulci's *Morgante* in which Charlemagne laments the deaths of his heroes at Roncisvalle and is described as a pelican whose young have been killed by a snake (27.213.1–5). Ariosto inverts Pulci's simile by establishing Orlando as he mourns Brandimarte, in the authoritative position of Charlemagne mourning Orlando in the *Morgante*. Ariosto's Orlando does for another what Pulci's Charlemagne had done for him—a macabre example of one poet out-imitating another.[34]

The realignment of Ariosto's imitative poiesis from the Ovidian to the Vergilian model indicates a change of tone in his intertextual poetics from tragicomic burlesque to epic grandeur. That he refracts this change through Pulci, a poet known for his humorous anti-epic strain, exemplifies Ariosto's uncanny ability to make the reader reinterpret the poem's sources in ways that contradict the typical sixteenth-century reception of those sources. Ariosto's final version of his simile takes the narrative out of the realm of romance and into the sphere of epic. But the excursion is only temporary, for the subsequent adventures of Rinaldo, the "snake-knight" of canto 1, are "steeped in a slithering mass of serpent imagery."[35] In the following cantos the snake as simile does not occur, but there are many references to snakes. Rinaldo even hears of an actual snake-man, Adonio, in 43.74–116. The *Furioso*'s return to romance in 42–43 mocks the epic thrust of the final quarter of the poem's narrative by maintaining the thematics of the serpent established over the course of the poem and by compromising the allusions to the serpent through the mixture of classical, biblical, and vernacular.

Ariosto: Quel Grandissimo Poeta: Un Dracone

When Torquato Tasso criticizes the *Furioso*'s narrative for its interposed episodes that disrupt the poem's continuity, he confuses the issue of the poem's construction by drawing attention to the snake simile and the snake-man. Indeed, the repetition of that simile (and the associated one of ivy) unifies the poem in an intratextual and intertextual network. Repeatedly Ariosto's allusions to literary models create a narrative unity by encouraging the reader to expect their recurrence with each version of the simile. And there is no question that Tasso's reading of the *Furioso* led him to appreciate this allusive unity of its design. But his praise was muffled at best.

Yet another passage in Tasso's criticism—this time outside the *Discorsi*—intensifies his ambiguous stance toward the *Furioso:* a gloss, the epigraph to this chapter, found in his private copy of Horace's *Ars poetica*.[36] In response to Horace's dictum that the work of art be *simplex dumtaxat et unum* (at least simple and uniform), Tasso notes: "Così il Trissino E qui ha peccato quel grandissimo poeta che io non nomino per veneratione, ma il suo peccato gli sarà perdonato dal giudice il più severo se fosse ancora un *Dracone* perchè ha partorito tante maravigliose e divine bellezze" (emphasis mine). (Thus Trissino. And here has sinned that very great poet whom I do not name out of veneration, but his sin will be pardoned him by the severest judge, were he even a Draco, because he has given birth to so many marvelous and divine beauties.)[37]

The gloss first addresses Trissino's *Italia liberata dai Goti* and its epic narrative that is consistent with neoclassical theory and practice. Tasso himself had already observed in the *Discorsi* (2:26) that copies of Trissino's poem were buried in the libraries of Europe while readers of all sorts eagerly sought Ariosto's. So much for obeying the rules of Horace.

The second, much longer, portion of the gloss contrasts the multiform nature of Ariosto's narrative to Trissino's. Ariosto, respectfully unnamed, "has sinned" by failing to create a poem that conforms to the Horatian rules of a simple and uniform narrative. The gloss's tone is noticeably Counter-Reformational: "his sin will be pardoned him by the severest judge." Tasso's comment concludes, however, with a literary cliché: seemingly he agrees with other sixteenth-century critics that in the *Furioso* Ariosto has given birth to "marvelous and divine beauties."

How does Tasso achieve this shift from a Counter-Reformational to a literary-critical tone? By way of a most curious observation in the mixed conditional, marked by ambiguous syntax: "but his sin will be pardoned him by the severest judge, were he even a Draco." The clause, "se fosse ancora un Dracone," is positioned such that it can be interpreted in at least two ways: either the judge who will pardon Ariosto is like Draco or Ariosto himself is like a kind of Draco. The former interpretation suggests that Ariosto would be pardoned by none less than the Athenian lawgiver, Draco, notorious for the harshness of his legislation. It is a rather erudite way and, I might add, a strikingly novel way, of saying that this poet could get away with anything. The latter interpretation—Ariosto himself as a kind of Draco—is even more novel. In this case "Dracone" stands for a capitalized form of the Italian word for "dragon," from Latin *draco* ("serpent" or "snake").[38] This latter possibility suggests once again the dimensions of Tasso's ambiguity toward Ariosto's achievement. Secretly in the margins of his Horace, in the private and confidential rhetoric of the annotator, Tasso metamorphoses Ariosto into the emblem of his narrative: a serpent. And he does so with a prophetic benediction: " . . . that very great poet . . . will be pardoned." For the creator of the *Gerusalemme Liberata,* Ariosto, the *Furioso,* and the snake had become unbearably indistinguishable, unbearably meaningful—and unbearably successful.

CHAPTER 5

Tasso's Allegory of the Source in Gerusalemme Liberata

Dice ancora Aristotele che . . . quella [la favola] de l'epopeia
è simile al vino troppo inacquato.

TASSO, *DISCORSI DEL POEMA EROICO*[1]

*I*n the previous chapter, we observed Torquato Tasso's troubled reaction to the fusion of sources in Ariosto's *Furioso.* In chapter 1, by contrast, we saw how Torquato's father, Bernardo, was able to accept the *Furioso* into his personal canon, despite its problematic confusion of romance and epic. Here I shall deal more directly with Torquato's ability and need to compromise sources in his own poem. In this reading of *Gerusalemme Liberata,* I argue that Torquato inscribed in the poem an allegory of imitative poetics, which provides the critic with a theoretical gloss on the poet's use of sources. Tasso develops an episode in the story line of canto 13 around a literal source of water—a spring in the desert outside of Jerusalem—to highlight a crisis in his use of literary sources for his intertextual narrative. The behavior of certain of his characters in response to a severe paucity of water stands allegorically for Tasso's treatment of his own sources. Torquato, we discover, is in many ways the ultimate compromiser.

Sources and the Drought

In canto 13 of the *Liberata,* Tasso's poem on the First Crusade, a Greek soldier deserts the Christian army under cover of darkness. Misconstruing the deserter's actions as exemplary, some of his fellow crusaders decide to imitate him. The sequence of events threatens to dissolve the uneasy Christian alliance mustered against the Saracen enemy, which has secured defensive positions inside Jerusalem. The desertion also threatens to end the crusade, for without a cohesive army the Christian forces have no chance against the entrenched infidel. The desertion, therefore, also challenges the very narrative of the poem: if too many soldiers follow the Greek deserter, the war effort ends and the poem becomes at best a narrative of the adventures of individual knights wending their way back to western Europe. But the alliance does not dissolve and the poem does not turn into a collection of separate odysseys. The First Crusade ends with a Christian victory. Why then is the episode of desertion included in the poem?

Tasso drew the material for canto 13 from the historical record. A certain Taticius, who had been sent to the alliance by the Byzantine emperor, Alexios I Komnenos, did indeed encourage soldiers under his command to desert the army. For the details of this crisis, Tasso consulted a variety of historical sources in composing the episode. But his account of the desertion indicates that he had ulterior motives for introducing the scene into his highly selective retelling of the First Crusade. Historical accuracy aside, his additional reasons for appropriating the factual record were poetic and theoretical. The episode of Tatino (the Italianized form of the deserter's name in Latin, Tatinus) gave Tasso the opportunity to theorize and allegorize his dependence on literary sources. The episode allowed Tasso to address the following questions: How was he to work sources of conflicting ideological content and form into the *Liberata*? How, in particular, was he to combine elements of classical epic and vernacular romance in a Christian context?

I have found no critic who satisfactorily discusses the second half of canto 13, let alone one who discusses it in terms of the conflict among its sources.[2] Most critics ignore the episode altogether as they rush from the favored scenes of Tancredi and Clorinda in 12–13 to Rinaldo on Armida's isle in 14–16. Fredi Chiappelli addresses the issue of the episode's sources, but disparagingly: "la descrizione della siccità è uno dei passi compositi della *Gerusalemme,* e non dei più riusciti" (551). (the description of the drought is one of the patchwork passages of the *Gerusalemme,* and not one of the most successful.) Chiappelli is aware of the many parts that make up the poetic whole—to use his image, the patchwork or "composite" whole—but he is critical of the art that binds the parts together. He continues more specifically: "La concezione generale dell'episodio è biblica . . . In questa concezione biblica si manifesta di tanto in tanto un accento personale, . . . Ma in generale, la condotta della narrazione vuol essere monumentale, e secondo la monumentalità classica, il solito tempio cristiano eretto con colonne e frantumi pagani, Santa Maria 'sopra' Minerva" (551). (The general conceptual framework of the passage is biblical. . . . In this framework every so often one becomes aware of an individualized accent. . . . But, in general, the conduct of the narration strives for monumentality, and, in accordance with classical monumentality, it strives to establish the usual Christian temple erected with pagan columns and fragments, Santa Maria "over" Minerva.) In Chiappelli's image the combination of sources creates a structure that is like a Christian church built over the site of a classical temple. So far, so good. But the critic errs, I believe, in assuming that Tasso endowed one of the components, a prominent allusion to the book of Exodus, with a priority over the others: " . . . convinto com'era il poeta della sua architettura ispirata all'*Esodo*" (551). (. . . convinced as the poet was in his architecture, which had been inspired by the book of Exodus.) Is the poet really "convinced" that the allusion to Exodus perfects his narrative? Rather, is he not forced to incorporate allusions to the Bible into his poem by literary critics authorized by the Church hierarchy? I shall argue below that this second question more accurately corresponds to the situation. Tasso's incorporation of the allusion to Exodus, however, is more subtle than it appears at first glance, for the poet compromises it with nonbiblical allusions. Chiappelli's architectural metaphor does not properly encompass the notion of rendering sources impure by mixing them together. And yet Tasso consistently blends sources—biblical, classical, and vernacular—and, consequently, tensions and incongruities fill his poetry, or, as I put it above, such tensions create conflicts of subject matter and poetic form. What distinguishes canto 13 is that Tasso resorts to allegory in an attempt to dramatize and resolve the narrative's intertextual conflicts.

Canto 13 is the thematic middle of the narrative, the fulcrum on which the poem's action turns.[3] Tasso reflects on this dramatic point in the narrative, both in the poem and in a letter in which he refers to the canto's centrality. In an oration near the end of canto 13, which I shall consider in more detail below, God declares to the faithful in heaven that the Christian army has suffered long enough. He commands a new order of events to unfold: "Or cominci novello ordin di cose" (13.73.5). (Now let a new order of things begin.) From this moment forward, the narrative moves inexorably toward a Christian victory. In a letter to one of his supporters, Scipione Gonzaga, Tasso gave a simple account for this change of circumstance: it derives from God's grace. In the letter he also discusses the centrality of canto 13, noting that Scipione has not yet come to the halfway point in the plot because he has read only through canto 10. Distinguishing the poem's "quanto" from its "favola," Tasso notes that 10 is halfway through the poem's twenty cantos, but that 13 is actually halfway through its plot.[4] In canto 13, the themes associated with the pagan successes of the first half of the poem come to an end and the thematic development of the plot turns to the Christians' advantage. As Tasso puts it, "Ma nel mezzo del terzodecimo le cose cominciano a rivoltarsi in meglio . . . e così di mano in mano tutte le cose succedono prospere."[5]

If the first half of the poem comes to an end, the second half must begin anew. Indeed the plot of the *Liberata* can be said to start over with the jussive subjunctives of God's speech, which establishes a new order by commanding, among other things, that Rinaldo be brought back into the Christian army (13.73.7). This new beginning of the poem is inaugurated thematically in canto 14, in which Carlo and Ubaldo seek out the magus of Ascalon, who instructs them on how to recover Rinaldo. Carlo and Ubaldo encounter the magus walking on the waters of a river that flows into the sea on the coast of southern Palestine. The magus leads them to his dwelling beneath the bed of the river, where he shows them the fountainhead of the world's water. The vision of the primeval aqueduct is mysteriously dramatic and sets an appropriate tone at the beginning of the quest for Rinaldo. But it is more than merely an overture to adventure. As David Quint has shown in his study on the source topos in Renaissance literature, Tasso's portrayal of the ultimate source has implications for his poetics.[6]

Such a reading of the scene in canto 14 depends on a close analysis of its intertextual dynamism. Analyzing in particular the allusions to the Book of Job and to the lunar episode in *Orlando Furioso* 34–35, Quint interprets the fountainhead in the magus's cave as a symbol of the limitations of human knowledge. Carlo and Ubaldo learn that the true source of knowledge, the Truth itself, is far above this magical place deep within the earth: God is the ultimate source and verification of all earthly sources. Tasso uses the symbol of the source, in Quint's reading, to reinforce his concept of God's relationship to creation.[7] Quint moves from a discussion of the literary sources of canto 14 to an analysis of the Counter-Reformation aesthetics that required Tasso to locate the authority for his poetic originality in the extratextual domain of the Christian God, far beyond the realm of the earthbound author. The discovery of God's ultimate power in canto 14 constitutes a turning in the poem that, for Quint, depends on Tasso's allusions to Ariosto and the Bible (102). But a complementary reading of cantos 13 and 14 might also consider how the *Liberata* itself moves intratextually toward the shift in canto 14. One might note, for example, how Tasso develops the narrative through his description of the dried-up sources in canto 13, which precedes the vision of the source of all earthly water in 14. We should now observe how the interplay of sources within the poem brings its first half to an end in canto 13, and how these literary sources contribute to the peripeteia of canto 14.

Canto 13 begins with a description of how Ismeno, the pagan wizard, infests the forest of Sharon with demons (1–16). It continues with a section on the magic forest (17–48) and the drought (49–69). The canto ends with God's response to Goffredo's prayer in the form of a saving rain that replenishes the dried-up sources on which the Christians depend for their water (70–80). There is a progression in the representation of marvelous elements in the canto, moving from the pagan bewitching of nature to God's successful overcoming of the pagans.

The black magic of the pagan wizard works against the Christian army. His demons terrify the army's heroes, Alcasto and Tancredi, who flee the forest. The forest, however, is the source of lumber, which the crusaders need to build their war machines in order to besiege Jerusalem. The campaign halts when Tancredi, admitting defeat, confirms Alcasto's report to Goffredo: "No, no, più non potrei (vinto mi chiamo) / né corteccia scorzar, né sveller ramo" (49.7–8). (No, no, I can do no more [I confess myself beaten], neither to split the bark nor pluck the bough.) Goffredo reacts predictably: he comes up with a plan to enter the forest on his own to fell the needed trees. It is not the first time that the captain has attempted to assume the role of foot soldier (cf. 11.54ff.). But Piero the Hermit intervenes to prevent the leader's rash act.

At stanza 51, Piero makes one of several prophecies about the end to come:

> "Lascia il pensier audace: altri conviene
> che de le piante sue la selva spoglie.
> Già la fatal nave a l'erme arene
> la prora accosta e l'auree vele accoglie;
> già, rotte l'indegnissime catene,
> l'aspettato guerrier dal lido scioglie:
> non è lontana omai l'ora prescritta
> che sia presa Sïòn, l'oste sconfitta."

> "Abandon your hardy plan; it falls to another to spoil the forest of its trees. Already the destined ship is beaching her prow on the solitary sands, and furls her golden sails; already, his most disgraceful fetters broken, the expected warrior weighs anchor from the shore. Now not far off is the fated hour when Sion can be taken, her host discomfited."

Piero foresees the defeat of the enemy at the poem's conclusion, so acquainted is he with the total vision of God. He foresees that the boat to rescue Rinaldo is already on its way ("già," 3). He knows that the crisis will be resolved sometime after the hero returns to the Christian camp. It is for Rinaldo to confront the enchanted forest upon reconciling himself with Goffredo. Thus Piero, the man of God, draws the lines of the second half of the plot.

But the prophecy serves another function at this crux in the narrative, for it echoes the critical vocabulary of generic conflict and resolution. In deterring Goffredo from entering the wood, Piero is warning the would-be epic hero against the dangers of romance. If Goffredo deviates from his course and enters the wood, he risks entanglement in unhealthy narrative patterns of the sort Tasso argues against throughout the *Discorsi* when he claims that romance is an aberration of epic. Piero's choice of vocabulary explains why the leader's intervention is not necessary. At 51.5, the verb that describes Rinaldo coming down from the beach, "scioglie," is the technical term used to denote narrative resolution. The same verb brings the entire narrative to its conclusion in canto 20 by marking Goffredo's fulfillment of his vow to retake Jerusalem (20.144.8).[8] When Piero says that the "chains" are already broken (51.4), he uses an equally connotative term. Sixteenth-century critics used "catena" to describe the interlaced structure of the typical romance narrative, as we saw in our discussion of Giraldi Cinzio in chapter 3. Piero means that the chains of Armida's control over Rinaldo have been broken; we, however, can also understand him to mean that the interlaced network of romancelike stories has been interrupted by the linear inevitability of the *Liberata*'s epic thrust. What Piero foretells is that the romance is over; we are at the beginning of something new in the design of the narrative. To be sure, this literary-critical prophecy is not without a touch of irony, for, although the romance has supposedly ended, we see its chains dismantled ever so slowly over the next seven cantos.

This sets the scene for the description of the drought, which, in spite of Piero's prediction of eventual victory, is suspenseful. Ismeno predicts the drought near the opening of canto 13 as he reports the progress of his magical endeavors to the king of Jerusalem, Aladino (13.13):

> Soggiunse appresso: "Or cosa aggiungo a queste
> fatte da me ch'a me non meno aggrada.
> Sappi che tosto nel Leon celeste
> Marte co 'l sol fia ch'ad unir si vada,
> né tempreran le fiamme lor moleste
> aure, o nembi di pioggia o di rugiada,

ché quanto in cielo appar, tutto predice
ardissima arsura ed infelice: . . ."

He added then: "To these things accomplished by me I add now a
matter that to me is no less pleasing. Mars is soon going to be in
conjunction with the sun, in the heavenly Lion, and no breezes or
clouds of rain or dew will be tempering their noisome flames; for
all the signs that appear in the heavens predict a most parched and
hapless drought . . ."

There is a structural parallel between the pagan prophet and his patron at
the beginning of the canto and Piero and Goffredo at midpoint. The parallel suggests the limitations of Ismeno's prediction, its shortsightedness
when compared with the all-encompassing vision of Piero the Hermit.
Nevertheless, Ismeno's prediction, based on his reading of the zodiac, is
accurate: the "arsura" descends with a consummate destruction upon the
Christians in the second half of stanza 52:

Ma nel Cancro celeste omai raccolto
apporta arsura inusitata il sole,
ch'a i suoi disegni, a i suoi guerrier nemica,
insopportabil rende ogni fatica.

But now the sun, being entered into Cancer, brings on unwonted
heat, inimical to his plans and to his soldiery, that renders every
task unbearable.

Tasso's outline of the events of the First Crusade is based, as I
noted above, on the historical record. His main source is *Belli sacri
historia,* an extensive chronicle written by the twelfth-century archbishop
William of Tyre. The first printed edition of the Latin work was published
in 1549, and it was quickly followed by numerous translations in the
vernacular, including an Italian version published in 1562.[9] The chronicle
details the problems the crusaders faced when they entered the deserts
of Palestine in the summer of 1097, overdressed and ill-prepared for
the intense heat and scarcity of water. While William never refers to an
actual drought, he repeatedly describes the destructive effect of the sun
and the consequent lack of water. At 13.53–58, Tasso follows more or
less the general description given in William's chronicle, where William
recounts how the invading forces dissipated their energies in Palestine
searching for drinking water. So also does Tasso depict his characters
exhausting themselves in search of relief. He embellishes this recasting

of the historical record with allusions to Vergil's *Georgics* and Lucretius's *De rerum natura* to compose a striking narration of the drought's effect on the terrain, on the crusaders' horses, and on the crusaders themselves.

William develops the narrative of his history with a clear sense of how an episode should begin and end. He prepares for the section on the summer of 1097 by commenting on the arid topography surrounding Jerusalem. He reproaches a postclassical historian, Solinus, for remarks in his *Polyhistor* about Jerusalem's geographical setting:

> The city lies in arid surroundings, entirely lacking in water. Since there are no rills, springs, or rivers, the people depend upon rain water only. During the winter season it is their custom to collect this in cisterns, which are numerous throughout the city. Thus it is preserved for use during the year. Hence I am surprised at the statement of Solinus that Judea is famous for its waters. He says in the *Polyhistor:* "Judea is renowned for its waters, but the nature of these varies." I cannot account for the discrepancy except by saying either that he did not tell the truth about the matter or that the face of the earth became changed later.[10]

William's revised estimation of the water supply in Jerusalem is conspicuous, and it might have caught Tasso's attention and quite possibly led him to create the center of his narrative around the drought. Tasso might also have appreciated William's skepticism toward his predecessor, a corrective attitude Tasso cultivates toward his sources, including even William. Tasso intentionally lodged the plot of the *Liberata* in a past event that was close enough to his own time to appear realistic and yet distant enough to allow the poet freedom to manipulate the historical sources.[11] At this point in his poetic version of the crusade, he follows William's account; later in the canto, however, he will make significant changes.

William describes how the Saracens used the drought and the heat of summer to their advantage. One of their strategies involved plugging all the springs in the vicinity of Jerusalem, thus blocking, as far as possible, the Christians from potable water (348).[12] In William's description, which he gives twice (at 8.4 and 8.7), the citizens of Jerusalem react immediately upon learning that the crusaders are near:

> cives, praecognito nostrorum adventu, ora fontium et cisternarum quae in circuitu urbis erant, usque ad quinque vel sex milliaria, ut populus siti fatigatus ab urbis obsidione desisteret, obstruxerant (8.4);[13]

The citizens, once our advance had been recognized, stopped up the mouths of the fountains and wells which were within a five- or six-mile radius of the city, so that thirst would exhaust our people and make them cease from laying siege to the town.

Canto 13 of the *Liberata* includes a narrative of a similar tactic (58.4–8):

> ma pur la sete è il pessimo de' mali,
> però che di Giudea l'iniquo donno
> con veneni e con succhi aspri e mortali
> più de l'inferna Stige e d'Acheronte
> torbido fece e livido ogni fonte.

[B]ut yet the thirst is the worst evil of all, for Judaea's wicked lord made every spring filthy and unwholesome with poisons and secretions more bitter and deadly than hellish Styx and Acheron.

There is, one notices immediately, a variant on the historical event in Tasso's version: whereas in William's account the pagans merely block the springs and wells, in Tasso's, the king of Jerusalem, Aladino, poisons the springs.[14] This strategy had already been announced at the beginning of the poem. In canto 1, Aladino ruins the countryside so that the Franks glean no sustenance as they invade: "turba le fonti e i rivi, e le pure onde / di veneni mortiferi confonde" (89.7–8).[15] ([H]e roils the springs and the streams and mingles their pure waters with death-dealing poisons.) Only in the context of the drought in canto 13 does that act, heretofore disregarded in the narrative, assume dire consequences for the Christian forces.[16]

Describing Aladino's act twice provides the poet the opportunity to lend some variety to the second version. Indeed, the passage in canto 13 reads like a schoolboy exercise in *variatio* in relation to that of canto 1: "le fonti" becomes "ogni fonte"; "turba" becomes "fece torbido"; "veneni mortiferi" becomes "veneni mortali." These superficial changes tend not to affect the content of the passage at all. There is, however, a notable addition to the description in 13 that invites further interpretation: "succhi aspri" (58.6). This phrase recalls the Lucretian allusion at the beginning of the poem in which poetry itself is likened to a mixture of bitter and sweet liquids (1.3):[17]

> Sai che là corre il mondo ove più versi
> di sue dolcezze il lusinghier Parnaso,

e che 'l vero, condito in molli versi,
i più schivi allettando ha persuaso.
Così a l'egro fanciul porgiamo aspersi
di soavi licor gli orli del vaso:
succhi amari ingannato intanto ei beve,
e da l'inganno suo vita riceve.

You know that the world flocks there where feigning Parnassus most
pours out her sweetnesses, and that the truth in fluent verses hidden
has by its charm persuaded the most froward. So we present to the
feverish child the rim of the glass sprinkled over with sweet liquids:
he drinks deceived the bitter medicine and from his deception
receives life.

Aladino pollutes the springs of Jerusalem with "bitter juices," as a
doctor coats the rim of a cup with sweet liquids to trick a sick child into
drinking the "bitter juices" of medicine within the cup.[18] At first glance
the analogy would seem to be turned on its head. Lucretius coats the bitter
with the sweet, but Tasso coats—in fact, he almost contaminates totally—
the sweet with the bitter. It has been argued—correctly, I believe—that
Aladin's contamination of the wells reflects Tasso's ambiguity about
literary pleasure and implies a potential threat to orthodox Christian
ideology.[19]

The mixing of water and poison is analogous to Tasso's mixing of
literary sources that conflict in their content and/or form. Stanza 58 does
not raise the issue of generic conflict, which we have already encountered
in the prophetic language of stanza 51, but it draws our attention to
a mixture of sources. First, Tasso must confront the historical source:
William of Tyre's chronicle. Second, there are the internal allusions Tasso
makes to the beginning of his own poem. Third, in line 7 the poet calls
on a classical commonplace to compare the poisoned springs around
Jerusalem to the infernal waters of the Styx and the Acheron—an image
brought into the Italian tradition by Dante's *Inferno*. And fourth, there is
the biblical source for Aladino's actions: 2 Chronicles 32:2–4 recounts
that a king of ancient Judah, Hezekiah, used a similar tactic when the
Assyrians once besieged Jerusalem.

The four sources of stanza 58 can be classified into two kinds
of allusions: *intra*textual and *inter*textual.[20] The intratextual is the one
made within the poem to the poem itself, for example, the allusion in
13.58 to 1.3. The intertextual allusions of stanza 58 are to texts beyond
the *Liberata,* which are historical, classical (perhaps filtered through a
medieval vernacular source), and biblical. The intratextual allusion in 58

focuses the reader's attention, somewhat paradoxically, on the essentially intertextual nature of the stanza. By inviting the reader to consider the stanza in theoretical terms (as the allusion to the beginning of the poem does), Tasso focuses the reader's attention on his sources and on the way in which he, like his character Aladino, mixes them.

The most noticeable detail in Tasso's mixture is the inherent opposition between Aladino and Hezekiah. Any significant parallel to Hezekiah must reverse the biblical model: Aladino, an infidel, who keeps the Christians from taking back what is rightfully theirs, is compared implicitly to Hezekiah, a man of God, who defends Jerusalem against the invading Assyrians. The parallel highlights what the two kings do not share, namely, a faith in the Judeo-Christian deity. Hezekiah's faith in God allows him to overcome his enemy, while Aladino's infidelity leaves him vulnerable to the Christian deity's machinations. At the end of canto 13, God answers Goffredo's prayer for rain and thus foils Aladino's strategy to defeat the crusaders by desiccation. Tasso's allusive recall of the Bible in stanza 58 sets up this later moment in his narrative.[21]

Poetic Allegories

A discussion of Tasso's sources in stanza 58—a microcosm of his poetics in the canto—leads one invariably back to the narrative of the drought in canto 13. The poet gives the reader a tour of the parched countryside and the languishing Christian army[22] before he shifts his focus to the drought's effect on the morale of the crusaders themselves (64):

> Così languia la terra, e 'n tale stato
> egri giaceansi i miseri mortali,
> e 'l buon popol fedel, già disperato
> di vittoria, temea gli ultimi mali;
> e risonar s'udia per ogni lato
> universal lamento in voci tali;
> "Che più spera Goffredo o che più bada,
> sì che tutto il suo campo a morte cada?"

So languished the countryside and in such state the wretched mortals lay in their affliction; and the faithful, having lost all hope of victory, began to fear extremity of evils; and on every side a universal complaint could be heard echoing in such words as these: "What more does Godfrey expect? or what is he waiting for—until his whole host drops dead?"

The speech, delivered by an unidentified narrative voice, continues in this troubled tone for three stanzas, dwelling on the inequity of the general situation. Its tone recalls the harangue of Thersites against Agamemnon in *Iliad* 2.212ff., and that of Drances against Turnus in *Aeneid* 11.336ff., although there are no points of direct linguistic imitation of these classical models.

Goffredo, however, is not suffering to the same degree as his men; indeed he hardly suffers at all (67):

> "Or mira d'uom c'ha il titolo di pio
> providenza pietosa, animo umano:
> la salute de' suoi porre in oblio
> per conservarsi onor dannoso e vano;
> e veggendo a noi secchi i fonti e 'l rio,
> per sé l'acque condur fa dal Giordano,
> e fra pochi sedendo a mensa lieta,
> mescolar l'onde fresche al vin di Creta."

> "Now look at the humane spirit, the compassionate care of a man
> who is called *the Good;* he forgets about the well-being of his men
> in order to preserve for himself a vain and destructive honor. And
> seeing the springs and the river dry for us, he has water fetched
> from Jordan for himself, and sitting at his cheerful feast with a few
> companions, he has cold water mixed with his Cretan wine."

The captain, mocked for his piety, has designed his own private water supply, which enables him to continue cutting his wine at dinner with fresh water in spite of the desiccated springs, on which his soldiers can no longer depend. The observation is articulated in the rhetoric of revolt, the masses with their collective pronoun "noi" versus the captain who is doing things "per sé." More exactly, Tasso's grammatical construction in line 6 indicates that Goffredo is not acting as a direct agent in all of this: "per sé l'acque condur fa dal Giordano." He has his water supplied from no less than the Jordan River. The detail is historically accurate. The crusaders often traveled as far inland as the Jordan to procure drinking water when droughts hindered the progress of their various campaigns.[23] But there is more at stake in the passage than historical accuracy.

Goffredo's exclusive water supply enables a curious mixture of water and wine. His use of the Jordan speaks for itself. The verbal attack in lines 5–8 implies that Goffredo is selfishly abusing the sacred water of the most holy river in Christendom. The plural "acque" (waters) suggests the exaggerated extent of the abuse. The very presence of wine on his table is a further indication of how little Goffredo suffers from the drought. The chroniclers recount how wine, a part of daily rations, became more scarce and costly as the water supply dwindled.[24] And why does he mix these waters with a "vin di Creta" (Cretan wine)? Tasso reports in his poem that the islands of Chios and Crete provided wine for the crusaders: "e Scio pietrosa gli vendemmi e Creta" (1.78.8) (and rocky Scio her vintages, and Crete). And the same passage in canto 1 clearly borrows from William of Tyre's description of the crusaders' march from Tripoli toward Jerusalem, during which friendly supply ships hugged the coast as the army proceeded southward.[25] But William does not go so far as to specify which wines the crusaders drank.

Nonetheless, Tasso's reference to Cretan wine is a realistic historical detail. Unlike mainland Greece, the island of Crete has a large supply of fresh water that makes it an effective agricultural region, for which it has been famous since antiquity.[26] Pliny the Elder, among others, praised the wines of Crete, especially its sweet raisin wines.[27] From as early as the second millennium B.C., the island's position at the eastern end of the Mediterranean basin made it an important commercial link among the economic centers of Italy, Greece, Egypt, Asia Minor, and the Levant.[28] Thus its wines were exported early on and continued to be shipped to other countries throughout its early history.[29] This is true for the period of Byzantine control over the island (961–1204)—at the time of the First Crusade—as well as for the era of Venetian dominion (1204–1669). The Venetians, as one might expect, excelled in marketing Cretan wine all over northern Europe.[30] By the time Tasso was writing, Pliny's sweet wine had come to be one of the favorite drinks of the English and French, which they called, respectively, "malmsey" and "malvesie," after one of the stops along the Venetian trade route from Crete to the north, Monemvasía. It seems likely that Tasso's participation in goliardic and courtly life during the 1560s and 1570s would have made him aware of the sociohistorical connotations of alluding to wine from Crete.

A literary rationale also coordinates the details in this passage, even to such a minute detail as the provenance of Goffredo's wine. When an Italian poet trained in the humanistic tradition, as Tasso was, refers to Crete, he conjures up the mythic legends associated with the island: Jupiter's birthplace, Minos, the Minotaur in Daedalus's labyrinth, and others. Moreover, these legends are refracted through well-known passages of Italian medieval literature in Dante, Petrarch, and Boccaccio.[31] Writers closer to his specific narrative tradition, Boiardo and Ariosto, also employ the myths of Crete.[32] Ariosto even comments on the need to cut the heavy wine of the "treacherous Greeks" in a humorous passage of his *Satire* 2.46–57.

Of greater interest for Tasso's reference to Crete in stanza 67, however, is a reference in one of Ariosto's last writings to wine from Candia, the Italian name for Crete. In the Marganorre episode added to the 1532 edition of the *Furioso,* the evil misogynist, Marganorre, develops his hatred for women in response to a deadly Cretan wine, for a poisoned "vin dolce di Candia" (sweet wine from Candia) kills Tanacro, Marganorre's son (37.67–75). The Cretan wine in the *Furioso,* like Goffredo's wine in canto 13, is introduced in a sacramental context. Ariosto's character, Tanacro, dies after having drunk the poisoned wine during the Eucharist celebration at his wedding mass. In both texts wine from Crete symbolizes the perversion of community: in Ariosto's episode the perversion leads to a dramatic coupled death (Tanacro and his unwilling fiancée, Drusilla, who prepared the poison, both die); in Tasso's episode, the perversion threatens the military alliance of the Christian side. Again, as with the historical details outlined above, there is no positive proof that Tasso's passage alludes to the *Furioso,* although, certainly, the two passages become mutually enlightened if taken together. In any case, the mixing of Greek wine possessed a significant cultural resonance for Tasso and his contemporaries.

Let us continue with our reading of canto 13. The Franks under Goffredo's immediate command criticize his mixture of wine and water. Because the Christian coalition he commands is formed of diverse crusaders from various parts of Europe, the potential for schism is great. While his own troops criticize him in words alone, other members of the coalition openly defy him and the alliance begins to crack along ethnic lines. The lone Greek leader, Tatino, who commands those soldiers sent personally by the Byzantine emperor, is the first to desert. Diverse chroniclers record that this desertion did indeed take place—however, not when the crusaders were besieging Jerusalem, but rather Antioch. Why then does Tasso change the locale? The answer lies in his willingness to alter the historical record for the sake of his poem's unified epic narrative.[33] Unity requires a concentration of disparate actions in one theater; Tatino's desertion had to be moved to the desert near Jerusalem.

Tatino is introduced in the catalog of the Christian troops in 1.50–51:[34]

Venian dietro ducento in Grecia nati,
che son quasi di ferro in tutto scarchi;
pendon spade ritorte a l'un de' lati,
suonano al tergo lor faretre ed archi;
asciutti hanno i cavalli, al corso usati,
a la fatica invitti, al cibo parchi;

ne l'assalir son pronti e nel ritrarsi,
e combatton fuggendo erranti e sparsi.

Tatin regge la schiera, e sol fu questi
che, greco, accompagnò l'arme latine.
Oh vergogna! oh misfatto! or non avesti
tu, Grecia, quelle guerre a te vicine?
E pur quasi a spettacolo sedesti,
lenta aspettando de' grand'atti il fine.
Or, se tu se' vil serva, è il tuo servaggio
(non ti lagnar) giustizia, e non oltraggio.

Behind them came two hundred born in Greece, who are almost
entirely free of any steel; crescent swords hang down at their sides;
quivers and bows rattle on their backs; wiry horses they have, inured
to running, tireless in effort, sparing in diet: they are quick to attack
and quick to sound retreat, and roving and scattered wage war by
taking flight. / Tatin rules the band, and he was the only one who,
being Greek, accompanied the Latin armies. Oh shame! oh crime!
were not those wars near neighbor to you, Greece? and yet you
sat, as at a spectacle, sluggishly awaiting the outcome of great
actions. Now, if you are a common slave, your servitude (make no
complaint) is a justice not an outrage.

The narrator uses the appearance of the Greek contingent to criticize the
country for its weak-willed effort. Although the war takes place near
Greece, the Greeks have dispatched only two hundred soldiers, merely a
pack of scouts to lead the crusaders through Asia Minor.[35]

Tasso's impassioned attack on Tatino has specific implications for
Greece as a whole. Filling the role of spectators at a drama (1.51.5–6), the
Greeks betray the cultural heritage they bequeathed to the West in their
refusal to campaign aggressively against the Saracens. The wording of
couplet 51.5–6 recalls Athenian tragedy, the cultural product of that brief
period of relative peace from 480 to 430 B.C., when the democratic and
cultural legacy of ancient Athens first took form. Subsequent references
to the evil emperor (1.69–70) also suggest that the present ruler of the
Byzantine empire has cynically disregarded the legacy of the Athenian
golden age. Only the European peoples are able to protect and preserve
what the Greeks no longer treasure.

Indeed, Tatino in canto 1 might at first appear an active exception
to Greek passivity. But any hope that this activity might result in some
heroic deed later in the narrative is in vain. Once again Tasso follows
William's historical narrative from the beginning to the point that satisfies
his own purposes. William foresees Tatino's desertion because of his

unreliability as an agent of the emperor. The rubric for the chapter in which he first mentions Tatino is direct: "One Tatino, a servant of the emperor, a very crafty man of notorious wickedness, becomes associated with our leaders."[36] He continues this description in a similar vein, reading into his physiognomy Tatino's moral shortcomings: "He was a wicked and treacherous man, whose slit nostrils were a sign of his evil mind" (150); the emperor is said to have "relied greatly upon his malice and unscrupulous duplicity" (150); and William declares from the outset that Tatino is responsible for "directing his nefarious schemes" (150). Clearly, for William the chronicler, Tatino is no shining star of probity.

The portrayal of Greeks as crafty masters of language is a topos of politicized rhetoric in the European Middle Ages. The literary archetype of clever Odysseus had long since become part of the common ground of Western culture. William's emphasis on the man as a liar is not out of order in this respect. During the Renaissance, leading up to Tasso's day, Italian culture continued to embrace the same stereotype of Greeks, probably for similar reasons. Ariosto provides a glimpse of this popular attitude in his play *I suppositi* (2.1.27–28), in which one character advises another: "Non ti fidare di lui, ch' egli è fallace e più bugiardo che se in Creta o in Affrica nato fusse."[37] (Don't trust him, because he's false and more of a liar than if he'd been born in Crete or Africa.) The stereotypes held firm through Tasso's lifetime, with a new villain of similar malicious qualities being added in the second half of the sixteenth century: the Turk. Ironically, the historical Tatino was probably not Greek but Saracen or Turk. Another chronicler of the crusaders' march through Asia minor, Anna Komnena, the emperor's daughter, claimed that the Byzantine army had captured Tatino's father in a battle and that the son, a kind of human war prize, had been raised in the imperial court.[38] But to return to Tasso's narrative, it mattered little whether Tatino was Greek, African (i.e., Saracen), or Turk. It mattered much more that he was not European and that he was untrustworthy.

In stanzas 64 through 67, the Franks criticize Goffredo's abundance of water. Tatino, however, is more direct (68–69):

> Così i Franchi dicean; ma 'l duce greco
> che 'l lor vessillo è di seguir già stanco,
> "Perché morir qui?" disse "e perché meco
> far che la schiera mia ne vegna manco?
> Se ne la sua follia Goffredo è cieco,
> siasi in suo danno e del suo popol franco:
> a noi che noce?" E senza tor licenza,
> notturna fece e tacita partenza.

Mosse l'essempio assai, come al dì chiaro
fu noto; e d'imitarlo alcun risolve.
Quei che seguir Clotareo ed Ademaro
e gli altri duci ch'or son ossa e polve,
poi che la fede che a color giuraro
ha disciolto colei che tutto solve,
già trattano di fuga, e già qualcuno
parte furtivamente a l'aer bruno.

So spoke the Franks; but the Greekish captain, who is already tired
of following their standard, said: "Why die here? and why let my
division grow weaker, along with me? If Godfrey is blinded in his
folly, let it be to his own hurt and that of the Frankish people: what
harm in that for us?" And without obtaining permission he made his
departure, in silence and by night. / The example caused a great stir
when it became known by light of day, and some resolve to follow it.
Those who were followers of Clothar and Adhemar and the other
captains that now are dust and bones—since that which releases
all has released the fealty that they swore to them—now consider
flight; and already some have departed secretly in the darkened air.

In stanza 68 Tatino speaks, presumably to himself; then he takes leave,
forsaking the camp by night. In an irrational sequence of tenses, the
Christian army learns of his action the following day: the preterite verb
forms "mosse" and "fu noto" shift unexpectedly to the dramatic present
of "risolve." The Greek leader has established an example in the past that
heightens the crusaders' resolve to imitate it.

Like stanzas 51 and 58, the opening couplet of 69 is striking for
its vocabulary drawn from the lexicon of sixteenth-century discourse
on *imitatio.* Contemporary Renaissance descriptions of poetic imitation
typically focus on one, usually modern, poet's imitation of a medieval or
classical text. The words, "essempio," "imitare," and "seguir," essential
to the critical discourse of imitation, suggest that Tasso wants to do more
with stanza 69 than merely further the plot through the description of
Tatino's desertion. The terminology, found throughout Tasso's *Discorsi
dell'arte poetica,* focuses our attention on the theoretical possibilities of
the episode.[39] But first we need to examine the reaction of Goffredo to
the exemplary Tatino, for our reading of Tatino's action is, of necessity,
refracted through Goffredo's reading.

Goffredo, ever consonant with his epithet "pio," prays for guidance
when confronted with Tatino's desertion. Although he entertains possible
violent responses to the soldier's bad example, his purposeful prayers
allow him to avoid such temptation. From his misadventure in canto 11 (of

which Piero reminds him in 13.51) he had learned the inappropriateness of intervening as a foot soldier. Rinaldo's murder of Gernando in canto 5 taught him that it would be dangerous for his troops to overreact at this point in the plot.[40] So at this turning point in the narrative, Goffredo shuns direct action and puts his faith in God (13.70):

> Ben se l'ode Goffredo e ben se 'l vede,
> e i più aspri rimedi avria ben pronti,
> ma gli schiva ed aborre; e con la fede
> che faria stare i fiumi e gir i monti,
> devotamente al Re del mondo chiede
> che gli apra omai de la sua grazia i fonti:
> giunge le palme, e fiammaggianti in zelo
> gli occhi rivolge e le parole al Cielo: . . .

> Godfrey hears it clearly and sees it clearly and could have had ready at hand the most stringent remedies; but those he shuns and abhors, and with the faith that could make the mountains move and the rivers stand, devoutly he prays the King of the universe that He open now the wellsprings of His grace: he clasps his hands and directs his eyes and his words aflame with zeal to Heaven: . . .

Goffredo's faithfulness in lines 3–4 has biblical overtones. In a phrase that recalls Jesus's own definition of faith, the narrator describes faith as empowering Goffredo's prayer so that it might "make rivers stand and mountains move."[41] Jesus preaches several times to his disciples about the efficacy of prayer, which can, through faith, effect miracles. Once he speaks to them of the withering of the fig tree: "Amen dico vobis, si habueritis fidem, et non haesitaveritis, non solum de ficulnea facietis, sed et si monti huic dixeritis: Tolle, et iacta te in mare, fiet. Et omnia quaecumque petieritis in oratione credentes, accipietis" (Matthew 21:21–22). (Truly, I say to you, if you have faith and never doubt, you will not only do what has been done to the fig tree, but even if you say to this mountain, "Be taken up and cast into the sea," it will be done. And whatever you ask in prayer, you will receive, if you have faith.) In a similar way, Goffredo's faith leads him to embrace the expectations of God, which are expressed repeatedly by Piero the Hermit. Here is Goffredo's prayer (71):

> "Padre e Signor, s'al popol tuo piovesti
> già le dolci rugiade entro al deserto,
> s'a mortal mano già virtù porgesti

romper le pietre e trar del monte aperto
un vivo fiume, or rinovella in questi
gli stessi essempi; e s'ineguale è il merto,
adempi di tua grazia i lor difetti,
e giovi lor che tuoi guerrier sian detti."

Our father and our Lord, if once you rained down the grateful dew
on your people in the wilderness; if once you placed the power in
mortal hands to break open the rocks and draw a living stream from
the riven mountain; now renew in these the same examples.[42] And
if their merit is unequal, supply their deficiencies with Thy grace,
and let it be to their profit that they be called Thy soldiers."

The narrator plays with the vocabulary and imagery of sources
when he describes the prayer in 70.6 as a request for God to open "the
wellsprings of His grace."[43] Tellingly, the prayer, given in full in stanza
71, actually requests water. But the request comes by way of an example.
Goffredo asks God to provide the crusaders with the same food he gave the
Israelites as they wandered in the desert, thus putting himself in a position
analogous to that of Moses. The mutinous crusaders, for their part, are
comparable to the grumbling Israelites. In effect, Goffredo prays for a
positive example to interpose between his army and Tatino's negative
example. Just as God rained down sweet dew and drew forth from the
rocks a living stream at Moses' request, so should he "now renew in these
[warriors] the same examples."

Goffredo is portrayed here as exhibiting a sincere parental concern
for his charges. But underlying the leader's request on behalf of his men
is the impinging vocabulary of literary imitation that shapes the scene.
At stake is the proper sort of exemplarity: Tatino's or God's. The men
of Clotareo and Ademaro (69.3), who can no longer follow their dead
Frankish leaders, are given two options: should they follow a Greek or
the God of the Old Testament? For the crusaders, there is a quick and
easy answer to this question; for the poet, inasmuch as the question also
applies to his imitative poiesis, the answer is much more complicated and
leads to the heart of Tasso's allegory of the source.

Goffredo's prayer is immediately effective. God responds with
a miraculous rainstorm and reaffirms Goffredo's authority, just as he
intervened several times to reaffirm the authority of Moses. And as
the threat of desertion ends, the second half of the poem begins. That
beginning is marked by God's language of inauguration in stanza 73,
which echoes Goffredo's remarks in 71. The divine proclamation on the
new beginning ("Or cominci novello ordin di cose," 73.5) corresponds

to Goffredo's request that God renew the examples witnessed by the Israelites ("or rinovella in questi / gli stessi essempi," 71.5–6). The implication of the comparison between Goffredo's request and God's reply is simple. to go forward one must first go back. The ancient past becomes an occasion to rewrite the present and shape the future. *Imitatio* is based on the same principle: one must go back (into literary history, into a literary source) in order to proceed.

Again, the issue of choice arises. In 71 the poet chooses to follow the Old Testament, strengthening the Christian underpinnings of the poem. The directness of Goffredo's reference to the Israelites has given rise to much enthusiastic criticism among Tasso's modern readers, as if the poet had triumphed by depending so obviously on a scriptural passage. De Maldè, for example, comments on how the passage in canto 13 and the story from Exodus are, with some minor exceptions, identical: " . . . tutto è identico nei due esemplari" (284). (. . . everything in the two texts is identical.) He then advances the forced claim that Moses and Goffredo are exact equivalents: "Mosè nel Vecchio Testamento fa perfetto riscontro a Goffredo nella *Liberata*" (284). (Moses in the Old Testament is a perfect counterpart to Goffredo in the *Liberata*.)

But can such a positive reaction, with its presupposition of an overt and unsophisticated imitation of a source, be accepted? Perhaps, but only by considering certain extra-poetic ideological demands. The technique of poets writing in the tradition of Tasso's vernacular humanism involves the cultivation of a deliberate elusiveness in the use of literary sources. A transparent allusion, moreover, is very probably obvious for a specific reason, that is, the decision to showcase a source can often be attributed to ideology. Writing under the tightening strictures of post-Tridentine aesthetics, Tasso became increasingly uncomfortable with the un-Christian qualities of the classical epic tradition that underlay much of the *Liberata*. The Roman censors, at least, were unhappy with the poem's un-Christian elements. Accordingly, the poet found himself in an awkward position. He reflects on his discomfort in many of the "lettere poetiche" written in 1575–76, the period when he was preparing the final draft of the *Liberata*. He openly had to demonstrate his commitment to Christian morals and aesthetics—whether or not that commitment might be central to his narrative. Perhaps, in his evocation of the famous passage from Exodus, Tasso intended to satisfy such an ideological requirement. To liken Goffredo to Moses was not really the point of the allusion; its purpose was to make Tasso resemble the kind of poet the Roman "revisori" demanded that he be.

No competent Christian reader would have failed to notice the source of Goffredo's prayer. If the ideologues were placated by its orthodoxy, all well and good. But if it is correct to interpret the allusion to Exodus as an ideological ploy on the part of Tasso, then the poet had his cake and ate it too. For no reader familiar with classical texts could avoid the additional fact that the context and the effect of the prayer are distinctly classical. When the prayer metamorphoses into a plural subject, "queste preghiere" (72.1), which fly up to God like winged birds, the learned reader recalls, among other classical motifs, the eagles of Zeus, who mediate between mortals and gods. Here as elsewhere in Tasso, such a plurality is antithetical to the ideal of Christian uniformity.[44] Once the prayers arrive at their destination, they evoke God's speech (73), which includes the very classical sounding verse already mentioned above: "Or cominci novello ordin di cose" (73.5). Indeed, God invokes the messianic rhetoric associated with many passages from the Bible, but at the same time he sounds remarkably similar to the narrator of Vergil's *Eclogue* 4.5: "magnus ab integro saeclorum nascitur ordo." (the great line of the centuries begins anew.)[45] Medieval and Renaissance readers interpreted the Vergilian passage as an example of the classical author's visionary, prophetic proto-Christianity. Therefore, in a sense, the literary culture of Tasso's day had already worked out this elaborate compromise for him. God speaks with a classical accent, yet it is a voice sanctioned by the ecclesiastical tradition.

Tasso's allusion to the Vergilian new order straddles and combines the realms of the biblical and the classical, only to be punctuated by one of the poem's most noticeable neoclassical touches, the majestic nod of the deity.[46] God, looking very much like Jupiter, effects his will with a cataclysmic shake of the head: "Così dicendo, il capo mosse . . ." (74.1). (Thus speaking, He nodded His head. . . .)[47] The un-Christian reaction of the deity undermines any aura of Christianity surrounding Goffredo's prayer. If in stanza 71 Tasso has appeased those readers who are eager to censure him, by stanzas 72 and 74 he is composing once again as he wills.

What is the point of the allegory of the source in *Liberata* 13? Before considering this question, first let me review the sequence of events in the episode of the drought. There are six principal moments: (1) the sources around the city of Jerusalem dry up and are poisoned; (2) while his troops languish, Goffredo enjoys wine cut with water brought from the Jordan; (3) Tatino, the Greek soldier, deserts the Christian army; (4) certain crusaders follow Tatino's lead; (5) Goffredo prays that God end the drought; (6) God responds to Goffredo's prayer.

One way to read these events allegorically might be as follows. A crisis confronts the poet in regard to his literary sources. The exact nature of the crisis is never specified, but one deduces that it involves these issues: which specific sources should the poet use; what is the appropriate context in which to mix sources; and to what extent should the poet mix sources? One option the text suggests involves the rejection of a model from the vernacular tradition of medieval romance in favor of a Greek model from the classical tradition. Tatino's lead is followed by those soldiers who served under Clotareo and Ademaro, leaders killed by Clorinda earlier in the narrative (11.43–44). On the one hand, Ademaro, a historical figure, and Clotareo, Tasso's invention, stand in the allegory as emblems of romance; on the other, Tatino stands for classical Greek sources.[48] The crusaders who desert the army in imitation of Tatino can no longer follow the leads of their medievalizing captains of romance. They follow a Greek leader instead. Classical epic, one may conclude, assumes a greater importance when romance falls short.

Another option, the one which I believe is favored by the plot, is to isolate different and better examples for literary models, which can be identified with the Christian tradition. When Goffredo, in open imitation of Moses, prays for rain, he acts the part of a readily identifiable Christian example. Thus, in the allegory of the source the sequence of possible models shifts from romance to classical to Christian.

Tasso designed this allegory, as I have discussed above, for public consumption. It represents his response to the crisis that the Counter Reformation caused for humanistically trained poets like himself. He nominally accepts and respects the dominant ideology of the Counter Reformation. Since the "revisori" working for the Church are critical of the inclusion of too much of the wrong sort of classicism, he controls his references to the pagan classics. And since the "revisori" require a stronger biblical underpinning for the text, Tasso satisfies that requirement by including traditional and obvious allusions to the Bible.

The full allegoresis is, however, more complicated than the reading outlined above would suggest. For what Tasso does with his sources in actuality—his poetic solution to the problem in conjunction with his ideological solution—does not conform neatly to the interpretation I have proposed. In other words, there is an alternate allegorical interpretation also at play, a poetic (and less public) solution to the crisis of his sources.

Having satisfied the "revisori," Tasso proceeds in the following way: as Aladino does with water and poison, and as Goffredo does with wine and water, so Tasso mixes his own different sources. One could say that he dilutes and cuts his sources even to the point of contamination, and, as I pointed out above, diluting and cutting might be considered "contamination" in the classical sense. In earlier chapters I have discussed how Boiardo and Ariosto engage in similar programs of imitative poiesis. Ariosto, in particular, thematizes the mixture of sources in his poem with the scene of Orlando muddying the spring in canto 23 of the *Furioso,* much as Tasso thematizes the mixture of his sources in canto 13. But neither Boiardo nor Ariosto had to confront the issue of Christian poetry and its appropriate sources as fully as Tasso did. The contaminated source does not have the same profound moral implications for poets writing before the Council of Trent.

Tasso's thematizing of his sources, therefore, must necessarily, at one level of reception or another, have moral overtones. Yet, to assert that Goffredo and Aladino are more realistic figures for the poet than Moses, who also creates his own sources anew, is a striking way of countering the Church's moral censorship. And although it may have smacked of blasphemy to some, the two soldiers do correspond more accurately as archetypes for Tasso than does Moses. It is not until the nineteenth century, with the rebellion against classicism, that readers' expectations require poets to be "new." Not until then will a poet have to draw forth from the rock, as it were, a hidden stream, a novel vein of poetry. Not until the nineteenth century will a kind of Mosaic creativity be forced upon poets.

Revising Humanistic Allegory in the *Conquistata*

What to make of the allegory of the source in canto 13 becomes a moot point in the drastically revised version of the poem published in 1593 and retitled *Gerusalemme Conquistata.* The principal motivation behind the revision was to align the poem with the requirements of the ecclesiastical "revisori," who had harassed the poet since the mid-1570s when the *Liberata* first came into circulation.[49] The *Conquistata,* then, represents the ideological capitulation of Tasso to those critics who were determined to have the poem conform to post-Tridentine literary doctrine.

In the revision of the *Liberata,* much of canto 13 is altered and cut. The second version of the poem increases the number of cantos from twenty to twenty-four, displacing the description of the drought in canto 13 of the *Liberata* to canto 19 of the *Conquistata.*[50] Noteworthy in this reshaping of the episode is the total excision of Tatino's desertion. By cutting stanzas 64–70 of *Liberata* 13, Tasso cuts the anonymous lament against Goffredo, which culminates with the description of the captain's mixing of the wine and water. Also cut are the stanzas that describe Tatino's reaction to Goffredo and the effect of the desertion on the crusaders. Gone, therefore, from the description of the drought in the *Conquistata* are all references to imitation and exemplarity. Even the Exodus-inspired request of Goffredo to "renew in these [warriors] the same examples [that were shown to the Israelites]" is recast significantly: "or rinnovella in questi / le grazie antiche" (19.134.6–7). (Now renew in these warriors the acts of ancient grace.) In the revised version of Goffredo's prayer, "examples" become "acts of ancient grace." The phrase in the *Conquistata* carries the same basic sense as the phrase in the earlier version, but it does not contain any of the seeds of the *Liberata*'s allegory of exemplarity. From the *Liberata*'s examples to the *Conquistata*'s grace, we move into a very different poem.[51]

Tasso cut the episode of Tatino for several reasons. In addition to reshaping the poem to suit the presiding morality of the Counter Reformation, Tasso's editing is an attempt to free himself from the agon between the genres of epic and romance, which gives the *Liberata* much of its energy. His editorial cutting heavily favors epic in the *Conquistata:* several scenes of epic inspiration are added to the final version, with extensive allusions made in particular to Homer's *Iliad.*[52] At the same time, much of what Tasso removes from the final version of the poem falls within the generic boundaries of romance. No longer, for instance, do we find the stories of Sofronia and Olindo, Erminia among the shepherds, and Armida's conversion of the Christian knights into fish.[53]

But the episode of Tatino was not excised because it is romancelike. It is absent, I believe, for two other reasons: (1) it contains an implicit critique of the Greek poetic tradition; and (2) it raises concerns about the moral efficacy of literary fictions. The story of Tatino impeded Tasso as he revised his poem into a composition that was to be a Christian-Homeric epic. I have argued that the allegory in *Liberata* 13 is in part a contest between Greek and biblical sources in which the Greek sources "lose." But Homer's *Iliad,* as noted above, becomes central to Tasso's redefinition of his Christian epic; and Homer's poem, needless to say, is a Greek source. Were the episode of Tatino remaining in the *Conquistata,* it would run glaringly counter to the poet's intentions in composing his new epic. For this reason alone, Tatino's episode had become painfully out of line.

The story of Tatino's desertion raises the issue of the moral efficacy of literature and the problem of exemplarity in general. Throughout this study, *imitatio* has referred to literary imitation almost exclusively, but the word, especially in Tasso's post-Tridentine world, has moral implications as well. Just as there may be limitations to the mimetic possibilities of a literary example, so may there be limitations to the behavior of a specific character within a literary work of art. Put simply, Tatino sets a bad example for conduct.

The disappearance of the Tatino episode from the *Conquistata,* however, does not signal an end to Tasso's critical posturing. In an essay that accompanied the publication of the revised poem, Tasso openly reflects on his rewriting of the *Liberata.*[54] "Ma perchè in quella [poesia] de' Toscani erano famosi i duo fonti di Merlino, de' quali uno accendeva Amore, l'altro l'estingueva, volli piuttosto, a guisa di emulo, che d'imitatore irrigare di nuovi fonti i campi della Poesia, derivandoli non dalle favole Francesche o Inglesi ma dalle sacre Lettere. . . ."[55] (But because in that poetry of the Tuscans there were two famous fountains of Merlin, one of which kindled Love, the other of which extinguished it, I wanted to irrigate the fields of Poetry with new springs, more like an emulator than an imitator, deriving them not from French or English stories but from sacred Letters. . . .) The mere fact that Tasso makes this claim and the way in which he does so are as important as what he says. In the *Conquistata* he prefers to depend on sacred literature instead of French or English "favole," filtered through poets writing in Tuscan like Pulci or, I believe, Ariosto. By this he means presumably that he is no longer dependent on the stories or plots that make up the two cycles of medieval romance, Carolingian or French, on the one hand, Arthurian or English, on the other. The choice of "favole" as noun in juxtaposition to "sacre lettere" points to the limitations of secular writing: it is as false as a fable. What Tasso means by "sacre lettere," however, only becomes clear as the passage from the "Giudizio" continues: " . . . ma dalle sacre Lettere, perciocchè nell'Opuscolo sessagesimo primo di S. Tommaso, nel qual si tratta *De dilectione Dei, & Proximi,* si legge di cinque fonti misteriosi, che possono significare i cinque generi della sostanza sensibile . . ." (141). (. . . but from sacred Letters, since in the sixty-first pamphlet of St. Thomas, in which is treated *De dilectione Dei, & Proximi,* one reads of five mysterious fountains, which can signify the five kinds of perceptible substance. . . .) "Sacred" in this context does not refer to the Bible or to the canonical texts of the earliest church fathers; rather, in a very medievalizing vein, "sacred letters" refers to the writings of Thomas Aquinas. Thus, in cantos 8 and 21 of the *Conquistata,* Tasso's example of a sacred literary source is appropriately an elaborate description of a literal source of water that he borrows from Aquinas's *De dilectione Dei:* a five-tiered fountain, which for Aquinas represents an allegory of the five elements that make up the medieval cosmos (earth, water, air, fire, and quintessence). The fountain, first described in canto 8 when seen by Tancredi, is the source that bestows holy wisdom upon the wayward Riccardo/Rinaldo in canto 21. Tasso's allegory of the fountain is Dantesque in its use of Thomistic philosophy to explicate the object as the font of eternal wisdom. It is, also, clearly a different kind of allegory from the humanistic one of poetic sources in canto 13 of the *Liberata.* The allegory of the fountain in the *Conquistata* culminates in God, not in poetry.

In order to highlight his dependence on the sacred sources of the Christian tradition, Tasso establishes a controversy between medieval vernacular literature and "sacre lettere." The controversy is similar to Tatino's allegorical episode, in which the Greek tradition is juxtaposed to the Judeo-Christian tradition to the detriment of the former. In the *Conquistata,* or at least in Tasso's description of the poem, a similar controversy is resolved once again in favor of religious tradition. One could say, perhaps, that the one contest replaces the other: the contest between Greek and sacred literature in the Tatino episode from the earlier version of Tasso's poem is replaced by a contest between medieval and sacred in the later one.

But there is much exaggeration in these implied agons. For all of Tasso's inclusions and omissions to suggest theoretical problems on the part of the poet, one must note the romance plots in the *Conquistata* that are not omitted.[56] Nor does he omit classical sources from the *Liberata* after the Tatino episode. As we have seen, he immediately resumes the narrative with a classical description of a nodding Jupiter who makes it rain on the crusaders. Both Tatino and the five-tiered fountain may easily appear to the reader as a superimposed poetics of intertextuality. And as such they become "declarations" that reveal as much about Tasso's strategies for composing as they do about his actual compositions. Tasso rationalized his contamination of sources, especially in his revision of the *Liberata* into the *Conquistata,* on the grounds of decorum, be it toward Christian poetic conventions or toward the requirements of classical epic. But his focus ultimately was limited to specific episodes of the poem and thus it allowed the poet to do what he wanted in other parts.

Throughout this chapter—indeed throughout this book—I have considered how a poet's choice of sources affects the organization of his poem's narrative. Tasso the poet, symbolized by the leader of the Christians, Goffredo, chooses and mixes his sources, sometimes from classical epic, sometimes from chivalric romance, sometimes from the Bible and its exegetical tradition. The result of this combination is a veritable Christianized "romance-epic." In the introduction I invoked this term to label the long poems of the Renaissance, although I simultaneously indicated the problematic, critical compromise it suggests. Let me add here by way of conclusion further comments on "romance-epic" and the literary beast the term aims to describe.

The epigraph to this chapter taken from Tasso's prose would not seem to have a direct impact on a discussion involving romance: "Aristotle goes on to say that . . . [the plot] . . . of epic is like excessively watered wine."[57] This observation from the final section of Tasso's *Discorsi del Poema Eroico* paraphrases Aristotle's *Poetics* 1462b. Tasso employs Aristotle's rivalry between tragedy and epic as a foil to conclude his own essay. The ending, however, is an ambiguous one. Tasso observes that Aristotle is for the most part critical of epic, especially its distended plot, which he contrasts with the more unified plot of tragedy. Tasso, for his part, appropriates Aristotle's argument against epic as a purely negative attack so that he might subvert or "revise" it. After all, epic narrative, with its compound plot, renders greater pleasure—a compounded delight, as it were—for the reader. He then concludes that the compounded narrative of epic, not the plot of tragedy, is the better: " . . . così aviene peraventura tra le favole che le più composte siano le migliori" (2: 382). (. . . thus it happens by chance among plots that the most compounded are the best.)[58]

While Tasso does not refer directly to romance in this final section of the *Discorsi,* it would seem that he is proposing an analogy that pertains to the vernacular genre: Aristotle deals with tragedy versus epic, much as Tasso deals with epic versus romance. Tasso's assertions about classical epic narrative can be applied to romance, the distended, amplified plot of which also yields a multitude of pleasures. Romance is certainly "among the most compounded" of all narratives. In this criticism, as in that regarding the sources of his poem, Tasso follows the widely known bare bones of Aristotle's arguments on tragedy and epic to deflect attention from his real concern in this analysis, the narrative designs of romance and epic. One reason for the theoretical decoy might be that, as the theorist in him could not completely condemn the counterclassical aspects of the romance narrative, so the poet in him could not totally abandon those same features. What we have, then, is a description of classical epic narrative in terms taken from the vocabulary of romance. We have confusion, yes, but it is, I believe, a calculated and literal "mixing together" of the genres in Tasso's theory.

Aristotle's image of watered-down wine complements the image of mixing water and wine in the *Liberata.* Aristotle writes: "If the epic poet takes a single plot, either it is set forth so briefly as to seem curtailed, or if it conforms to the limit of length it seems thin and diluted" (1462b). But Tasso, unlike Aristotle, is not critical of the mixture of sources in his plot qua mixture; his problem is with what kinds of sources get mixed together in the first place. His difficulty is the combining of epic and romance elements in a Christian context. We could say that he is trying to baptize a hybrid made out of Aristotle's Homer and Ariosto: "Ariostotle," if you will. I employed Tasso's image of the *Furioso*'s narrative as a misshapen beast in discussing Ariosto's poem in chapter 4; Tasso's *Liberata* is certainly no less bizarre in its configuration, for the theoretical boundaries that circumscribe the *Liberata*'s creation delimit a literary gerrymander of gargantuan complexities.

Tasso spent his career trying to resolve the demands of Aristotelian criticism without denying the romance heritage of his father, Ariosto, Boiardo, and Pulci, among others. It is appropriate that Torquato leave Aristotle behind while trying to recuperate the epic plot, which he interprets as a good plot to the degree that it contains intermingled and compounded parts characteristic of romance. His final metaphor for disregarding Aristotle's position on epic narrative is that of the traveler:

> Concedamisi dunque ch'in questa ed in alcune altre poche opinioni lasci Aristotele . . . perciò che in questa diversità di parere io imiterò coloro i quali ne la divisione de le strade sogliono dividersi per breve spazio, e poi tornano a congiungersi ne l'amplissima strada, la qual conduce a qualche altissima meta o ad alcuna nobilissima città piena di magnifiche e di reali abitazioni ed ornata di templi e di palazzi e d'altre fabriche reali e maravigliose. (2: 383)

> Let me then be permitted to part company with Aristotle on this and some few other matters. . . . In this divergence of view I shall imitate those whom a branching of the road separates for a brief while; later they return and meet on the broad highway that leads to some lofty destination, some noble city, filled with magnificent regal dwellings, and adorned with temples and palaces and other majestic architectural marvels.

As Tasso takes his leave of Aristotelian authority, even as he proposes, promises, to join Aristotle further down the theoretical road, he reveals his undiminished and abiding attraction to the genre of romance. For where else is that traveler headed but into the world of romance, that literary realm of fantastic and wondrous fabrications? It is a civilized and urbane, even decorous, view of romance, to be sure, but romance no less. It is, one might say, a classically correct romance. Ever the compromiser, Tasso came to the end of his life still somewhere between the first and last phrases of the *Discorsi del Poema Eroico,* somewhere between the opposing poles of "i poemi eroici" and "altre fabriche reali e maravigliose."

Conclusion
Ivy: Column: Romance: Epic

The Vine

I dreamed this mortal part of mine
Was metamorphosed to a vine;
Which crawling one and every way,
Enthralled my dainty Lucia.
Me thought, her long small legs and thighs
I with my tendrils did surprise;
Her belly, buttocks, and her waist
By now soft nervelets were embraced: . . .

ROBERT HERRICK[1]

*I*n book 4 of the *Institutio Oratoria* (4.1.77), Quintilian, writing just two generations after Ovid, provides the locus classicus for criticizing the narrative of the *Metamorphoses:*

> Illa vero frigida et puerilis est in scholis adfectatio, ut ipse transitus efficiat aliquam utique sententiam et huius velut prestigiae plausum petat, ut Ovidius lascivire in Metamorphosesin solet, quem tamen excusare necessitas potest res diversissimas in speciem unius corporis colligentem.

> There is indeed a pedantic and childish affectation in vogue in the schools of marking the transition by some epigram and seeking to win applause by this feat of legerdemain. Ovid is given to this form of affectation in his *Metamorphoses,* but there is some excuse for him owing to the fact that he is compelled to weld together subjects of the most diverse nature so as to form the semblance of a whole. (adapted from Butler)

Quintilian criticizes the transitions in the poem as affected, but in the same sentence he excuses Ovid on the grounds that his poem

170

is a collection of varied material held together in the semblance of a whole. Quintilian's observations inform many subsequent discussions of the poem. Critics frequently begin with an observation on the narrative of the *Metamorphoses,* as Quintilian does with his comment on transitions, only to proceed with a reference to the poem's unity (or lack thereof).[2] Discussing the poem's nature as a unified work often leads critics to the vexed question of the poem's genre, although Quintilian does not address this issue because it is not within the scope of his survey.

Hercules Ciofanus, a native of Sulmona, Ovid's birthplace, formulated a critical response to the *Metamorphoses* under the influence of Quintilian's remarks.[3] Writing at the end of the sixteenth century, Ciofanus's criticism suggested a countertrend to the typical interpretation of classical epic. An observation on the poem's narrative leads Ciofanus to discuss its unity, but his conclusions are different from Quintilian's. In the preface to his commentary on the *Metamorphoses,* Ciofanus asks the following rhetorical question and then provides an answer:

> quid dicam de modo illo singulari ac prope divino connectendi fabulam cum fabula? in quo ita excelluit, ut nihil artificiosius, nihil praestantius, nihil denique ornatius aut dici aut fieri possit: quod res diversissimas tractans adeo ingeniose eas connexuit, ut una materia plane videatur.[4]

> What am I to say concerning that exceptional and nearly divine way he [Ovid] has of connecting story with story? He excels to such an extent that there is nothing more artful, more outstanding, indeed nothing more ornate that can be said or done. This is because he has brought together subjects of a most diverse nature and connected them ingeniously with the result that a single subject clearly may be seen. (my translation)

The passage is indebted to Quintilian's remarks on the *Metamorphoses.* But where the classical critic refers to the Ovidian transition as *frigida et puerilis . . . adfectatio,* Ciofanus writes about *modo illo singulari ac prope divino connectendi fabulam cum fabula.* The adjectives *singularis ac divinus* counter the negative judgment contained in the Roman critic's phrase *frigida et puerilis.* There is a clearer instance of Ciofanus challenging Quintilian's criticisms in the clause *quod . . . videatur.* The clause recalls, indeed it invites comparison with, Quintilian's *res diversissimas in speciem unius corporis colligentem.* Ciofanus adopts Quintilian's phrase "things of a most diverse nature," but he then states that those things are connected into *una materia* and not *in speciem unius corporis.* Whereas Quintilian describes the subject matter of Ovid's poem as collected "into the semblance of a whole," Ciofanus states that Ovid has organized his poem "with the result that one totality may clearly be seen." Ciofanus deliberately replaces "speciem," the essential qualification in Quintilian's remarks, with "plane," and in so doing he shifts the emphasis from Ovid the author to the reader of Ovid's poem. "Ovid has organized his poem with the result that it may clearly be seen by his reader as a unified work of art," to paraphrase Ciofanus's observation.

A passage in Ciofanus's commentary provides a glimpse of how a reader like himself may have cultivated an appreciation for the *Metamorphoses* through the reading of an Italian classic. Ciofanus's commentary on the *Metamorphoses* is primarily a collection of textual emendations and parallel passages from other Latin poets. There is, however, one lengthy note on the acanthus plant in which the commentator refers to Ariosto's *Furioso*.[5] This is the only reference to a vernacular work in Ciofanus's entire commentary, a uniqueness suggesting that Ariosto's poem had achieved the status of an esteemed classic for Ciofanus. The critic locates the *Furioso* among other classical poems, establishing a canon of authorities on the acanthus plant that ranges from Vergil's golden epic, through Statius's silver poetry, to Columella's didactic work on horticulture, *De re rustica*. The list establishes generic boundaries that delimit a variety of possibilities within the category of epic: Vergil's canonical epic, Ovid's anti-epic, and Statius's non-epic *Silvae* (which Poliziano promoted, we may recall from chapter 1, as a model of anti-Vergilian narrative arrangement). It is impossible to determine where Ciofanus would rank the *Furioso* in such a catalog; however, the passage in question, which arose during the discussion in chapter 4, bespeaks the generic ambiguity of Ariosto's poem that has prompted critics from Ciofanus's day to our own to try to find the right place for it in the canon. The passage is from a sexually charged scene of mistaken gender and identity in *Furioso* 25.69.5–8:

> Non con più nodi i flessuosi acanti
> le colonne circondano e le travi,
> di quelli con che noi legammo stretti
> e colli e fianchi e braccia e gambe e petti.

> Never did twisting acanthus entwine pillars and beams with more knots than those which bound us together, our necks and sides, our arms, legs, and breasts in a close embrace.

The speaker, Ricciardetto, describes his encounter with Fiordispina, after a water nymph—so he tells it—has transformed him from a woman into a man. (No summary can do this incredible story justice: read the "fabula" [25.27.5] for yourself!) The alleged metamorphosis, one of several Ovidian references in the passage,[6] permits Ricciardetto to consummate his desire, which he portrays in terms of the simile of the vine clinging to the column. This episode, particularly the way in which the embrace is described, drew the criticism of Torquato Tasso in his *Discorsi del Poema Eroico* (1: 154). But that should come as no surprise to us now that we have reviewed his mixture of repugnance for and fascination with Ariosto's ivy and snakes in chapter 4. Girolamo Ruscelli, an editorial entrepreneur who was working in the second half of the sixteenth century, claims that Ariosto intended to excise octaves 68 and 69 from canto 25.[7] Such rhetoric aside, I hope to have made a strong case earlier in the book for the necessary logic of the sequence of ivy and snake similes in the *Furioso:* Ariosto knew better than to delete this passage.

Ciofanus, perhaps inadvertently, cites a passage in canto 25 that leads one back, by an appropriately twisting path, to the center of Ariosto's poem, which is where this book began. In the middle chapters of the book, I argued that ivy (synonymous here with acanthus) symbolizes romance, both in the sense of an amorous embrace and in the sense of the generic mode of the romance narrative. Ivy clinging to a column, I would now like to add, is an apt symbol for the reciprocity and interdependence not only of lovers in Ariosto's story but also of the interdependent generic modes of romance and epic narrative. Such entanglement characterizes Boiardo's Herodotus and Vergil, Ariosto's Ovid, and Tasso's Dante and Ariosto, as we have seen at various points in this study. It also characterizes the imitative process through which the modern poets refer to sources in their respective poems. At the beginning of the book, I used Ariosto's image of Orlando contaminating the spring in *Furioso* 23 to emblematize the poetics of allusion, to symbolize these poets' intertextual references to the disposition of other poets' narratives. I noted that Orlando dumps Medoro's pastoral poem into the spring, along with other bits of the land-scape, including, presumably, the grotto's ivy-covered entrance (23.106). That emblem of narrative continuity is dismantled and churned up with the rest of the mix. I made a case for the viscous spring as a figure for the product of sources brought together, "compromised" in the etymological sense of the word, and subsequently reassessed in their new contexts. It is fitting to conclude with this same murky image from the center of the *Furioso,* for this is the place, figuratively speaking, where Ariosto's poem renews its ambiguous self. That romance ivy, along with the sturdy column of epic to which it clings, is bound to resurface sooner or later, in the work of one poet or another.

Notes

Introduction

1. "Don Juan in Hell" 81.
2. David Quint, whose work I consider at various points throughout this book, focuses on how Ariosto and Tasso engage the classical topos of the source in *Origin and Originality in Renaissance Literature.*
3. Theorists in classical antiquity schematized the art of rhetoric into five parts: in addition to *inventio* and *elocutio,* the parts include *dispositio, memoria,* and *actio.* These moments in the creation and presentation of an oral work are usually translated as invention or discovery of the subject matter, style, arrangement, memory, and delivery. While the first three may be a factor in one poet's imitation of another, the last two pertain to public oratory. The earliest theoretical discussion of narrative arrangement is Aristotle, *Rhetoric,* Book 3, chapters 13–19. But, as George A. Kennedy has pointed out, much of classical rhetoric, including the arrangement of an oral narrative, is already evident in Homeric poetry (9–15, 60–81).
4. I am aware of the standard etymological interpretation of "compromise"— that it derives from *promittere* and *cum,* meaning "to promise mutually."
5. Lawrence F. Rhu discusses how Torquato Tasso treats Homeric poetry in this way in the *Liberata* in *Genesis* 20–22.
6. *Proclaiming a Classic.*
7. This is not the only place in the poem where Ariosto thematizes his dependence on sources in a metacritical way. An analogous scene occurs at *Furioso* 1.25–31, as the complexities of the interlaced narrative of the first canto become apparent to the reader. Ferraù, having lost his helmet in a stream, aggressively searches the flowing waters for it with a large tree limb. His research ("ricerca") is suddenly interrupted by the appearance of

a ghostly figure rising out of the water to chest height. The ghost, Argalia, reprimands Ferraù for failing to keep a solemn promise that he would cast Argalia's helmet into the stream several days after the warrior's death.

The scene is neatly woven into the narrative, more so than these few details can suggest. Its thematic relevance depends in large part on its connection to the poem of Ariosto's predecessor at the court of the Estense, Boiardo's *Innamorato*. In fact, one might say that Argalia emerging from the flowing stream is a figure for the Ariostan character emerging from its source in Boiardo. The scene is the continuation of a passage at the beginning of Boiardo's poem (1.3.53–68) in which Ferraguto (his name in the earlier text) swears to Argalia, whom he has mortally wounded in a duel, that he will bury his corpse in full armor in the river. He does not keep his word, but the ghost gets his helmet back through the intervention of uncanny chance (and the workings of the interlaced narrative).

8. A particular kind of source, which I do not discuss, is medical. Marina Beer examines how Ariosto's use of medical sources parodies intellectual tendencies in the Estense court (83–108).

9. The 1532 edition includes four new episodes, approximately 5,600 lines. A useful guide to the different versions of the poem is the "Tavola comparativa delle tre edizioni originali del *Furioso*" in *I frammenti autografi dell'*OF, ed. Santorre Debenedetti. For a general discussion of Ariosto's rewriting, see Gianfranco Contini, "Come lavorava l'Ariosto." More recently Alberto Casadei has addressed the historical circumstances of Ariosto's rewriting in *La strategia delle varianti* and *Il percorso del* Furioso.

10. Millicent Marcus, "Angelica's Loveknots" 39.

11. I follow the text of the *Furioso* established by Debenedetti and Segre, as it is reported in Emilio Bigi's edition.

12. I generally follow or slightly adapt, as I have done here, Guido Waldman's translation of the *Furioso*.

13. Ascoli's comment on Orlando's "violent 'deconstruction'" of the cave and garden suggests an allegorical way of reading the episode, but the critic does not explore how Ariosto problematizes sources in the scene (*Ariosto's Bitter Harmony* 231). On interpretive violence, see Mazzotta, *Dante, Poet of the Desert* 188–90; see also Bàrberi Squarotti, *L'artificio dell'eternità* 481–507.

14. The narrator reports (calling on another set of four words) that Orlando was filled with "hate, anger, wrath, and madness" (129.7) when he set upon the grotto. The 1516 edition emphasizes this quartet by repeating it in a slightly different order at 134.1: "In ira, in odio, in rabbia, in furor venne." The poet changed this, however, in the poem's final version: "In tanta rabbia, in tanto furor venne" (134.1). Gareffi analyzes such details in his treatment of the scene's stylistic development in *Figure dell'immaginario* (121–56), but he has nothing to say about Ariosto's sources.

15. I have found no critic who makes this point, although Durling goes so far as to say that Orlando's destructiveness is analogous to the poet's use of "denunciation (destruction of reputation)" (*Figure of the Poet* 174).

16. For a discussion of the term in the Quattrocento, especially in relation to Poliziano's poetry, see Thomas M. Greene, *The Light in Troy* 156–62. Ariosto's remarks in the prologue to his comedy, *I Suppositi*, recall a passage from the opening of Terence's *Andria*, in which the Roman playwright explains that he has combined two of Menander's comedies into his own. Terence's image for this combination of sources is *contaminatio* (prologue, 16), the mixing of multiple models through imitation. While he does not translate Terence's passage exactly, it is clear from the context that Ariosto is familiar with the original passage.
17. Maria Cristina Cabani tracks the repetition of "sasso" in her thorough study of the *Furioso*'s "memoria interna" (166–70).
18. Carne-Ross is good on Olimpia and Orlando as types of the same character: "In her passionate dedication she is a type of Orlando and can thus in Canto IX 'replace' him, developing in her own new terms the thematic content of his scene in Canto VIII. She can do this because Orlando is not so much the main character in the poem as the one who most fully embodies its theme" ("The One and the Many" [1976] 154). Miranda Johnson Haddad discusses how the Medusa legend (and these passages on "sasso") affect the intertextual relationship between Ariosto and Dante (218–21).
19. Wiggins does not support his tantalizing statement, "It is particularly ironical that Medoro's ode . . . should be modeled on a Latin poem" (130). Which Latin poem?
20. I discuss the translation of "commodità," which Waldman renders "indulgence," in some detail below. Gilbert, emphasizing the Latin etymology of "commodità," translates this line, "for the convenient place you have given me." In his Elizabethan version, Harington recasts the word as "great pleasures": "I, poor Medore, can yield but praise and thanks / For these great pleasures found amid your banks." Rose translates it, "For the convenient harbourage you gave, . . ."
21. Rosenmeyer discusses the trope of the "inventory" (his term) in classical pastoral (257–58). Cf. the catalogs in Petrarch, *Canzoniere* 35.9–10, 126.1–13. For Petrarchan allusions in Medoro's poem, see Bigi's ed., *OF* 995. See also Bigi's essay, "Petrarchismo ariostesco," in which he discusses the Petrarchan influence on the linguistic alterations between the first and third editions of the *Furioso*.
22. Vergil's first eclogue deals with the shepherds' reaction to the threat that their pastures will be confiscated. Vergil was the first poet to introduce nonpastoral concerns into bucolic poetry, enlarging the scope of the Theocritean idyll (Rosenmeyer). The most provocative discussion of Vergil's transformation of Greek pastoral may still be Bruno Snell's (281–309). But see Alpers (5) for a contextualization of Snell; Alpers's close reading of Vergil's text, for its part, is superb. For the development of politically aware pastoral in the Renaissance, see Marinelli's "The Nearness of Sparta," in his *Pastoral* 57–74.
23. Ronald Martinez has noted another important Petrarchan detail of the place

itself: "Angelica's bower of bliss . . . exemplifies the Petrarchan transformation of the lady's body into the landscape" ("Ricciardetto's Sex" 27).

24. He describes the sylvan setting as a "solitary and comfortable little wood." Rodomonte thinks of the area around Montpellier as beautiful and comfortable: "sì commodo gli parve il luogo e bello" (28.94.2).

25. In the sphere of rhetoric, Cicero uses the word to mean "aptness" or "suitability." See the second definition for the entry in the *Oxford Latin Dictionary.*

26. Ariosto's comedies are full of words from the family of "comodo." See, e.g., *I Suppositi* (prosa) 1.2.33; (versi) 2171; *La Cassaria* (versi) 2797; *Il Negromante* (2nd red.) 175, 458, 517, 1790, 2041; *La Lena* 269, 324, 337. This is a very unscientific list of such words; there are no doubt many more to be found. The greatest confirmation of Ariosto's familiarity with and dependence on the family of "comodo," however, may be *La Scolastica,* which his brother, Gabriele Ariosto, composed to complete the play he left unfinished at his death, *I Studenti.* In trying to write like his brother (he describes this reverential imitative process in the "Prologo" to *I Studenti*), Gabriele uses variations of "comodo" eight times in Act 5 alone (416, 425, 463, 519, 653, 701, 713, 985). Gabriele may even pun on the similarity of "commodo" (in his spelling) and "comedia" when Bartolo says, "Faremo quasi una comedia dupplice" (980), to which Lazzaro responds, "facciàn commodo / A messer Bartol" (985–86).

27. For Ariosto's comments on the revival, see *I Suppositi* (prosa), "Prologo" 27–32, *Lena* 590–91, and *Satire* 6.143–44.

28. See, e.g., Caretti, 2: 998. Another critical tack is exemplified by A. Bartlett Giamatti's discussion of "commodità" as an example of "the language of the marketplace" ("Sfrenatura" 35).

29. I explore the notion of narrative opportunism in more detail in chapter 3.

30. See Plautus, *Menaechmi* 137 + 140; *Miles Gloriosus* 1134 + 1383; *Persa* 255; *Epidicus* 614; and Terence, *Phormio* 841–42.

31. Ascoli is good on the understated presence of tragedy in the poem, beginning with his analysis of its title (*Ariosto's Bitter Harmony* 59–60).

32. Thomas R. Hart addresses the issue of pastoral in the *Furioso* in his *Cervantes and Ariosto: Renewing Fiction.* Pastoral is without question more extensive in *Don Quixote* than in the *Furioso,* but Hart's Cervantean perspective encourages him to force the degree of the difference: "The pastoral affords Cervantes an opportunity to deal with a theme of central importance in *Don Quixote* that does not appear in *Orlando furioso:* the way books can change their readers' lives" (5). Readers of the *Furioso* may take exception to this part of Hart's thesis, for Ariosto does subject the pastoral genre to a definite critique, in, for example, the episodes of Alcina's garden (6–7), Atlante's castle (12), and most noticeably the episodes that culminate with Orlando's madness (23–24).

33. For a discussion of the romance mode, see Parker, *Inescapable Romance;* Quint, *Epic and Empire;* and Zatti, *Il* Furioso *fra epos e romanzo.*

34. On this simile as a gloss on Orlando's heroism, Bigi notes: "L'impiego di

una così lunga similitudine mitologica in sede di proemio, non risponde, come in altri casi, ad un intento di stilizzazione umoristica . . . ma piuttosto alla volontà di sottolineare il carattere eroico e drammatico della figura di Orlando, in coerenza con la rappresentazione che l'A. aveva dato del personaggio nell'episodio di Olimpia" (479). (The use of such a lengthy mythological simile in place of a proem does not indicate, as it does elsewhere, any humorous intentions. Rather, it is indicative of the author's wish to underline Orlando's dramatic heroism and to make it consistent with the portrait that he had given of the character in the episode of Olimpia.) So far, so good. But surely it is unusual to describe him as a heroic *woman*. Nevertheless, Ariosto confirms the comparison later in the narrative's first glimpse of Orlando mad when he uproots trees (23.134.8–135.2), much as Demeter does in canto 12.

35. The description of the fight between Orlando and Mandricardo (23.83.6–8) may allude to Valla's prose version of Homer's *Iliad* 12.421–24. See Bigi on the passage (985). In the Homeric original and in Valla's version of it, the two farmers fight over property lines; Ariosto adds to this scenario the phrase "nel partir acque" (23.83.7) to have them fighting over water rights as well. Is it mere coincidence that the poet introduces a squabble over water just before the scene at the center of the poem on what is essentially poetic water rights? If so, it is felicitous!

36. Wiggins 112.

37. Carne-Ross paraphrases Boiardo's title with wit: "Orlando—of all people!—in love" ("The One and the Many" [1966] 222). For a discussion of the literary-historical context of the title, see Eduardo Saccone, "Il 'soggetto' del *Furioso*" 206–09.

38. Wiggins makes this comment in his reading of Orlando's dream in *Furioso* 8 (113).

39. Recent work on the relationship between gender and genre, how a culture's notion of the former category can affect its understanding of the latter, has demonstrated that Ariosto's poem played an important part in the sixteenth-century debate on the status of women, the *Querelle des femmes* (Benson, Shemek, Finucci, Migiel, and Schiesari). For a review of important recent works on the *Querelle*, see Shemek, "Of Women, Knights, Arms, and Love," notes 2 and 3. Marianne Shapiro discusses narrative repetition as it involves two of Ariosto's heroines, Bradamante and Marfisa, but she does not elaborate her claim that the design of the narrative is informed by "the male-female controversy in dialectical form" (181). For an Italian perspective on Ariosto and women, see Mario Santoro's collection of essays, *Ariosto e il Rinascimento,* esp. chapters 3, 7, 12, and 13.

40. Robert Durling, as in many instances, is the exception, for he does discuss the allusion to Horace in the context of his thesis on the unifying role of the poet-persona in the *Furioso*. But Durling, in my opinion, does not develop the insight as fully as he might. See his *Figure of the Poet* 165–66.

41. See *Le fonti* 393–408. See also Giulio Bertoni's comments on Ariosto's

imitation of the madness of Tristan in *L'OF e la Rinascenza a Ferrara* 104–06.

42. He writes: "dei quali [atti], del resto, si può anche penetrare l'origine" (403). (of which actions, furthermore, one can also penetrate the origins.)

43. Feminist critics, e.g., Annette Kolodny, have done this with Harold Bloom's rhetoric in *Anxiety of Influence.*

44. For a list of the synonyms, see Horace, *The Satires,* ed. Edward P. Morris, 170. On the vocabulary of madness, Niall Rudd (298) refers the reader to D. M. Paschall, "The Vocabulary of Mental Aberration in Roman Comedy and Petronius."

45. For text and translation I follow H. R. Fairclough's edition.

46. I have adapted Fairclough's translation.

47. Recall Horace's conflation of literary and literal construction in his ode "Exegi monumentum" (3.30).

48. Several readers have explored the analogue between Orlando and Hercules, without, however, making quite the point that I am making: namely, that the wood of error is as classical in its origins and essence as it is medieval. Rajna (citing Lando and Pigna) mentions Ariosto's allusion to Seneca's Hercules (*Le fonti* 66–67). Eduardo Saccone discusses the parallel in much detail in "Il 'soggetto,' " esp. 201–23. Ascoli does as well, analyzing in particular the intertextual parallels between the *Furioso* and Seneca's *Hercules Furens* in *Ariosto's Bitter Harmony* 59–62.

49. Clare Carroll explores the connections between Ariosto and Stoicism in her reading of the *Furioso* as a Stoic comedy. See also Giuseppe Mazzotta, "Power and Play: Machiavelli and Ariosto."

50. Carne-Ross discusses Ariosto's use of this prepositional phrase as a leitmotiv for the circular motion of the quest throughout both his *Arion* articles. Zatti's recent "L'inchiesta, e alcune considerazioni sulla forma del poema" (chapter 2 of *Il* Furioso *fra epos e romanzo,* esp. 49–51) extends Carne-Ross's observations to include many variants of the prepositional phrase.

51. Horace uses the image of the muddied literary source elsewhere. Kirk Freudenburg, in an examination of Horace's Callimachean aesthetics, discusses the dual image of the muddy river and clear stream in *Satires* 1.1.54–60 (*The Walking Muse* 185–90). While I find no direct allusion to this satire in *Furioso* 23, I suspect that Ariosto would have been aware of this thematization of the source in Horace's writing.

52. For the reception of the term "spy" ("Überasschung," "spia") by Italianists, see Dante Isella's essay "La critica stilistica."

53. Thomas M. Greene, "Poliziano: The Past Dismembered," in *The Light in Troy* 147–70.

54. "Nella fusione perfetta dell'elemento romanzesco con l'elemento classico sta . . . la principale novità dell'*Orlando furioso*" (*L'OF e la Rinascenza a Ferrara* 120). In a provocative essay, Remo Ceserani also questions the "perfect fusion" of narrative models in Ariosto's poem; see his "Due modelli culturali."

Chapter 1

1. "Sources should not be multiplied beyond necessity." This quote is mentioned by Maria Corti, *La felicità mentale* 65; she does not give the exact source for it in the works of Boethius of Dacia, nor can I find it!

2. For a brief history of Ariosto's translations (I mean of his bones, not his words), see Virgilio Ferrari, "Le case degli Ariosti in Ferrara," esp. pp. 71ff. For the speeches made to celebrate the removal of his mortal remains to the library in 1801, see Turri's pamphlet "Tre rogiti che furono celebrati in Ferrara nel 1801 per trasporto delle ossa di Lodovico Ariosto . . ."

3. "Progetto di raccogliere tutti gli oggetti appartenenti all'Ariosto in una sala della biblioteca" 3.

4. I have benefited from the discussions of positivism in Abbagnano, Cecchini, Simon, and Charlton.

5. Carlo Cattaneo (1801–69) and Giuseppe Ferrari (1811–76) saw Saint-Simon and Comte as continuers of Viconian philosophy. For Cattaneo, see Sestan; for Ferrari, see Bertino.

6. The university's "Facoltà di Lettere" (its combined departments of humanities) sponsored the publication of the journal.

7. Antonio D'Andrea quotes these passages from the *Programma* 1 (1883), p. 2, in his commendable essay, "Il 'metodo storico' ": "lavoro paziente e minuto dei molti" vs. "larghe divinazioni dei pochi" (446).

8. Cultural, or at least regional, politics contributed to the attack on the aesthetic tendencies of De Sanctis and his school. Critics from northern Italy were prejudiced against the Neapolitan and his followers.

9. I discuss the work of these critics in detail throughout the following chapters, esp. chapters 3 and 4.

10. I discuss specific critics of Boiardo and Tasso in chapters 2 and 5, respectively.

11. See the opening pages of the "Introduction" above. See also Rajna, *Le fonti* IX.

12. My translation.

13. Trans. Ainslie 66.

14. "Introduzione," *OF,* pp. v–lv.

15. Now collected in *Ariosto e il Rinascimento.*

16. "Un repertorio linguistico e stilistico dell'Ariosto: La *Commedia.*"

17. One can trace an analogous development in the criticism of Dante's *Commedia,* with Maria Corti's work on the Tuscan poet paralleling Segre's on Ariosto. In *La felicità mentale,* she rigorously analyzes Dantesque intertextuality, proposing a useful, if simple, distinction between direct and indirect sources ("fonte diretta" and "fonte indiretta"). A direct source is one that corresponds to the imitating text on a linguistic, stylistic, or intellectual level (i.e., in the development of an argument or a line of reasoning), while an indirect source is merely a less exact imitation. Corti then makes the tantalizing, albeit unexplored, suggestion that recourse to different kinds of sources bespeaks a creative crisis on the part of the author (67–70). Despite her many useful observations, she concludes on a note

of frustration that betrays a positivist bent: "ma una registrazione della autentica intertestualità rimane illusoria e il nostro lavoro decorosamente mutilo" (71). (but to record genuine intertextuality is still an illusory goal and the work we produce remains a dignified mangle.)

18. The full title is "Intertestuale-interdiscorsivo: Appunti per una fenomenologia delle fonti." He also outlines his phenomenology of sources in "Pio Rajna: le fonti e l'arte dell'*OF.*"

19. The full sentence reads: "A lui [Rajna] interessa quella che chiama invenzione (p. IX), cioè l'elaborazione dei materiali diegetici" ("Pio Rajna: le fonti e l'arte" 318).

20. Segre calls such sources "fonti formali" (formal sources); see "Appunti sulle fonti dei *Cinque Canti*" 418. Resuming the debate between Rajna and Croce, Segre argues that since contemporary scholarship is especially interested in stylistic analysis, it should pay close attention to sources that determine the form of the poem in question. He tries to resolve this debate between Croce's idealism and Rajna's positivism by suggesting that literary scholarship concern itself with formal issues, but in a scientific way.

21. "Appunti per una fenomenologia delle fonti" 22.

22. For a brisk history of recent theories of intertextuality, see the introductory chapter in Clayton and Rothstein, "Figures in the Corpus" 3–37.

23. It behooves me to register my debt to several classical philologists from whose work I have learned much about the poetry of allusion, although I do not refer to them often in these pages: Conte, Farrell, La Penna, Pasquali, and Thomas.

24. David Quint's work in *Epic and Empire* on the charged ideology informing the choice of certain sources opens the discussion of imitation in useful ways. Daniel Javitch also confronts the issue of the fullness of poetic *imitatio* in much of his work on Ariosto, especially in "The Imitation of Imitations in the *OF.*" Javitch avoids focusing on merely a pair of poets, the imitator and the imitated, by examining Ariosto's allusions to Vergil's allusions to Catullus. Guido Baldassarri (*Il sonno,* 3–58), Barbara Pavlock (170–86), and Eduardo Saccone (161–200) similarly have discussed Ariosto's allusive recall of Statius's reading of Vergil in the episode of Cloridano and Medoro (*OF* 18–19), which Latin models in turn allude to scenes from Homeric poetry. While the analysis of such telescoping of allusions does indeed avoid a reductive dyadic study, it is limited to specific passages in the Renaissance poem.

25. *Adone* 2: 89.

26. "Stoff" is the German term used by literary critics to refer to subject matter and themes; its study is called "Stoffgeschichte." See the article by Guyard and Weisstein, "Stoffgeschichte."

27. Rhu, *Genesis* 101. For Tasso's text, see Mazzali's ed., *Scritti* 1:6.

28. For the historical background on this debate, see Izora Scott, *Controversies Over the Imitation of Cicero in the Renaissance* 14–22.

29. For a list of all the courses Poliziano offered (as accurately as can be

determined), see Vittore Branca, *Poliziano e l'umanesimo della parola* 86, n. 22.

30. I follow the text of the "Oratio" established by Eugenio Garin in *Prosatori latini del Quattrocento* 870–85.

31. The text from Cicero's *Orator* 3.11 is "reprehendent, quod inusitatas vias indagemus, tritas relinquamus." ([Readers] will criticize us for leaving the well-trodden paths and searching for unusual ones.) (adapted from Hubbell's trans.)

32. Poliziano uses the metaphor to describe Statius's preparation of the *Silvae* for publication (874). He concludes the oration by claiming that Quintilian will lead the young writers down a fast path to excellence in oratory (884).

33. For text and translation I follow the edition of Williams 54–55.

34. In an illuminating article, Antonio La Penna discusses the suggestiveness of many of Vida's terms, such as *furta* and *alludere,* without, however, touching on these passages from book 2; see "La teoria dell' 'arte allusiva' nel *De arte poetica* di Girolamo Vida."

35. Numbers are to the lines in Sherberg's edition.

36. Bernard Weinberg discusses the reception of Aristotle's *Poetics* in detail throughout his *A History of Literary Criticism in the Italian Renaissance.* In more recent research, Enzo Turolla argues convincingly that Aristotle's *Poetics* had no impact on the development of aesthetic criticism before the 1540s. See his article "Aristotele e le poetiche del Cinquecento."

37. For a discussion of the crisis in narrative theory in the Cinquecento, see William W. Ryding, *Structure in Medieval Narrative* 9–12; see also Charles Altman's review of Ryding, "Medieval Narrative vs. Modern Assumptions: Revising Inadequate Typology."

38. Most sixteenth-century theories of epic narration were extrapolated from remarks in Aristotle's *Poetics* on the narratives of tragedy (1450b–53a) and epic (1459a–b).

39. Lodovico Dolce likens Ariosto to Vergil in the dedicatory sonnet to the 1542 Giolito edition of the *Furioso* with rhetoric that is typical of the comparison: "Spirto Divin; ne le cui dotte carte / Fra bei concetti al gran Virgilio eguali . . ." (Divine spirit, in whose learned pages among whose beautiful conceits equal to Vergil . . .) The sonnet was reprinted frequently in the Cinquecento.

Girolamo Ruscelli comments on the similar linguistic achievements of Ariosto and Homer in "Mutationi, et miglioramenti, che M. Lodovico Ariosto havea fatti metter nell'ultima impressione del *Furioso*": "Et oltre à ciò l'Ariosto . . . volle in questo suo poema Eroico usar tutti i modi di dire communi nella Italia, come fece Omero nel suo di quei della Grecia sua" (621). (Furthermore, Ariosto wanted to use all the expressions common in Italy in this epic poem of his, just as Homer used all those of Greece in his.)

40. Pigna makes this claim in his "Vita" of Ariosto, one of the important paratexts that was frequently reprinted with the *Furioso* in the Cinquecento; for the

exact passage, see the edition printed by Felice Valgrisi, 1587, p. 5 (not numbered).

41. For the dating of events in Tasso's life and for his biography in general see Edward Williamson, *Bernardo Tasso*. A useful discussion of the literary ambience during Tasso's life is found in Albert N. Mancini, *I Capitoli Letterari di Francesco Bolognetti*. Mancini edits and analyzes poems and correspondence exchanged among Bolognetti, Tasso, Giraldi, and others.

42. This is a synthesizing interpretation of various observations by Tasso, which I discuss below. He never actually defines "rhapsodic."

43. Recently two Italian critics have broached this topic. Donatella Rasi, in "Breve ricognizione di un carteggio cinquecentesco," observes that Tasso believed the chivalric romance to have had "un'origine in qualche modo 'classica' " (7) (in some sense a 'classical' origin)—a point she does not develop but which is borne out by an analysis of his references to rhapsodes. Riccardo Bruscagli discusses Giraldi's contribution to this conversation on rhapsodes in "Vita d'eroe: l'*Ercole*." While he and I come to some similar conclusions concerning Giraldi's focus on the rhapsode, Bruscagli's emphasis is ultimately a different one from mine. His thesis is that Giraldi writes the *Discorsi* to make a critical space for his own poem *Ercole*. In this process Giraldi stresses more the importance of thematic content ("le azioni di un uomo solo" [Ercole]) than narrative artistry (16).

44. References in parentheses are to volume and letter number in *Delle lettere di M. Bernardo Tasso;* letters cited directly are given by the volume and page(s). Seghezzi's edition is the standard edition of letters published up to 1733; see "Appendix I: A Bibliography of the Works of Bernardo Tasso," in Williamson's *Bernardo Tasso* 151–57.

45. *Lettere* 1: 193–94. Rasi assumes this letter was written in March (6); but see Williamson's note on the problems of that specific chronology (109). Scholars agree that it was written sometime in the first half of 1556.

46. Ariosto himself contributes to the confusion, for despite his occasional gestures to the oral tradition, he also describes the composition of the poem in terms of writing: *OF* 15.9.5–8 and 33.128.7.

47. Camillo Guerrieri Crocetti superficially examines the correspondence between the two men in *G. B. Giraldi ed il pensiero critico del secolo XVI* 35–45.

48. *Lettere* 2: 197.

49. I follow the text in *Scritti critici* 48.

50. The text of the first edition of the letter also reads "forse" and thus further qualifies the conditional: "Ma se questi tali considereranno, che questa sorte di Poesia *forse* potrebbe essere quella istessa . . ." (my emphasis), *Delle Lettere* (1560–62) 2: 210.

51. For some interesting observations on a "cantastorie" who was one of Ariosto's contemporaries, see Giuseppe Frasso, "Un poeta improvvisatore." For a singer from Tasso's day, see Alfonso Lazzari, "Un improvvisatore."

52. *Scritti critici* 48.

53. Marina Beer (207–15) is helpful on Giraldi's rhetoric of exclusion in the *Discorso*.

54. At an earlier stage of the *Amadigi*'s composition Tasso intended to write an epic. In a letter to Sperone Speroni written in 1543 (1: 82), Tasso defends his decision to use the octave stanza, a decision that countered the advice of Sperone, who had urged him to use the more heroic "versi sciolti." Without applying precisely this terminology, Tasso argues that his poem in its narrative design is epic, and therefore, by implication, heroic, in spite of its dependence on the stanzaic meter of romance: "Nè mi par che questa [the plot of the *Amadigi*] sia altro, che una perfetta azione d'un uomo non meno che sia quella d'Omero nell'Odissea, e di Virgilio nell'Eneida. Nella qualità, e maniera del verso sarò simile all'Ariosto: nell'ordine, e nelle altre cose alla disposizione appartineti, Virgilio, e Omero, quanto basteranno le forze mie, procurerò d'imitare" (1: 169). (Nor does it seem to me that the plot of the *Amadigi* is anything other than a totally complete action of one man, no less than Homer's plot in the *Odyssey* and Vergil's in the *Aeneid*. In the quality and in the manner of the verse I shall be similar to Ariosto; in the organization and in the other things that have to do with the narrative disposition, I shall try to imitate Vergil and Homer, as much as my powers will allow.) Torquato Tasso recounts how his father was forced to reconceptualize the *Amadigi* as a romance narrative instead of an epic after a botched dramatic reading of the first draft (*Apologia* 125–27).

55. *Lettere* 2: 221; the letter is dated 8 August 1556.

56. For the *Furioso* as a woven work of art, see the discussion in chapter 3.

57. Tasso studied Greek under the tutelage of Demetrio Calcondila in Bergamo (Williamson 3).

58. Scholars have debated the etymology of the word, tracing it either to the art of stitching songs together or to the Greek noun *rabdos,* "staff," which referred to the staff with which a bard kept time as he chanted epic verses. See Tarditi, "Sull'origine e sul significato della parola 'rapsodo.'"

59. *Lettere* 2: 305–06. Weinberg briefly examines this letter in *A History of Literary Criticism* 1: 140–42; see also Rasi 15–18.

60. *Lettere* 2: 134, pp. 452–53.

61. *Opere di M. Sperone Speroni* 5: 521.

62. *Lettere* 2: 116, p. 325.

63. *Lettere* 2: 116, p. 325.

64. Giraldi has nothing favorable to say about Pulci. Here is a typical remark: "Di quelle [repetitions] che mostrano poco giudicio se n'hanno gli esempj nel Pulci nel suo *Morgante,* il quale comincia con le medesime parole spessissime volte molte stanze; Il che reca un fastidio incredibile a chi legge" (*Scritti Critici* 113). (There are examples in Pulci's *Morgante* of those sorts of repetitions that demonstrate little judgment; Pulci begins many stanzas very frequently with the same words, which is unbelievably boring for the reader.)

65. It did not prevail, although the poem continued to be performed into the

twentieth century. In his travelogue, Augustus Hare describes hearing the *Furioso* read (not sung) in Chioggia in 1900: "Cut off from the rest of the world by water, the life here is still of centuries ago, and Ariosto is even now read publicly in the evenings in the principal street, by a regular reader to a large and delighted audience" (54). Pio Rajna dedicated an entire essay to rhapsodes in nineteenth-century Naples, not all of whom sang their material; see his "I 'Rinaldi' o i cantastorie di Napoli," where he observes of a performer: "Egli legge declimando, e non china gli occhi sulle carte, se non quanto è necessario" (567). (He reads as he declaims, only casting his eyes down over the page as much as is necessary.)

Chapter 2

1. For Schama, see his article "Clio Has a Problem" 32; the epigraph from Twain is cited in Detlev Fehling, *Herodotus and His "Sources"* 175.
2. There was also a body of "cantari" that dealt with classical material, especially the stories associated with the Trojan legends. See Francesco A. Ugolini, *I cantari d'argomento classico.*
3. Boiardo tends to populate his poem with Carolingian heroes; however, he situates them in Arthurian places. Charles S. Ross makes this observation in his article, "Boiardo," in *The Spenser Encyclopedia.*
4. Robert Durling discusses these seemingly medieval characteristics of the *Innamorato* in the chapter on Boiardo in *Figure of the Poet* 91–111. Andrea Di Tommaso is good on the tension between "Word Heard and Written" (his phrase) in his chapter on "The Poet and His Audience" (esp. 22–30).
5. See, e.g., 2.31.48, where the narrator, nearing the end of Book 2, aptly mixes his metaphors: "A questo libro è già la lena tolta." (The breath of this book has expired. [Ross's translations, here and throughout.]) And at 1.2.68, the narrator acknowledges that his audience includes readers: "Gran meraviglia e più strana ventura / Ch'odisti mai per voce, o per scrittura." (Great marvels and more strange adventure / Than you have ever heard or read.) Michael Sherberg presented a paper on this topic at the Columbia University conference on Boiardo (1994), which will be published in the conference proceedings.
6. I have not been able to read Cristina Zampese's *La cultura classica nell'OF,* so I speak here with some reservation. I am led to believe that her study deals primarily with thematic classical sources. My understanding of Zampese's work derives from the author's synopsis of her book in *Il Boiardo* 2 (1993): 17.
7. There are many signs that this may change in the near future. The excellent translation of the *Innamorato* by Charles Stanley Ross has made the poem more accessible to non-Italianists. (I follow Aldo Scaglione's text of the *Innamorato,* as reported in Ross's translation.) A useful concordance on microfiche has appeared: *OI: Concordance, rimario & tables,* edited by David Robey and Marco Dorigatti. Riccardo Bruscagli has completed a commentary on Boiardo's poem (Einaudi, 1995); see his exploratory article

"Prove di un commento." Finally, textual bibliographers working in Italy, including Antonia Tissoni Benvenuti and Cristina Montagnani, on the one hand, and Neil Harris, on the other, have begun publishing works that will culminate with a definitive edition of the *Innamorato*, to be edited under Tissoni Benvenuti's direction. Much work has come to light following the 1994 and 1995 conferences in Italy and North America that commemorated Boiardo's death in 1494.

8. For a useful introduction to Gravina that emphasizes his role in the development of Italian literature, see the following articles by Gustavo Costa in *Dictionary of Italian Literature:* "Arcadia" 17–19; "Enlightenment" 194–97; "Gravina" 261–62; and "Neoclassicism" 351–52.

9. *Ragion Poetica* 152. For a modern ed., see *Scritti critici e storici* 195–327. Quondam mentions Gravina's awareness of Boiardo's classicism in *Cultura e ideologia* 261–62.

10. See Carlo Dionisotti, "Regioni e letteratura" 1391.

11. For a good, brief introduction to the court of the Este with an extensive bibliography see "The Court of Ferrara," in Felton Gibbons, *Dosso and Battista Dossi* 3–23. Two important books have come out since Gibbons wrote his: Luciano Chiappini, *Gli Estensi,* and Werner Gundersheimer, *Ferrara: The Style of a Renaissance Despotism.* The former presents an elaborate genealogical history of the family; the latter, a detailed study of the impact of Estense rule in the Quattrocento and early Cinquecento, has recently been translated into Italian with a new introduction by the author: *Ferrara Estense.* For a brief discussion of the devolution of Ferrara as papal fief to the States of the Church in 1598, see Bonner Mitchell, *1598: A Year of Pageantry in Late Renaissance Ferrara.*

12. For a discussion of the impact of the court on society, with many references to Ferrara, see Sergio Bertelli et al., *Italian Renaissance Courts.* The most recent general treatment of chivalry and Italian courts is Aldo Scaglione, *Knights at Court.*

13. For my remarks in this and subsequent paragraphs I am indebted to the studies of Trevor Dean, *Land and Power in Late Medieval Ferrara,* and Richard M. Tristano, "Vassals, Fiefs, and Social Mobility in Ferrara."

14. Jane Bestor discusses the technicalities involved in maintaining the Estense rule in "The Problem of Bastardy in the Estense Succession."

15. The council was transferred to Florence in 1439 because of a plague in Ferrara, hence it is generally referred to as the Council of Ferrara-Florence.

16. *The Civilization of the Renaissance in Italy* 31. The most authoritative modern study of Rossetti bears Burckhardt's claim out; see Bruno Zevi's critical biography, *Biagio Rossetti, architetto ferrarese, il primo urbanista moderno.*

17. I have consulted a version of Feltrino's biography recorded in the seventeenth-century ms. in Modena, Biblioteca Estense, γ.E.3.10, *Vita del Cavalier Feltrino Boiardo, già Signore di Rubiera, et di Scandiano, anni: 50, scritta latina da Bartolomeo da Prato. Sopra questa volgare da G.D.Z.* The narrator remarks that Feltrino went to Jerusalem, "ove conforme al

voto con somma devotione al sepolchro, rese ringratie à Dio" (25). (where
having satisfied his vow with profound devotion at the sepulcher, he gave
thanks to God.)

18. Dean 165–66.
19. *Le Satire* in *Tutte le opere di Ludovico Ariosto* 3: 35.
20. Trans. Wiggins 61.
21. For information on Guarino's life see Remigio Sabbadini, *Guariniana*. Schol-
    ars who have continued Sabbadini's work on Guarino include Giulio
    Bertoni, *Guarino da Verona fra letterati e cortigiani a Ferrara (1429–
    1460);* William H. Woodward, *Vittorino da Feltre and Other Humanist
    Educators;* Renate Schweyen, *Guarino Veronese;* and Eugenio Garin, who
    discusses the role of Guarino's school in the development of humanism
    across Europe in a useful book, *L'educazione in Europa 1400/1600;* see
    also his "Guarino Veronese e la cultura a Ferrara." More recently, Paul F.
    Grendler has discussed Guarino's seminal position in education in Italy:
    Schooling in Renaissance Italy 126–29. Finally, see the work of Grafton
    and Jardine discussed below.
22. Sabbadini 2: 37–38.
23. Anthony Grafton and Lisa Jardine have recently exposed Guarino's aggres-
    sive campaign of propaganda through which he promoted the achievements
    of his students and curriculum. See the first chapter of their study, "The
    School of Guarino: Ideals and Practice," in *From Humanism to the Hu-
    manities* 1–28.
24. Sabbadini 1: 140.
25. On this moment in Guarino's career, see Deno John Geanakoplos, *Greek
    Scholars in Venice* 28–30.
26. Sabbadini 2: 35. The students were expressly prohibited from reading Ovid's
    Ars amatoria: Guarino Veronese, *Epistolario* 3: 422. Garin discusses the
    curriculum of Guarino's school in *L'educazione in Europa 1400/1600* 127–
    36.
27. On the function of translations in Guarino's classroom, see Joseph R. Berri-
    gan, "The Latin Aesop of Ermolao Barbaro" 141–48.
28. Riccardo Truffi, "Erodoto tradotto da Guarino Veronese."
29. See the conclusion of Grafton and Jardine 26–28.
30. Guarino in turn sent his sons to the school of Vittorino. See Grendler 130.
31. For an account of student life in Ferrara see "Ludovico studente," in Michele
    Catalano, *Vita di Lodovico Ariosto* 1: 86–103. Nicola Maria Panizzato (d.
    1529), a lifelong friend of Ariosto (mentioned in *OF* 46.14.8), was a student
    of Battista and eventually became a teacher of Latin and Greek at the *Studio.*
    Ercole Strozzi, Boiardo's cousin and friend of Ariosto, also studied under
    Battista. See Mario Cosenza, *Biographical and Bibliographical Dictionary
    of the Italian Humanists* 5: 438.
32. Ariosto was probably tutored from 1486 to 1489 by Luca Ripa (fl. 1480s), who
    taught at the school during these years. Domenico Catabene (fl. 1480s), a
    law student at the *Studio* and a boarder in the Ariosto household in 1485,
    also may have tutored Ariosto. See Catalano 1: 88–89.

33. Garin cites Agricola's letter, which lists over twenty areas around Italy and Europe from which Guarino's students had come in search of learning (*L'educazione* 127–29).

34. Jo Ann Cavallo argues that the *Innamorato* has an ethical dimension, which reflects in part the influence of Guarino's school on Boiardo (*Boiardo's* OI 3–6).

35. An example of Borso's interest in maintaining the feudal cast to his dukedom was his continued use of the elaborate ceremony of knighthood. He regularly knighted his dependents on St. George's Day; see Dean 148.

36. Giulio Bertoni provides this inventory in *La biblioteca estense* Appendix 1.

37. *Borsias,* ed. W. Ludwig.

38. Marina Beer in *Romanzi di cavalleria* discusses the vast quantity of minor chivalric works available to readers (and their audiences) in the lifetimes of Boiardo and Ariosto. She is also part of a team that has recently brought forth many of the texts of such works in a four-volume set, *Guerre in ottava rima.*

39. Tissoni Benvenuti reviews the contents and dating of this inventory in "Il mondo cavalleresco e la corte estense" 18–21.

40. See Bertoni, *La biblioteca estense,* Appendix 3.

41. Many of the translations still exist in the Biblioteca Estense in Modena in lavish dedication copies. See, e.g., the manuscript of Boiardo's translation of Xenophon's *Cyropaedia* in the Biblioteca Estense, alpha G.5.1.

42. The version of Cornelius Nepos's *Lives* is the only translation that has been reprinted in a full edition in modern times: in Zottoli's edition of 1936–37, which also gives the prologues Boiardo wrote for the translations. Boiardo's Nepos was also reprinted in a private edition by O. Guerrini and C. Ricci (1885).

43. Boiardo's version of Apuleius has recently been the subject of a serious examination by Edoardo Fumagalli, *Matteo Maria Boiardo volgarizzatore dell'*Asino d'Oro. Fumagalli considers the cultural background and the literary implications of Boiardo's translation, but his focus is more directed toward Apuleius's critical reception than toward the translation's importance in Boiardo's development as a literary artist.

44. Boiardo's version of Xenophon's *Cyropaedia* has not been edited once for publication, not even in the Renaissance.

45. See the comments by J. S. Phillimore in "The Greek Romances" 94–95.

46. See John Herington, "The Poem of Herodotus." For a more traditional discussion of Herodotean narrative, see Henry R. Immerwahr, *Form and Thought in Herodotus.* More recently, Donald Lateiner has discussed the historian's narrative artistry in *The Historical Method of Herodotus,* esp. chapter 1, "A New Genre, A New Rhetoric" 13–51. Quintilian anticipated many of the comments of these scholars with his reflections on history as a kind of prose poem (10.1.31).

47. Carlo Dionisotti is the most noticeable exception. He discusses the lack of interest in Boiardo's translations in "Tradizione classica e volgarizzamenti,"

now in *Geografia e storia della letteratura italiana,* ed. 1980, 158–61. Eugenio Ragni and Antonia Tissoni Benvenuti also have commented on the need for a serious treatment of Boiardo as a translator. There has been some paleographical work done on the various Renaissance manuscripts and the early printed editions of the translations (Bertoni, Frati, Reichenbach). Several critics who have considered Boiardo's translations evaluate them negatively for philological and stylistic shortcomings (Albini, Rossi, Tincani). All is not negative, however. Michael Murrin, in "Agramante's War" (reprinted as chapter 3 of *History and Warfare*), gives an intelligent reading of Boiardo's imitation of Herodotus's councils of war in book 2 of the *Innamorato.* He provides a useful appendix based on his scrutiny of the Herodotean original, Valla's prose trot, and Boiardo's version. Maria Acocella updates the bibliography in her thoughtful essay in *Schifanoia.* And, finally, an entire session was devoted to the translations at the international conference "Il Boiardo e il mondo estense nel Quattrocento," 13–17 September 1994. The proceedings will include the presentations of E. Fumagalli, D. Looney, G. Ponte, A. Scarsella, and A. Soffientini.

48. Ed. Ferruccio Ulivi, *Opere di Matteo Maria Boiardo.*
49. Edoardo Fumagalli has produced a smart desktop edition of an excerpt from *Storie* I, 95–130, which recounts the early days of Cyrus. This useful edition includes an introduction with a summary of the text's history. It would be wonderful to have, if not an edition of the entire text, at least a facsimile of the 1533 editio princeps.
50. 1533, 1538, 1539, 1553, 1565.
51. I follow Zottoli's edition of the prologue.
52. So Giulio Reichenbach argues in *Matteo Maria Boiardo,* 193–95. And, more recently, Edoardo Fumagalli has argued along the same lines in his edition of *Nascita . . . di Ciro il Grande* viii.
53. See Murrin's appendix to "Agramante's War" for passages that show Boiardo's use and divergence from Valla (now also "Appendix 2" in his *History and Warfare*). In a subsequent study I intend to explore in more detail the relationship among Boiardo's *Erodoto,* Valla's version, and the original.
54. For an example of Boiardo's use of the verb "comporre" in regard to his own poem, see his letter to Isabella d'Este, 8 August 1491 (*Opere volgari* 238, letter no. 86).
55. The most lucid definition of the phenomenon is in Quintilian, *Institutio Oratoria* 9.3.23: "*interpositio,*" a grammatical figure of speech, "consists in the interruption of the continuous flow of our language by the insertion of some remark." I follow the text and translation of H. E. Butler 3: 458–59. Subsequent theoreticians who applied Quintilian's grammatical category to the discussion of narrative included Fortunatianus and Martianus Capella. See Heinrich Lausberg, *Handbuch der Literarischen Rhetorik* 1: 167 + 399.
56. William V. Harris notes the following: "There seems to be no fully adequate discussion of Herodotus' place in the transition from oral culture to partly

literate culture (but see F. Hartog, *Le miroir d'Hérodote* [Paris, 1980], 282–97); even the basic question abut his variation between the verbs *graphein* and *legein* needs further investigation" (*Ancient Literacy* 80, n. 74).

57. Trans. Cavalchini and Samuel.

58. See, e.g., Mazzali 2:381, n. 6; and Cavalchini and Samuel 204, n. 3.

59. Indeed Conti's translation is based on a manuscript tradition that had currency until the nineteenth century. Only then did Valckenaer propose the now-accepted emendation of "Hesiod" for "Herodotus."

60. *Athenaei Dipnosophistarum sive Coenae sapientum.* Libri xv. Natale de Comitibus Veneto nunc primum à Graeca in Latinam linguam vertente. . . . Venetiis apud Andream Arrivabenum ad signum Putei. M D L V I. The marginal note cited is on p. 254. The presence of Tasso's personal copy of this translation allows one to correct the misleading note in the translation of Tasso's *Discourses on the Heroic Poem* by Cavalchini and Samuel: "Tasso evidently misreads Athenaeus . . . substituting Herodotus for Hesiod and Hermodotus for Hermophantus" (p. 204, note 3).

61. On Berni's "rifacimento" see Elissa Weaver's essay, "Riformare l'*OI*," Bruscagli, *I libri* 117–44. Carlo Téoli notes the fate of Boiardo's work in his edition of Apuleius: "I fiorentini sommersero la sua fama; il Berni fa che non si legga il suo *Orlando;* il Firenzuola, che non si legga il suo *Asino*" (xiii). (The Florentines submerged his fame; Berni sees to it that no one reads his *Orlando;* Firenzuola, his *Asino.*)

62. Murrin observes that both Boiardo and Valla omit Herodotus's discussion of tyrants at 1.96–100 and 7.10g.2 (*History* 251). But at another passage in the translation Boiardo includes some remarks on tyranny in Athens; see his version of H5.65–66 at B171r–v. Is this a case of sloppy self-censorship or a veiled criticism of the patron's politics buried deep enough in the work to avoid too much scrutiny?

63. "B" refers to the 1533 edition of Boiardo's translation; "H" to the Loeb edition of Herodotus. Compare the following passages in the translation for other examples of the "lasciare-tornare" formula: B135v (H4.96), B194r (H6.55), B203r (H6.93), B249v (H7.171).

64. For the passages translated directly from Herodotus here and below, I have followed, with slight changes, the translation of A. D. Godley. J. Enoch Powell's *A Lexicon to Herodotus* has been useful as a concordance.

65. I have altered the Loeb translation to remove the idiomatic "it is the business of my history," a phrase that introduces a metaphor in English where the Greek verb *epidizēmai* has none. For another passage where Boiardo uses the formula (with "seguire" in place of "seguitare"), see B221r (H7.26).

66. In recent decades classicists have debated the issues raised by such passages, asking, in general, whether Herodotus is more aptly considered the father of history, as Cicero puts it, or the father of lies. The two camps are represented by W. Kendrick Pritchett and Detlev Fehling. Kwintner, in her excellent review of Pritchett's *The Liar School of Herodotus,* calls his book "a refutational commentary on the work of Detlev Fehling" (*BMCR* 94.4.10, first screen). See her review for a record of the dispute.

67. See Giuseppe Albini, "I versi nell'*Erodoto* del Boiardo."
68. See Craig Kallendorf, *In Praise of Aeneas.*
69. Cf. Milton's deliberate re-creation of a poetic career modeled on Vergil's as he progressed from lyrics to his epic.
70. The definitive outline of the relationship between Boiardo and the works of Vergil is now Eugenio Ragni's entry on Boiardo in the *Enciclopedia Virgiliana* 1: 518–21.
71. For a discussion of Boiardo's use of the Vergilian subtext in his bucolic poetry, see Ignacio Navarrete, "Boiardo's *Pastorali* as a Macrotext."
72. See *OI* 2.6.12, based in part on *Georgics* 1.356–64.
73. The fundamental article on this aspect of Boiardo's Vergilian imitation is Ettore Paratore, "L'*OI* e l'*Eneide.*"
74. "Casella, Palinuro e Orfeo. 'Modello narrativo' e 'rimozione della fonte.' "
75. See Aelius Donatus's influential *Vita,* para. 21.
76. *Virgil, A Study in Civilized Poetry* 215–382. See also G. N. Knauer's essay, "Vergil's *Aeneid* and Homer," full of meticulous detail.
77. David Quint, "The Boat of Romance and Renaissance Epic." Quint refers directly to Boiardo's rewriting of *Aeneid 10* in *Epic and Empire* (34–36), where he proposes that Vergil suggests an analogy between Turnus and Cleopatra. Although I do not see that particular analogy, I owe much to Quint's critical understanding of the relation between epic and romance. He writes masterfully on the ideologies that shape generic forms and on how those forms interact. My argument differs from Quint's in its emphasis on passages in Boiardo (and Ariosto and Tasso) that confuse one's perception of the generic forms or modes of epic and romance. My thesis that these poets deliberately compromise classical sources by incorporating them into chivalric forms highlights the similarities between epic and romance—rather than the differences discussed by Quint—in these Renaissance rewritings of classical authors.
78. Quint, "The Boat of Romance" 179.
79. Quint, "The Boat of Romance" 179. See also *Epic and Empire,* esp. chapters 1 and 6.
80. Nohrnberg briefly compares the Vergilian episode with Homeric precedent (*Analogy* 8–11) and with Boiardo's allusions to it in his opening chapter's meditation on the generic differences between romance and epic narratives.
81. I have found no critic who makes this precise claim, although Lyne has a useful note on the verb *obeo* at 10.641, which means "to die" (110–11). Several critics comment on the romancelike quality of Turnus's chase after the phantom; see Gransden's remark on the passage as "weirdly effective" (150); Quinn's reference to it as an attempt "to re-establish the fairy-tale atmosphere" (*Virgil's* Aeneid 228); and Nohrnberg's description of "Virgil's more magical treatment" (*Analogy* 10). The sort of foreshadowing of book 12 I see in *Aeneid* 10, Quinn calls, interestingly, "interweaving" (*Latin Explorations* 212–16).
82. José Luis Colomer, "Translation and Imitation."
83. I follow the text of R. A. B. Mynors.

84. Trans. Fairclough.
85. Thomas M. Greene traces this motif from its origins in classical literature into the Renaissance in *The Descent from Heaven.*
86. I have adapted the translation of S. J. Harrison.
87. For further examples of such irony, see Harrison's commentary, pp. 228–29.
88. Gransden is good on the parallel between the descriptions of Turnus in *Aeneid* 10 and 12 (150–51).
89. Pöschl notes, "The whirlwind that drives him over the water is a suggestive symbol of his helplessness in the face of blind forces" (108).
90. Later in the continuing saga of Angelica and Ranaldo, the lady and the horse are crudely equated when Angelica offers Ranaldo Baiardo (the horse had come into her hands) in exchange for his love; he, however, refuses! See 1.28.42–47.
91. Ariosto does not seem interested in maintaining any allusions to Boiardo's Vergilian model, perhaps because he saw only superficial parody in his predecessor's treatment of Vergil and did not want to engage in the same.
92. See the article by Guido Fusinato, "Un cantastorie chioggiotto" (182).
93. Michael Sherberg discusses the development of Ranaldo/Rinaldo in the literary tradition before Boiardo through Ariosto and Tasso; see *Rinaldo: Character and Intertext.*

Chapter 3

1. I follow Perella's text and translation of *Pinocchio* 128–29: "So many things can happen!"
2. I have adapted Gilbert's translation.
3. Ariosto was uncertain of the spelling of the adjective; in the earlier editions of the poem he regularly spelled it correctly with the double consonant, "*opp*ortuno."
4. I borrow "narrative opportunism" from a statement James Nohrnberg made in a lecture delivered to the NEH Summer Institute on Ariosto and Tasso at Northwestern University, 26 July 1990. Nohrnberg used the happy phrase in reference to the passage in Boiardo's *Innamorato* where Orlando takes charge of his destiny by seizing the forelock of fortune worn by the Fata Morgana (2.9.17). More recently, Nohrnberg developed this idea in a paper, "Orlando's Opportunity," delivered at the Columbia University conference on Boiardo (1994).
5. Cited by Susan Courtney in a note on Maurice Ravel; see *Debussy/Ravel Quartets.*
6. The critical debate on the role of Astolfo, in particular, foregrounds the issues of fortune and control of one's future. See the respective discussions of Ascoli (*Ariosto's Bitter Harmony* 281ff.) and Marinelli (*Ariosto and Boiardo* 148–65). There is still room for further critical exploration of the interplay between fortune and narrative development—of the narrative's future, as it were.

7. Mario Di Cesare points out that the "three possibilities reflect the unnatural, the natural, and the supernatural" (316).
8. Ed. William S. Anderson. I generally follow Miller's translation. In the notes I refer to the *Metamorphoses* as *Met.*
9. E.g., *Met* 4.543–62.
10. Javitch, *Proclaiming a Classic* 71–85. I also have done some work along these lines in my dissertation, "Ovidian Influence on the Narrative of the *OF*" (U. of North Carolina, 1987).
11. A typical sixteenth-century reaction to the *OF,* that of Giason Denores, is quoted in Bernard Weinberg, *A History of Literary Criticism in the Italian Renaissance* 2: 957:

> nunc loquitur de totius operis, et omnium poematis partium inter se dispositione, quae omnis in hoc maxime posita est; ut partes inter se cohaereant, ne disiunctae videantur: quod quidem in Ludovico Ariosto reprehenditur: cum nihil in eo sit, quod simul componi possit, sed ita omnes partes in eo opere disiunctae: ut lectoris animum, et memoriam confusa narratio vehementer offendat.

> He [Horace] now speaks of the disposition of the whole work and of all the parts of the poem among themselves, a disposition which consists above all in this, that the parts should hang together with one another and should not seem to be disconnected. This is a defect which should indeed be reproved in Ludovico Ariosto, since there is nothing in him that is susceptible of composition, but all the parts in his work are so disjoined that his confused narrative violently displeases the mind and the memory of the reader. [Weinberg's translation.]

The locus classicus of criticism on the narrative of the *Met* is in Quintilian's *Institutio Oratoria* 4.1.77; I discuss this passage in the conclusion to the book. For a list of readers who criticize Ovid's poem for its lack of unity, see L. P. Wilkinson, "World of the *Met*" 231–32.
12. Antoine Du Verdier, *Prosopographie* 2409–10: the *OF* equals and sometimes surpasses the *Met* "pour le regard de la liaison de ses fables, qu'il a fait suivre avec un merveilleux artifice . . ." (quoted in Fatini 73). (for the concern for the connection of the tales, which he makes work with wondrous artifice . . .) Montesquieu made the same comparison; see *Pensées et fragments* 2: 45, 47, 49, 88; quoted in Fatini 359. A classicist, Giovanni Patroni, compares their narratives and concludes: ". . . e lo studio di certo il secondo [Ariosto] aveva fatto del primo . . ." ("Rileggendo le *Metamorfosi*" 308; quoted in Fatini 466). (. . . the study which the latter had certainly made of the former . . .) The most authoritative and emphatic statement comes from Romizi: " . . . ad Ovidio, più che ad alcun altro poeta dell'antichità, si appressò il nostro Lodovico . . . a lui somigliò per la rapidità e varietà delle scene e per l'abilità dei trapassi . . ." (*Le fonti*

latine 96). (. . . to Ovid, more than to any other poet of antiquity, our Lodovico came near . . . he resembled him in the rapidity and variety of the episodes and in the competence of the transitions.) But Croce, I should note, objected to the comparison Ariosto-Ovid in his essay *Ariosto, Shakespeare e Corneille* (68–69).

13. On the specific connection between Ovidian and Ariostan narrative, see Daniela Delcorno Branca, *L'OF e il romanzo cavalleresco medievale* 9; William J. Kennedy, *Rhetorical Norms in Renaissance Literature* 130–50; and C. S. Lewis, *Major British Writers* 97–98. Robert M. Durling has noted the similarity between the voice of the Ovidian *praeceptor amoris* and the Ariostan narrator in *Figure of the Poet* 257–58. Daniel Javitch has compared episodes in the narratives: "Rescuing Ovid from the Allegorizers," "The *OF* and Ovid's Revision of the *Aeneid*," "The Imitation of Imitations in the *OF*," and in his book *Proclaiming a Classic*. Barbara Pavlock examines Ariosto's use of Ovid in the Olimpia episode in her chapter, "Ariosto and Roman Epic Values." Mary-Kay Gamel Orlandi studies Ovidian narrative voice in Ariosto's poetry, but she does not consider the structure of the narrative in her "Ovid True and False in Renaissance Poetry." Several other recent works treat the issue of Ovidian influence on medieval and Renaissance authors: John M. Fyler, *Chaucer and Ovid;* Richard J. DuRocher, *Milton and Ovid;* and Sara Sturm-Maddox, *Petrarch's Metamorphoses.* While Fyler and Sturm-Maddox deal mainly with thematic influences, DuRocher addresses the question of the non-Aristotelian Renaissance epic, which he dubs the contrast-epic (152ff.). See also Charles Martindale, *John Milton and the Transformation of Ancient Epic.*

14. Catalano 1: 261–80; Segre, "La biblioteca dell'Ariosto" 45–50. Catalano provides ample documentation for his reconstruction of Ariosto's library, whereas Segre is more speculative in his approach, but both scholars come to many of the same conclusions. Another scholar, Denys Hay, suggests that many men of Ariosto's position would have owned or had access to editions of Ovid's poetry: " . . . the order of popularity of Latin classics remains in the sixteenth century as reported by Dr. Scholderer (for the fifteenth). Cicero was easily the most popular author, especially his *Letters,* and is followed by Ovid, Vergil, Terence and Horace in that order . . ." (38).

15. Catalano 1: 265.

16. Brand, *Ariosto* 15–17; Segre, "La poesia dell'Ariosto" 14. Ariosto's most obvious Ovidian poem is perhaps also his best Latin work, "De diversis amoribus," which takes its inspiration from Ovid's *Amores.* For the poem see Ariosto's *Lirica* 222–24.

17. Ascoli reads this satire in conjunction with the presentation of Brunetto Latini in *Inferno* 15 and argues convincingly for the implicit critique Ariosto makes of humanist education (*Ariosto's Bitter Harmony* 107–20). There is, for example, an important usage of the noun "umanista" in the poem (6.25), but any positive value associated with this relatively new word in the Italian

language is negated by its context: "Few humanists are without that vice which did not so much persuade, as forced, God to render Gomorrah and her neighbor wretched!" (6.25–27) By impugning humanists as sodomites, Ariosto, as Ascoli shows, suggests that the typical humanistic education is deficient and sterile. This criticism is borne out in the development of Ruggiero's character in the *Furioso*—he who is destined to be none less than the founder of the Ferrarese House of Este and progenitor of Ariosto's (sometime) patrons. Humanism, then, came with its discontents, which shed some light on what is, ultimately, Ariosto's idiosyncratic use of the classics.

18. I disagree with the translation of Snuggs, "order and texture," which undermines the precision of Giraldi's imagery. See *Giraldi Cinthio on Romances* 15.

19. Ariosto refers to the poem as a woven work of art in *OF* 2.30.5–6, 13.81.1–2, and 22.3.5. For a general discussion of how the theme of weaving is developed in the poem, see Susan Perry Alexander, "The Poet's Craft"; Durling's comments on the poet as weaver, *Figure of the Poet* 117–18; and Ascoli's points, many of which are in his helpful and full notes (*Ariosto's Bitter Harmony* 161ff.). See also the analyses of Brand ("L'entrelacement"), Dalla Palma, Pampaloni, and Weaver, all of which document the tight construction of the poem's narrative.

20. C. S. Lewis's annotations to his reading copy of the *Furioso* are worth noting here. Lewis writes across the top of several pages the following: "Knight errantry gives Ariosto's heroes an irresponsible freedom wh. those of Homer cannot have [12]; This admittedly excludes from the poem any teleological unity of the Homeric type [13]. But the comic (which has close connections with pantheism, scepticim, and pessimism) must be the negation of teleological unity [14]. All that a comic poem demands is Concatenation i.e. that apparent unity wh. veils, but does not hide, its essential discord. The *Furioso* has a serious surface and a comic depth [15]." While this is essentially a running commentary on Vincenzo Gioberti's introductory essay to Lewis's text, it is valuable for showing what interested Lewis as a reader of Ariosto, e.g., the issue of "concatenation." The copy is part of a cache of approximately one hundred books that belonged to Lewis, including works by Dante, Boiardo, Spenser, and many classical authors, housed in the Rare Book Collection of the Louis Round Wilson Library, University of North Carolina at Chapel Hill. They are all deserving of further study.

21. *Etude sur le* Lancelot en prose 17. See also Eugene Vinaver, *The Rise of Romance* 72ff.; Rosemond Tuve, *Allegorical Imagery: Some Medieval Books and Their Posterity;* and Daniela Delcorno Branca, *L'OF e il romanzo cavalleresco medievale.* An early attestation of the verb "to interlace" in English is found in Thomas Lodge's Ovidian epyllion, *Scillaes Metamorphosis: Enterlaced with the unfortunate love of Glaucus* (1589). There is no reason to believe that Lodge was referring to a narrative

technique with this usage. I cite the title of his poem merely to show how easily the figurative sense of the word lends itself to the critical terminology developed by readers like Lot.

22. *The Works of Geoffrey Chaucer* 357, lines 156–57.

23. Ascoli, rev. of *L'OF e il romanzo cavalleresco medievale.*

24. Waldman's translation here is wanting, for he only uses the adverbial "too"; Gilbert renders the phrase "at the very same time".

25. Two articles deal with the implications of the weaving imagery at the beginning of the poem: Grundy Steiner, "Ovid's *Carmen Perpetuum*"; and C. D. Gilbert, "Ovid, *Met* 1.4." Other works that specifically discuss the structural organization of the narrative of the *Met* include J. Tolkiehn, "Die Bucheinteilung der *Met* Ovids"; Frank J. Miller, "Some Features of Ovid's Style: Ovid's Methods of Ordering and Transition in the *Met*"; Walther Ludwig, *Struktur und Einheit der* Met *Ovids;* Ernst Jurgen Bernbeck, *Beobachtungen zur Darstellungsart in Ovids* Met; J.-M. Frécaut, "Les transitions dans les *Met* d'Ovide"; Brooks Otis, *Ovid as an Epic Poet;* Robert Coleman, "Structure and Intention in the *Met*"; Douglas A. Little, "The Structural Character of Ovid's *Met*"; E. J. Kenney, "The Style of the *Met*"; and G. Karl Galinsky, *Ovid's* Met: *An Introduction to the Basic Aspects.* More recently, Leonard Barkan has discussed the poem as a tapestry and the artist's creative act of representation as the ultimate metamorphosis in *The Gods Made Flesh,* throughout but especially 1–18.

26. *Deducere* also implies the movement of a ship into harbor and the act of leading someone down into the forum. All these senses are operative in the opening passage; I am merely focusing on one of them.

27. Joseph B. Solodow has made a keen reading of the poem's organization in *The World of Ovid's* Met. See especially his opening chapters on "Structures" (9–36) and "The Narrator" (37–73).

28. Two noticeable errors: Atlas holds the heavens at 2.296 but does not receive the burden until 4.632; Hercules, apotheosized at 9.229, attacks Troy at 11.213.

29. For a survey of criticism on the theme of metamorphosis, see Barkan 295, n. 2.

30. *Introduction* 67.

31. See the commentary of Michael von Albrecht, *Die Parenthese in Ovids* Met *und ihre dichterische Funktion,* and especially the table at 29–35.

32. For a discussion of secondary narrators see Eleanor Winsor Leach, "Ekphrasis and the Theme of Artistic Failure in Ovid's *Met.*"

33. Many critics have written about Ariosto's transitions. Two analyses worth reading are those by Bruscagli, " 'Ventura' e 'inchiesta' fra Boiardo e Ariosto" (*Stagioni* 87–126), and Zatti, "L'inchiesta, e alcune considerazioni sulla forma del poema" (*Il* Furioso *fra epos e romanzo* 39–68).

34. A good example of this kind of reading is Carne-Ross, "The One and the Many." Zatti, following Carne-Ross to some extent, also reads the poem in this way; see his "L'inchiesta, e alcune considerazioni sulla forma del poema" (*Il* Furioso *fra epos e romanzo* 39–68).

35. E.g., James T. Chiampi, "Angelica's Flight and the Reduction of the Quest in the *OF.*"

36. *Ludovico Ariosto's* OF 589.

37. See the informative chapter on Harington's efforts at normalizing the reader's experience of the text in Javitch's *Proclaiming a Classic* 134–57.

38. A manuscript of the work still survived in the eighteenth century. Ariosto's son Gabriele refers to the work in the *Epicedio* he composed after his father's death (ll. 221–23): "Nec tantum dederas haec laudis signa futurae / Sed puer et Tysbes deducis carmen in actus, / Parvaque devincis praecoci crura cothurno." (Nor had you yet given these signs of future glory / but still a boy you led down the song of Thisbe to the stage, / and you bound up your little legs in precocious boots of tragedy.) Cited in Catalano 1: 124–25.

39. *Allegorical Imagery* 363.

40. There are allusions to episodes of the Theseus sequence throughout the *Furioso,* including the Minotaur legend (*OF* 25.36–37), the story of Pirithous and Persephone (*OF* 44.56), and the recognition scene involving Medea, Aegeus, and Theseus (*OF* 46.59); the point of greatest dependence, however, is the scene of Isabella and Orlando in *Furioso* 13.

41. Rajna (following Fausto, Lavezuola, and others) goes into great detail about the Apuleian source underlying the characters and the setting in *Furioso* 13 (*Le fonti* 227–34). The cave, the robbers, Gabrina, and Isabella all have their corresponding match in Apuleius, *Metamorphoses,* book 4, which slipped the attention, one assumes, of Florence M. Weinberg, *The Cave: The Evolution of a Metaphoric Field from Homer to Ariosto.* Weinberg discusses the Apuleian cave (99–102) and concludes her study with a brief look at Merlin's cave in *Furioso* 3 (274–79). She makes no mention of the Apuleian/Ovidian cave in *Furioso* 13.

42. Nancy Zumwalt, "*Fama Subversa.*"

43. Zumwalt 214–15.

44. Robert Coleman, "Structure and Intention in the *Met*" (474–75), gives a good account of the parody of Homeric epic in Nestor's description of the battle.

45. Is there perhaps an allusion here to Odysseus and Polyphemus?

46. Orazio Toscanella ignores the Ovidian allusion in his remarks on the passage, arguing that Orlando uses a "stizzone" instead of a sword, in compliance with chivalric codes: "Et non fa, che metta mano alla spada; che sarebbe stato contro il decoro della persona; e contra le regole della cavaleria; perchè un cavaliere dee risentirsi con arme con i pari suoi; e adoperare il bastone; o cosa simile contra i plebei, e i vili, e infami" (*Bellezze del Furioso* 111–12). (And he doesn't even touch his sword because it would would have been against the decorum of his character and against the rules of chivalry to do so, for a knight must express his anger in weapons with his equals and he must use the stick or something similar against the plebeians, the base and loathsome.)

47. Compare Ascoli's interpretation of Orlando as both Hercules and Anteus (*Ariosto's Bitter Harmony* 58–63).

48. See the article by Annabel Patterson, "Intention."
49. My translation.
50. See Mack's excellent discussion of this Ovidian technique (*Ovid* 127–30). For an analysis of Ariosto's similar treatment of "heroic" stuff, see Javitch's "Imitation of Imitations."
51. Bigi, in his commentary on the *Furioso* (200), surveys the references to Turpin in Italian romance. Durling has good points to make on the role of Turpin in the larger issue of poetic truth (*Figure of the Poet* 120ff.). See, more recently, the fine essay by Sergio Zatti, "Il ruolo di Turpino: Poesia e verità nel *Furioso*," in *Il* Furioso *fra epos e romanzo* 173–212.
52. The relationship between the *OF* and the *Met* in these passages is the most developed form of imitation, called "dialectical imitation" by Thomas M. Greene, in *The Light in Troy* 40–45.
53. See Tasso's *Lettere* 2: 48.

Chapter 4

1. Tasso's unpunctuated gloss on the passage from Horace is found in Horace, *Opera* (Florence: per Antonium Miscominum, 1482) in the John Hay Library of Brown University. See the discussion by Rudolph Altrocchi, "Tasso's Holograph Annotations to Horace's *Ars Poetica*." The line from Horace translates, "In short, be the work whatever you will, let it at least be simple and uniform" (trans. H. R. Fairclough 453). I discuss Tasso's gloss, which I have examined in microfilm, at the end of this chapter.
2. I am adapting Lawrence Rhu's translation of Tasso's *Discorsi* in Rhu, *Genesis* 119–20. For the passage from *Inferno* 25.58–60, I follow Singleton's translation 263. For the text of the *Discorsi* here and below, I follow the 1977 rpt., ed. Mazzali, *Scritti* 1: 28.
3. Giovanni Battista Pigna makes a similar observation about romance narratives in *I romanzi* . . . 45: "Ma che diremo di questo Romancio, che vien a essere un animale sproporzionato?" (But what shall we say of this romance that is like a disproportionate animal?) For several modern observations on Pigna's comparison, see Margaret Ferguson, *Trials of Desire* 208, n. 2; and David Quint, "The Figure of Atlante" 85–87.
4. Tasso was very aware of Ariosto's allusions to the *Inferno,* as the annotations to his private copy of the *Commedia* make clear. For example, in a gloss on the Pier della Vigna episode in *Inferno* 13, Tasso accuses Ariosto of stealing from Dante the image of a soul encased in a tree for his episode of Astolfo in *Furioso* 6. The gloss reads, "furto dell'Ariosto" (theft of Ariosto). See Torquato Tasso, *Postille alla* Divina Commedia 57.
5. The *Furioso* makes at least eight direct verbal allusions to *Inferno* 25: 2.5.4 and 5.62.3 allude to 25.31; 7.29.1–2 alludes to 25.58–59; 11.12.1 to 25.94–97; 12.48.2–4 to 25.85–86; 15.69.8 to 25.61; 16.75.6 to 25.27; and 18.36.5–6 to 25.79–81. Segre classifies these allusions into different categories in "Un repertorio linguistico e stilistico dell'Ariosto: La *Commedia*."

6. Dante's ivy probably alludes most directly to Ovid's *Met* 4.361–65. For a thorough and witty discussion of the presence of Ovid in *Inferno* 25, see Madison U. Sowell, "Dante's Nose and Publius Ovidius Naso: A Gloss on *Inferno* 25.45." Sowell has also edited a volume on Dante's reading of Ovid: *Dante and Ovid: Essays in Intertextuality.* Leonard Barkan, as we saw in chapter 3, writes about *Inferno* 24–25, highlighting the Ovidian origins of much of the material Dante transforms (154–55).

7. While it is impossible to pin down the exact dates of Tasso's literary chronology, scholars have determined that he wrote the *Discorsi* in the early 1560s and the bulk of the *Liberata* in the decade from around 1565 to 1575. See C. P. Brand, *Torquato Tasso,* chaps. 1 and 3. See also Guido Baldassarri, "Introduzione ai *Discorsi dell'arte poetica* del Tasso."

8. Boiardo uses this same verb in reference to Herodotean narrative; see the discussion above in the third section of chapter 2. Pietro Bembo uses "traporre" to describe the way Boccaccio inserts popular speech into his artful prose (31).

9. I follow Lanfranco Caretti's text of the *GL.*

10. I cite from the translation of Ralph Nash.

11. This is not to belittle Tasso's Neoplatonism, for which see Annabel Patterson, "Tasso and Neoplatonism."

12. Sergio Zatti discusses the textual dynamics of the dispersal and retrieval of the Christian army in *L'uniforme cristiano e il multiforme pagano.* David Quint presents the historical and cultural problems to which Tasso's thematics of dispersal and retrieval refer in "Political Allegory in the *GL*" and in *Epic and Empire.*

13. In an unpublished paper, "Ricciardetto's Sex and the Castration of Orlando: Anatomy of an Episode from the *OF,*" Ronald L. Martinez makes a convincing case for the centrality of Ricciardetto's interlude with Fiordispina.

14. I have adapted Nash's translation 390.

15. Ascoli has discussed some of the connections among these similes in *Ariosto's Bitter Harmony.* Although Kristen Olson Murtaugh does not deal in detail with any of the examples of the snake simile, her essay, *Ariosto and the Classical Simile,* has been a helpful guide. Surprisingly, Ariosto's great positivist readers do not have too much to say about the sequence: see Rajna, *Le fonti* 549–50; and Romizi, *Le fonti latine* 90 and 97–98.

16. On the significance of the horse and lack thereof for the knight, see Giamatti, Dalla Palma, and Ascoli's response to both these scholars in *Ariosto's Bitter Harmony* and in a keen review of Dalla Palma.

17. See, e.g., the Saracen ship that blows to shore just in the nick of time to provide the Christian triumvirate with weapons and a horse for the duel on Lipadusa (41.23–29); Brandimarte dies in the subsequent gladiatorial duels because the horse was not an adequate defense (41.79).

18. In the "palio di San Giorgio" (or "pallio" as Ariosto spells it in the 1532 ed.), prostitutes and Jews, similarly marginalized yet necessary elements of the civic fabric, were forced to race through town scantily clad. For a full

discussion, see Deanna Shemek's essay "Circular Definitions: Configuring Gender in Italian Renaissance Festival."

19. Carne-Ross (acknowledging Durling) has observed that the chiastic arrangement of the tenor and vehicle in the double simile has an Horatian elegance; see "The One and the Many" (1996) 201.

20. For Angelica's place in the canto, see Peter V. Marinelli, "Shaping the Ore: Image and Design in Canto I of *OF*." For Angelica's role in the poem, see Carne-Ross's first and second essays, Shemek's "That Elusive Object of Desire," and Santoro's "L'Angelica del *Furioso:* fuga dalla storia," in *Ariosto e il Rinascimento* 111–33.

21. See his "Brieve dimostratione," first printed to accompany the *Furioso* in Giolito's ed. of 1542, and reprinted frequently in the sixteenth century.

22. Ovid, *Fasti,* ed. and trans. Sir James George Frazer 57 + 59. I have adapted Frazer's translation at certain points below.

23. "Osservationi . . . sopra il *Furioso*" 2: "Coloro . . . affermano l'Ariosto haverlasi presa [la comparatione] da quella di Vergilio . . . Ma non s'accorgono, che le parole dell'Ariosto non vi s'adattano puntalmente. . . . Questa imitatione dunque si vede chiaramente esser fatta da quel distico d'Ovidio nel secondo de' *Fasti*." (Some [i.e., Dolce and Ruscelli] claim that Ariosto took the simile from Vergil . . . but they fail to realize that Ariosto's words don't exactly fit Vergil's text. . . . This imitation then is clearly seen to derive from that distich in the second book of Ovid's *Fasti*.)

24. Daniel Javitch has noted that Dolce consistently highlights what he takes to be a principal source at the expense of any others, whereas Lavezuola is usually attuned to the multiple allusions behind a given passage of the *Furioso*. He is more attuned at least than Dolce to Ariosto's habit of imitating literary passages that in themselves are also imitations of previous works. See Javitch's "Sixteenth-Century Commentaries on Imitations in the *OF*."

25. See Sara Mack's discussion of the *Fasti* as literary art in *Ovid*.

26. Wiggins refers in passing to Ruggiero as "a Hercules under Omphale's power" (110).

27. This view of the hero as a Faunus complements Ascoli's discussion of Orlando as Silenus; see the chapter in *Ariosto's Bitter Harmony,* "Oneness in Nonsense" 331–60.

28. Another early commentator of the *Furioso,* Orazio Toscanella, makes the obvious but nonetheless valid point that the double simile in the stanza respects the gender of each character: " . . . comparing the male to a person or thing that is masculine and the female to a person or thing that is feminine. Since Rinaldo's gender is male, he compares him to a masculine person, a half-naked farmer. And just below, coming up with a simile for Angelica whose gender is female, he compares her to a feminine person, a shepherdess." The Italian text reads: " . . . il comparare il maschio, à persona, ò cosa maschia; et la femina; à persona, ò cosa feminile; essendo Rinaldo di sesso maschile, lo compara à persona maschile; cioè ad un

villan mezo ignudo: et poco più giù comparando Angelica, che è di sesso feminile, la compara à persona di sesso feminile; cioè ad una pastorella." In "Bellezze del *Furioso*" 11.

29. For a reading of the episode of Orlando's madness that focuses on the semiotics of his disrobing, see Francesca Savoia, "L'abito e la pazzia d'Orlando."

30. Ariosto alludes to this Ovidian episode in several passages of the *Furioso;* for example, when Bireno abandons Olimpia (10.15.1–4), the poet editorializes by borrowing a comment from the description of Tereus (*Met* 6.472–74).

31. Ariosto is reserving the topos of the "pallido nocchiero" for a passage later in the narrative (40.29).

32. This is not to contest Elissa Weaver's observation that the snake in 23 calls to mind the biblical serpent and the theme of problematic knowledge; that allusion is all the more present in 39. See her "Lettura dell'intreccio dell'*OF.*"

33. See Ascoli, *Ariosto's Bitter Harmony* 346–48.

34. The proem of *Furioso* 42 also borrows from Pulci (*Morgante* 27.212). The Ariostan narrator reflects on the inevitability of revenge when a friend, a lord, or a relative is injured before one's eyes. The proem's appropriateness becomes immediately clear as Orlando, who holds Brandimarte even closer than a relative (15.8), avenges his death by killing Agramante. The threat of the serpent creates a curious sense of family: Sobrino, the remaining pagan warrior, surrenders only to become like a relative (19).

35. Ascoli, *Ariosto's Bitter Harmony* 348. At least two snake similes in Boiardo's *Innamorato* are used for Ranaldo, the precursor of Ariosto's Rinaldo: 1.23.38.1–4 and 1.27.13.1–4.

36. Altrocchi (see chapter 4, note 1 above) uses internal and external evidence to conclude that Tasso annotated his copy of Horace in the mid-1580s.

37. Altrocchi's translation 935. I have removed Altrocchi's incorrect "also."

38. The proper Italian is "dragone," from the Latin *draco* and from the Greek *drakon.* "Dracone" is a linguistic variant, used, especially in the Christian tradition, as a synonym for "serpent"; e.g., Rev. 12:9: "draco ille magnus, serpens antiquus" (that great dragon, the ancient serpent).

Chapter 5

1. *Scritti* 2: 379. For the passage from Aristotle, see *Poetics* 1462b1–2.

2. There are several studies on Tasso's sources, all dating from the era of positivist criticism: Vincenzo Vivaldi, *Sulle fonti della GL, Prolegomeni ad uno studio completo sulle fonti della GL,* and *La GL studiata nelle sue fonti;* Salvatore Multineddu, *Le fonti della GL;* and Ettore de Maldè, *Le fonti della GL.*

3. This is not to contest Walter Stephens's argument that the poem's midpoint comes at the beginning of canto 11, with the scene of the Eucharist on the Mt. of Olives (11.1–15). The calculus of a poem that tries to be at once

classical, romance, and biblical will allow for the reckoning of different midpoints.

4. In his introduction, Raimondi, in a similar vein, notes that canto 13 represents the symbolic center of the poem with its idealized geography in encapsulated form: forest and city with desert in between (pp. lxv–vi).

5. The full text in question reads: "Voglio però che sappia, che questa è più tosto metà del quanto, che de la favola; perch'il mezzo veramente de la favola è nel terzodecimo, perchè sin a quello le cose de' cristiani vanno peggiorando. . . . Ma nel mezzo del terzodecimo le cose cominciano a rivoltarsi in meglio: viene, per grazia di Dio, a' prieghi di Goffredo la pioggia; e così di mano in mano tutte le cose succedono prospere" (*Le lettere di Torquato Tasso* 1: 66). (But I want you [Scipione Gonzaga] to know that this is half of the poem's length, rather than its plot. The true middle of the plot is in the thirteenth canto, because up to that canto the situation for the Christians worsens. . . . But in the middle of the thirteenth canto the situation begins to change for the better: the rain, by the grace of God, comes in answer to Goffredo's prayers. And in this way, bit by bit, their situation works out favorably.)

6. *Origin* 92–117.

7. Tasso invokes a similar notion in a passage from the *Discorsi* to account for the relationship between the artist and his own aesthetic creation. See the concluding pages of *Discorso* 2 (*Scritti* 1: 41–42).

8. For an acute discussion of the poem's ending, see Ascoli, "Liberating the Tomb," especially pp. 171ff., where he considers the meaning of "sciogliere."

9. For a recent biography of William, see Peter W. Edbury and John Gordon Rowe, *William of Tyre: Historian of the Latin East*. The editio princeps of William's history was published in Basil (1549) by N. Brylingerum. Giuseppe Horologgi's translation in Italian was published in Venice by V. Valgrisi (1562).

10. William of Tyre, *A History of Deeds Done beyond the Sea* 1: 346–47. See also 347, n. 25: "Solinus *Polyhistor* xxxv. William's critical attitude here toward this postclassical writer is that of a modern scholar. In this chapter he tests his source, both by the observed facts of geography and by his knowledge of ancient history. The contrast between William's acceptance of so much legendary material in the previous book—probably written about 1171—and the more critical attitude displayed in this chapter—probably written in 1182—reflects his growth as an historian."

11. See his remarks on the "vero alterato" in *Discorso* 2 (*Scritti* 1: 20). In *Discorso* 1 (*Scritti* 1: 11–12), he goes into some detail on the liberty a poet should take with the historical record when necessary.

12. Other accounts of the First Crusade similarly describe the problems caused by the lack of water. See *Gesta Francorum* 19, 88, 100; also Peter Tudebode, *Historia de Hierosolymitano Itinere* 114–15.

13. I follow the Latin text cited in the notes of Maier's ed. of the *Liberata* (39). The translation is my own.

14. William of Tyre does not refer to the poisoning of the water supply; *pace* Chiappelli (554, n. 58.3).
15. It is worth noting that the old shepherd, the former courtier who hosts Erminia, revels in the pure drinking water of his sylvan hideaway "che non tem'io che di venen s'asperga" (7.10.6) (and I have no fear lest it be mixed with poison).
16. I am assuming that at 13.58.5–8, Aladino does not repeat the action described in 1.89.7–8, namely, that he does not repoison the springs. I take the passage in 13 to be the same action merely described for a second time, although I am aware of its temporal ambiguity. Had Tasso wanted to be clear he could have used the pluperfect tense, "aveva fatto," rather than the preterite form, "fece," at 13.58.8.
17. Michael Murrin suggests that Tasso may have been inspired to use the Lucretian analogy by the argument of Maximus of Tyre, a Platonist of late antiquity whose lectures Tasso was studying as he revised the *Liberata* (*Allegorical Epic* 98–100).
18. The adjectives "aspro" (13.58.6) and "amaro" (1.3.7) are synonymous.
19. Sergio Zatti, in a comparative reading of these passages, adduces other lexical parallels to interpret the mixture of bitter and sweet in the poisoned springs of 13 as a gloss on the mixture of sweetened medicine in canto 1. He reads 13 as a passage about literature in which the mixture of water and poison is like the mixture of sweet liquids and medicine, of truth and lies, of fact and fiction in stanza 3 of canto 1 (*L'uniforme cristiano* 157–63).
20. For more on this distinction see the discussion above in the introduction and chapter 4.
21. The biblical books of 2 Kings and 2 Chronicles describe how Hezekiah prepared his kingdom for a massive invasion by the Assyrians. Concluding that the citizens of Jerusalem had sufficient water to withstand a long siege, Hezekiah contrived to stop up all the springs near Jerusalem. The reference to the "Siloè" in Tasso's text (59.1) alludes to the spring of Gihon that flows into the Pool of Siloam (or "Siloè"). It also calls to mind the career of Hezekiah, who had a tunnel drilled seventeen hundred feet through the rocky bluff on which Jerusalem rests to serve as a conduit from a spring outside the city to a reservoir inside the city walls called the Pool of Siloam. The tunnel, a kind of hidden aqueduct, was an incredible feat of engineering in its day. For a description of Hezekiah's Tunnel, as it came to be called, see *The Westminster Historical Atlas to the Bible* 486. Other passages on the tunnel are 2 Kings 20:20, Ecclesiasticus 48:17, and Isaiah 22:9–11. The tunnel also figures prominently in certain manuscript readings of the text of 2 Samuel 5:6–9, which recounts how David used the aqueduct to sneak into Jerusalem in order to capture it from the Jebusites. Hezekiah's various accomplishments are recorded in several books of the Bible in addition to the passage from 2 Chronicles cited above. Of note for Tasso's image of the poisoned source is Proverbs 25:26, a passage rabbinical tradition attributes to scholars in Hezekiah's court. The proverb in question takes the corrupted spring as its symbol for the honest man who falters when

confronted with injustice: "Fons turbatus pede et vena corrupta, Iustus cadens coram impio." (Like a muddied spring or a polluted fountain is a righteous man who gives way before the wicked.) The passage suggests further that Hezekiah is associated with the kind of imagery Tasso develops over the course of canto 13.

Tasso's scene alludes to this passage from 2 Chronicles: "Quod cum vidisset Ezechias, venisse scilicet Sennacherib, et totum belli impetum verti contra Ierusalem, inito cum principibus consilio, virisque fortissimis ut obturarent capita fontium, qui erant extra urbem: et hoc omnium decernente sententia, congregavit plurimam multitudinem, et obturaverunt cunctos fontes, et rivum, qui fluebat in medio terrae, dicentes: Ne veniant reges Assyriorum, et inveniant aquarum abundantiam" (2 Chronicles 32:2–4). (And when Hezekiah saw that Sennacherib had come and intended to fight against Jerusalem, he planned with his officers and his mighty men to stop the water of the springs that were outside the city; and they helped him. A great many people were gathered, and they stopped all the springs and the brook that flowed through the land, saying, "Why should the kings of Assyria come and find much water?")

22. In *L'uniforme cristiano,* Zatti notes that Tasso colors his description of the drought with the vocabulary of sexual languor. He correctly points out that "languir" (62.1, 63.1, 64.1), "vaneggiar" (56.4), and "bramare" (57.8) are part of the poem's lexicon of desire. He concludes that repressed sexual desire is rearing its head in the encamped army and in the landscape of the desert itself (159). But the desire, which no one denies, need not be understood only in Freudian terms. In the *Liberata* there is as much longing for textual integrity, for sources that can be brought together into one whole, as there is for sexual fulfillment.

23. Marshall W. Baldwin, *The First Hundred Years* 1: 335.

24. See, e.g., *Gesta Francorum* 62.

25. *A History of Deeds Done beyond the Sea* 1: 329–30.

26. See Linda Rose, "Crete."

27. See Pliny, *Naturalis Historia,* XIV, 11, 81: "passum a Cretico Cilicium probatur et Africum." (Next after the raisin-wine of Crete those of Cilicia and of Africa are held in esteem.) For text and trans. see Rackham's ed., 4: 240–41.

28. William Addison Laidlaw, "Crete" 242.

29. See the remarks of Eliyahu Ashtor, *Levant Trade in the Later Middle Ages* 364.

30. John Julius Norwich, *A History of Venice* 269–70.

31. Dante associates Crete with the Minotaur (*Inf* 12.25). Petrarch refers to the island as the place of superstitions: "Creta, vetus superstitionum domus, aliis vivit" (*Fam* 15.7.14). Boccaccio refers to Cretan legends throughout his work; see, e.g., his entry on Europa, "Cretensium regina," in *De mulieribus claris;* see also *Genealogia* 2.62; *Teseida* 5.17.

32. Boiardo refers to myths associated with Crete in *Innamorato* 2.8.16; likewise Ariosto in *Furioso* 20.23; 25.36–37.

33. Tasso also rewrote the historical record because he wanted the role of deserter to be filled by a Greek. He could have chosen, e.g., Ugone of Vermandois, brother of Philip I, king of France, who also deserts the army at a crucial juncture in the campaign. But Tasso not only disregards this detail of the historical record; he accords Ugone a place of honor in the catalog of the troops in 1.37.

34. The same stanzas with slight changes also occur in the *Gerusalemme Conquistata* 1.71–72.

35. Tasso revises the Greek contribution to one thousand soldiers in the *Conquistata,* but he remains critical of Greek lethargy.

36. *A History of Deeds Done beyond the Sea* 1: 150.

37. For the stereotype of Greeks as liars, also see *OF* 29.18.8.

38. *A History of Deeds Done beyond the Sea* 1: 150, n. 35.

39. See, e.g., in *Discorso* 2, Tasso's remarks on Trissino and Ariosto: " . . . ove il Trissino, d'altra parte, che i poemi d'Omero religiosamente si propose d'imitare" (*Scritti* 1: 26) (. . . Trissino, on the other, who proposed to imitate the poems of Homer devoutly); " . . . giudico nondimeno che [Ariosto] non sia da esser seguìto nella moltitudine delle azioni" (*Scritti* 1: 27) (. . . I myself still think that Ariosto should not be imitated in the matter of multiple plots).

40. David Quint discusses the allegorical implications of the trouble within the Christian alliance in "Political Allegory in the *GL,*" now in *Epic and Empire* 213–47.

41. Although there are many passages in the Bible where faith is glossed as the ability to move mountains (e.g., Matthew 17:19, 1 Corinthians 13:2), I find no biblical passage in which faith is defined as the ability to stop the flow of rivers. Matthew 17:19 reads: " . . . si habueritis fidem, sicut granum sinapis, dicetis monti huic: Transi hinc illuc, et transibit, et nihil impossibile erit vobis." (. . . if you have faith as a grain of mustard seed, you will say to this mountain, "Move hence to yonder place," and it will move; and nothing will be impossible to you.) Paul repeats the image at 1 Corinthians 13:2: " . . . et si habuero omnem fidem ita ut montes transferam, charitatem autem non habuero, nihil sum." (. . . and if I have all faith, so as to move mountains, but have not love, I am nothing.)

42. I have adapted Nash's translation of this clause.

43. In poetic or archaic Italian the masculine "i fonti" denotes the figurative use of "source"; contrast Tasso's use of "le fonti" for actual springs of water (1.89.7). For a list of examples of the figurative use, see the entry in the Crusca dictionary, para. 6.

44. For a full study of the dynamics of the one and the many in the poem, see Zatti, *L'uniforme cristiano* 9–44.

45. Trans. Fairclough.

46. Salvatore Multineddu (*Le fonti* 147–48) compares Tasso's scene with the description of Zeus's nod in *Iliad* 1.488–533. I think it is more likely that Tasso is invoking the topos rather than the specific passage in Homer.

47. Tasso's description of the effect of the nod is also classical in its detail,

as one of Tasso's earliest commentators, Guastavini, notes: "i Romani gli augurî da sinistra avevano per felici" (cited in Caretti 2: 440). (The Romans considered omens from the left auspicious.)

48. In this interpretation one might argue that Tatino stands for classical sources in general. Indeed, the textual tradition of the poem is ambiguous enough on the spelling of Tatino's name that some editors read "Latino." This in turn has caused many commentators, e.g., Chiappelli (64, n.51.1), to warn against confusing Tatino with the character, Latino, of 9.27. Tasso's autograph manuscripts suggest that he himself was indecisive about the character's name. See Solerti's discussion of these textual problems (1: 53).

49. C. P. Brand discusses some of the other reasons for the revisions, such as Tasso's stylistic maturity, his greater focus on Homer as a structural model, and his long-standing desire to reduce the episodic part of the plot; see his *Torquato Tasso* 123–32.

50. The reordering is as follows (with some additions and much editing): *GL* 13.1–52 → *GC* 16.1–56; *GL* 13.53–63 and 71–80 → *GC* 19.120–30 and 134–43; stanzas 64–70 of canto 13 are cut from *GC*. See the schematic comparison of the two narratives by Angelo Solerti, "Ragguaglio della favola . . ." in *Gerusalemme Conquistata,* ed. Luigi Bonfigli 2: 385–409.

51. In *Writing from History,* Timothy Hampton discusses the transformation of Tasso's rhetoric of exemplarity in the *Liberata* into a rhetoric of martyrdom in the *Conquistata.*

52. The Homeric scenes, however, are not all successful. As Brand has noted, "Tasso's attempt to add epic grandeur by means of new episodes mostly imitating Homer also fails to add artistically to the poem: the battle of the ships, the death of Ruperto, the reactions of Riccardo, are unnecessary complications in an already over-laden military action" (*Tasso* 128).

53. These examples and several others are listed by Brand, *Tasso* 125.

54. The full title of the essay is "Del giudizio sopra la *Gerusalemme* di Torquato Tasso da lui medesimo riformata" in *Opere* 4: 129–76.

55. "Giudizio" 141.

56. E.g., he does not remove the sultry description of Armida's garden and its bathing nymphs in *GL* 16.

57. *Discourses on the Heroic Poem* 202–03.

58. Cavalchini and Samuel translate: " . . . , so among fables the most composite are the best." I prefer to render "favole" here as "plots" rather than "fables".

Conclusion

1. The conceit discussed below, of lovers entwined like ivy, is fully developed in Herrick's poem on an erotic dream. For its dramatic conclusion, see "The Vine" in *Erotic Poems* 95.

2. Solodow, who discusses Quintilian's criticism (27), is now a major exception to this unfavorable reception of Ovid's narrative.

3. There is some inconsistency in the spelling of his name: I use the Latin.
   For a brief sketch of his life, see the article by Vera Lettere. Ettore Paratore provides more information on Ciofanus's intellectual development,
   especially on the Roman circle in which he moved, in "Ercole Ciofano."
   See also Giuseppe Papponetti, "Geminazione della memoria: l'*Ovidio* di
   Hercole Ciofano," for a study of the manuscripts and editions Ciofanus
   used and for a description of the texts he produced, including a note on his
   commentary on Ovid (168–69). Finally, Papponetti and Adriano Ghisetti
   Giavarina discuss the impact of Ciofanus's early education in Sulmona on
   his scholarship in "Un'effige quattrocentesca di Ovidio."
4. "Ovidii Defensio, et *Met* Laus," ed. N. E. Lemaire 8: 296.
5. See the note on *Met* 13.700–701 in *Herculis Ciofani Sulmonensis In omnia
   P. Ovidii Nasonis opera observationes* 253–55. After discussing the cultivation of the acanthus plant (the scholar reports that he has studied several
   varieties), Ciofanus creates the anthology of passages:

> Virgilius. I. Aeneid.
> > *Et circumtextum croceo velamen Acantho.*
> Quod ad fructum referri debet. Item illud Statij lib. III. Sil. in Hercule
> Surrent. *Hic tibi Sidonio celsum pulvinar Acantho Texitur.* Illud
> eiusdem Virg.
> > *Mistàq ridenti Colocasia fundet Acantho.*
> Rectè exponit Servius, *id est, laeto.* Quoniam, cùm florescit, spec-
> tantibus quandam affert hilaritatem. Sic etiam dicuntur *Prata ridere.*
> Epitheta *Flexus, & Mollis.* quae in tribus his eiusdem poëtae versibus
> sunt:
> > *—aut flexi tacuissem vimen Acanthi.*
> > *Illa comam mollis iam tum tendebat Acanthi.*
> > *Et molli circum est ansas complexus Acantho.*
> Item illud Columellae lib. X. *Pallida nonnonquam tortos imitatur
> Acanthos.* & illud Ariosti: *Non con piu nodi il flessuoso Acantho.*
> Ad id referri debent, quod, quo quis vult, contorquetur, flectitur, ac
> porrigitur.

> Vergil. *Aeneid* 1.
> "And a robe woven around the edges with yellow acanthus." [1.649]
> Which must refer to the plant's [yellow] fruit. Likewise that verse
> from the third book of Statius, *Silvae.* On Hercules in Sorrento
> [to Pollius Felix]. "Here for you is the raised couch woven with
> Sidonian acanthus." [3.1.37–38] That verse, again, of Vergil.
> "And [the earth] will flow with [gifts] the Egyptian bean mixed with
> the smiling acanthus." [*Ec.* 4.20]
> Servius explains correctly, "that is, happy." Because, when it blos-
> soms, it conveys a certain cheerfulness to those who look upon
> it. Similarly "fields" are also said "to smile". Its adjectives are
> "twisting" and "pliant". Which occur in these three verses of the
> same poet:

"nor would I have kept quiet about the vine with a twisting acanthus." [*Geor.* 4.123]

"Then she braided her hair with the twisting acanthus." [*Geor.* 4.137, a line with variants in the edition Ciofanus used]

"And he [Alcimedon, an artisan] has clasped the handles with pliant acanthus." [*Ec.* 3.45]

Likewise that verse of Columella, book 10. [10.241] "And sometimes [the artichoke] is pale like the twisted acanthus." And that line of Ariosto: "Never did twisting acanthus with more knots." They [the epithets] must refer to this quality, namely that it bends, it is twisting, and it stretches out where anyone wants.

6. For a discussion of Fiordispina's lament (25.34–37), which is modeled closely on the lament of Iphis (*Met* 9.726–63), see Ferroni 148–52. Ronald Martinez discusses this Ovidian allusion and much more in his unpublished essay, "Ricciardetto's Sex." The passage in Ovid to which the simile of the ivy alludes most directly is "utve solent hederae longos intexere truncos" (4.365). (Or as the ivy often weaves itself around great trunks of trees.)

7. As far as I know, there is no verifiable basis for Ruscelli's claim. He writes: "[Ariosto] havea cassate, et tolte via in tutto quelle due stanze . . . perche in effetto sono alquanto troppo disoneste da leggersi in un libro" (Ruscelli, ed., 1587, pp. 618–19). ([Ariosto] had struck and removed those two stanzas . . . because they are somewhat too inappropriate to read in a book.)

Bibliography

Abbreviations of works cited frequently:

POEMS
GL = *Gerusalemme Liberata*
Met = Ovid, *Metamorphoses*
OF = *Orlando Furioso*
OI = *Orlando Innamorato*

SECONDARY MATERIALS
DBI = *Dizionario Biografico degli Italiani*
GSLI = *Giornale Storico della Letteratura Italiana*
JMRS = *Journal of Medieval and Renaissance Studies*
MLN = *Modern Language Notes*
PMLA = *Publications of the Modern Language Association*
TAPA = *Transactions and Proceedings of the American Philological Association*

Primary Sources

Alighieri, Dante. *The Divine Comedy.* Trans. and comm. Charles S. Singleton. 6 vols. Princeton: Princeton UP, 1977.

Ariosto, Ludovico. *Cinque Canti.* Ed. Lanfranco Caretti. Turin: Einaudi, 1977.

———. *I frammenti autografi dell'OF.* Ed. Santorre Debenedetti. Turin: Chiantore, 1937.

———. *Lirica.* Ed. Giuseppe Fatini. Bari: Laterza, 1924.

———. *Opere minori.* Ed. Cesare Segre. Milan: Ricciardi, 1954.

———. *OF.* Ed. Emilio Bigi. 2 vols. Milan: Rusconi, 1982.

———. *OF.* Ed. Lanfranco Caretti. 2 vols. Milan: Ricciardi, 1954.

———. *OF.* Ed. Santorre Debenedetti. 3 vols. Bari: Laterza, 1928.

———. *OF: Secondo l'edizione del 1532 con le varianti delle edizioni del 1516 e del 1521.* Ed. Santorre Debenedetti and Cesare Segre. Bologna: Commissione per i testi di lingua, 1960.

———. *OF.* Trans. Allan Gilbert. 2 vols. New York: Vanni, 1954.

———. *OF.* Trans. William Stewart Rose. Ed. Stewart A. Baker and A. Bartlett Giamatti. Indianapolis: Bobbs-Merrill, 1968.

———. *OF.* Ed. Girolamo Ruscelli. Venice: F. Valgrisi, 1587.

———. *OF.* Ed. Cesare Segre. 1964. Milan: Mondadori, 1976.

———. *OF.* Trans. Guido Waldman. 1974. New York: Oxford UP, 1983.

———. *Le Satire.* Ed. Cesare Segre. *Erbolato.* Ed. Gabriella Ronchi. *Lettere.* Ed. Angelo Stella. Milan: Mondadori, 1984. Vol. 3 of *Tutte le opere di Ludovico Ariosto,* gen. ed. Cesare Segre.

———. *The Satires of Ludovico Ariosto: A Renaissance Autobiography.* Trans. Peter DeSa Wiggins. Athens: Ohio UP, 1976.

Aristotle. *The Poetics.* Trans. W. Hamilton Fyfe. 1927. Cambridge: Harvard UP, 1973.

Bembo, Pietro. *Prose della volgar lingua.* Ed. Carlo Dionisotti-Casalone. Turin: UTET, 1931.

Beni, Paolo. *Comparatione di Homero, Virgilio e Torquato: Et in particolare si fa giudizio dell'Ariosto.* Padua: Lorenzo Pasquati, 1607.

[Bible.] Biblia sacra iuxta vulgatam clementinam. Ed. Alberto Colunga, O.P., and Laurentio Turrado. Biblioteca de Autores Cristianos series. Madrid: BAC, 1977.

The Oxford Annotated Bible. New York: Oxford UP, 1962.

Boiardo, Feltrino. *Vita del Cavalier Feltrino Boiardo, già Signore di Rubiera, et di Scandiano, anni: 50, scritta latina da Bartolomeo da Prato. Sopra questa volgare da G.D.Z.* MS γ.E.3.10. Biblioteca Estense, Modena.

Boiardo, Matteo Maria. *L'asino d'oro di Lucio Apuleio volgarizzato da Agnolo Firenzuola con l'aggiunta della novella dello sternuto.* Tradotta da Matteo Boiardo. Ed. Carlo Téoli. Milan: Daelli, 1863.

———. Herodoto Alicarnaseo Historico, *Delle guerre de Greci et de Persi.* Tradotto di greco in lingua italiana per il conte Mattheo Maria Boiardo. Venice: Nicolini di Sabbio, 1533.

———. "Lettere inedite di Matteo Maria Boiardo." Ed. Giulio Reichenbach. *GSLI* 64 (1914): 163–71.

———. *Opere di Matteo Maria Boiardo.* Ed. Ferruccio Ulivi. Milan: Mursia, 1986.

———. *Opere volgari.* Ed. P. V. Mengaldo. Bari: Laterza, 1962.

———. *OI.* Leipzig: Fleischer, 1840.

———. *OI.* Ed. Giuseppe Anceschi. Milan: Garzanti, 1978.

———. *OI.* Ed. Riccardo Bruscagli. Turin: Einaudi, 1995.

———. *OI.* Trans. Charles Stanley Ross. Berkeley: U of California P, 1989.

———. *OI; Amorum Libri.* Ed. Aldo Scaglione. 2 vols. 1951. Turin: UTET, 1976.

———. *OI: Concordance, rimario & tables.* Ed. David Robey and Marco Dorigatti. Oxford: Oxford UP, 1989.

———. *Tutte le opere.* Ed. Angelandrea Zottoli. Milan: Mondadori, 1936–37.

Boiardo ed Ariosto. *Opere.* Ed. Antonio Panizzi. 9 vols. London: Pickering, 1830–39.

Borsias. Ed. W. Ludwig. Leiden: E. J. Brill, 1977.

Chaucer. *The Works of Geoffrey Chaucer.* 2nd ed. Ed. F. N. Robinson. 1933. Oxford: Oxford UP, 1957.

Cicero. *Brutus.* Trans. G. L. Hendrikson. *Orator.* Trans. H. M. Hubbell. 1939. Cambridge: Harvard UP, 1962.

Ciofanus, Hercules. *Herculis Ciofani Sulmonensis In omnia P. Ovidii Nasonis opera observationes.* 3 vols. in 1. Antwerp: Plantin, 1581–83.

———. "Ovidii Defensio, et *Met* Laus." *Publius Ovidius Naso: Opera omnia.* Ed. N. E. Lemaire. 8: 295–97.

Collodi, Carlo. *Le Avventure di Pinocchio.* Trans. and ed. Nicolas J. Perella. Berkeley: U of California P, 1986.

Denores, Jason. *Poetica di Iason Denores.* Padua: Paulo Meietto, 1588.

Dolce, Lodovico. "Brieve dimostramento di molte Comparationi et Sentenze Dall'Ariosto in Diversi Autori Imitate." *OF.* Venice: Giolito, 1542.

———. *Le Trasformationi di Lodovico Dolce tratte da Ovidio.* Venice: Francesco Sansovino, 1568. Rpt. New York: Garland, 1979.

[Donatus.] *Vitae Vergilianae Antiquae.* Ed. Colinus Hardie. Oxford: Clarendon P, 1966.

Du Verdier, Antoine. *Prosopographie au déscription des personnes illustres tant chrestiennes que prophanes.* Lyon: Frelon, 1605.

Erotic Poems. Ed. Peter Washington. New York: Knopf, 1994.

Gesta Francorum. Ed. and trans. Rosalind Hill. London: Nelson, 1962.

Giraldi Cinzio, Giovambattista. *Discorsi . . . intorno al comporre dei Romanzi, delle Comedie, e delle Tragedie, e di altre maniere di Poesie.* Venice: Giolito, 1554.

———. *Giraldi Cinthio on Romances: Being a Translation of the* Discorso intorno al comporre dei romanzi. Trans. Henry L. Snuggs. Lexington: U of Kentucky P, 1968.

———. "Lettera a Bernardo Tasso sulla poesia epica." B. Weinberg, *Trattati di poetica* 2: 453–76.

———. *Scritti critici.* Ed. Camillo Guerrieri Crocetti. Milan: Marzorati, 1973.

Gravina, Vicenzo. *Di Vicenzo Gravina Giurisconsulto della Ragion Poetica Libri due.* Naples: De Bonis, 1731.

———. *Scritti critici e storici.* Ed. Amedeo Quondam. Bari: Laterza, 1973.

Guarino Veronese. *Epistolario.* Ed. Remigio Sabbadini. 3 vols. 1919. Turin: Bottega d'Erasmo, 1969.

Guerre in ottava rima. Ed Marina Beer et al. Modena: Panini, 1989.

Harington, John, trans. *Ludovico Ariosto's OF.* Ed. Robert McNulty. Oxford: Clarendon P, 1972.

Herodotus. *Histories.* Trans. A. D. Godley. 4 vols. 1920. Cambridge: Harvard UP, 1981.

Horace. *The Satires.* Ed. Edward P. Morris. 1939. Norman: U of Oklahoma P, 1968.

———. *Satires, Epistles, and Ars Poetica.* Trans. and ed. H. R. Fairclough. Cambridge: Harvard UP, 1970.

Lavezuola, Alberto. "Osservationi . . . sopra il *Furioso* nelle quali si mostrano tutti i luoghi imitati dall'Autore nel suo poema." *OF.* Venice: Francesco dei Franceschi, 1584.

Lewis, C. S. "Annotations to *OF.*" Classici Italiani. Milan: Istituto Editoriale Italiano, 1930. Lewis's personal copy: PQ 4567 A2 1930 v. 1. Rare Book Room, Louis Round Wilson Library, University of North Carolina at Chapel Hill.

Malatesta, Gioseppe. *Della nuova poesia ovvero delle difese del* Furioso. Verona: Sebastiano delle Donne, 1589.

Marino, Giovambattista. *Adone.* Ed. and intro. Giovanni Pozzi. 2 vols. Milan: Mondadori, 1976.

Montesquieu, Baron de. *Pensées et fragments de Montesquieu.* Ed. Gaston de Montesquieu. 2 vols. Bordeaux: G Gounouilhon, 1901.

[Ovid] Naso, P. Ovidius. *Amores; Medicamina faciei femineae; Ars Amatoria; Remedia Amores.* Ed. E. J. Kenney. Oxford: Clarendon P, 1961.

———. *Fasti.* Ed. and trans. Sir James George Frazer. Cambridge: Harvard UP, 1976.

———. *Heroides.* Ed. Arthur Palmer. 1874. Hildesheim: Georg Olms, 1967.

———. *Met.* Ed. William S. Anderson. Leipzig: Teubner, 1977.

————. *Met.* Ed. Otto Korn, Moritz Haupt, Rudolf Ehwald, and Michael von Albrecht. 2 vols. Berlin: Weidmann, 1966.

————. *Met* Libri XV. Ed. Hugo Magnus. Berlin: Weidmann, 1914.

————. *Met.* Trans. A. D. Melville. Comm. and ed. E. J. Kenney. Oxford: Oxford UP, 1986.

————. *Met.* Trans. Frank Justus Miller. 2 vols. 1916. Cambridge: Harvard UP, 1971.

————. *Met* 6–7. Comm. Franz Bömer. Heidelberg: Winter, 1976.

————. *Opera omnia.* Ed. Petrus Burmannus. 4 vols. Amsterdam: Changnion, 1727.

————. *Opera omnia.* Ed. N. E. Lemaire. 9 vols. Paris: Dondey-Dupré, 1824.

————. *Ovid's* Met: *Books 6–10.* Ed. William S. Anderson. Norman: U of Oklahoma P, 1972.

————. *Tristium Libri Quinque; Ibis; Ex Ponto Libri Quattuor; Halieutica; Fragmenta.* Ed. S. G. Owen. 1915. Oxford: Clarendon P, 1951.

Pigna, Giovanni Battista. *I romanzi, divisi in tre libri, ne' quali della poesia, et della vita dell' Ariosto con nuovo modo si tratta.* Venice: V. Valgrisi, 1554.

————. "Vita." Venice: V. Valgrisi, 1556.

Pliny. *Natural History.* Ed. H. Rackham et al. 10 vols. Cambridge: Harvard UP, 1938–63.

Plutarch. *Plutarch's Lives.* Ed. and trans. Bernadette Perrin. 11 vols. London: Heinemann-Putnam, 1914–26.

Poliziano, Angelo Ambrogini. "Oratio." *Prosatori latini del Quattrocento.* Ed. Eugenio Garin. Milan: Ricciardi, 1952. 870–85.

————. *Prose volgari inedite e poesie latine e greche edite e inedite.* Ed. Isidore del Lungo. 1867. Hildesheim: Olms, 1976.

————. *Le Stanze, l'Orfeo e le Rime.* Ed. Giosuè Carducci. Bologna: Zanichelli, 1912.

Pulci, Luigi. *Il Morgante.* Ed. Giuseppe Fatini. 2 vols. 1948. Turin: UTET, 1984.

Quintilian. *Institutio Oratoria.* Ed. and trans. H. E. Butler. 4 vols. 1921. Cambridge: Harvard UP, 1976.

Ruscelli, Girolamo. "Mutationi, et miglioramenti, che M. Lodovico Ariosto havea fatti metter nell'ultima impressione del *Furioso.*" *OF.* Venice: Felice Valgrisi, 1587. 615–21.

Speroni, Sperone. *Opere . . .* 5 vols. Venice: D. Occhi, 1740.

Tasso, Bernardo. *Delle lettere . . .* 2 vols. Venice: Giolito, 1560–62.

————. *Delle lettere di M. Bernardo Tasso . . .* Ed. Anton-Federigo Seghezzi. 2 vols. Padua: Giuseppe Comino, 1733.

Tasso, Torquato. *Apologia del S. Torquato Tasso, In difesa della sua* GL . . . Ferrara: Baldini, 1586.

———. "Del giudizio sopra la *Gerusalemme* di Torquato Tasso da lui medesimo riformata." *Opere* 4: 129–76.

———. *Discourses on the Heroic Poem.* Trans. Mariella Cavalchini and Irene Samuel. Oxford: Clarendon P, 1973.

———. *Gerusalemme Conquistata.* Ed. Luigi Bonfigli. 2 vols. Bari: Laterza, 1934.

———. *GL.* Ed. Lanfranco Caretti. Milan: Mondadori, 1957.

———. *GL.* Ed. Fredi Chiappelli. Milan: Rusconi, 1982.

———. *GL.* Ed. Marziano Guglielminetti. Milan: Garzanti, 1974.

———. *GL.* Ed. Bruno Maier. Intro. Ezio Raimondi. 1963. Rpt. Milan: Rizzoli, 1982.

———. *GL.* Trans. Ralph Nash. Detroit: Wayne State UP, 1987.

———. *GL.* Ed. Angelo Solerti. 3 vols. Florence: Barbèra, 1896.

———. *Le lettere di Torquato Tasso . . .* Ed. Cesare Guasti. 5 vols. Naples: Rondinella, 1857.

———. *Opere.* 6 vols. Florence: S.A.R. per li Tartini e Franchi, 1724.

———. *Postille alla* Divina Commedia. Ed. Enrico Celani. Città di Castello: Lapi, 1895.

———. *Rinaldo.* Ed. Michael Sherberg. Ravenna: Longo, 1990.

———. *Scritti sull'arte poetica.* Ed. Ettore Mazzali. Milan: Ricciardi, 1959. Rpt. 2 vols. Turin: Einaudi, 1977.

———. "To Maurizio Cataneo." Letter in *Apologia in difesa della* GL. Ferrara: Cagnacini, 1585.

Toscanella, Orazio. *Le bellezze del* Furioso *di M. Lodovico Ariosto . . .* Venice: Pietro dei Franceschi, 1574.

Tudebode, Peter. *Historia de Hierosolymitano Itinere.* Trans. with intro. and ann. John Hugh Hill and Laurita L. Hill. Philadelphia: American Philosophical Society, 1974.

Valvassori, Clemente. "Prefatione su l'*OF.* A chi legge." Venice: G. A. Valvassori detto Guadagnino, 1554.

Varchi, Benedetto. *L'Ercolano.* 2 vols. Milan: Società Tipografica de' Classici Italiani, 1804.

Vergil. *Aeneid.* Comm. T. E. Page. London: Macmillan, 1964.

———. *Aeneid 10.* Intro., trans., and comm. S. J. Harrison. Oxford: Clarendon P, 1991.

———. *Opera.* Ed. R. A. B. Mynors. Oxford: Oxford UP, 1969.

———. *Virgil with an English Translation:* Eclogues, Georgics, Aeneid. Trans. H. Rushton Fairclough. 2 vols. Cambridge: Harvard UP, 1922.

Vida, Marco Girolamo. *De arte poetica.* Ed., trans., and comm. Ralph G. Williams. New York: Columbia UP, 1976.

William of Tyre. *A History of Deeds Done beyond the Sea.* Trans. and ann. Emily Atwater Babcock and A. C. Krey. 2 vols. New York: Columbia UP, 1943.

Secondary Sources

Abbagnano, Nicola. "Positivism." *Encyclopedia of Philosophy.* New York: Macmillan, 1967.

Acocella, Maria Antonietta. "Alcune considerazioni su Boiardo traduttore." *Schifanoia* 11 (1991): 63–79.

Agnelli, Giuseppe, and Giuseppe Ravegnani. *Annali delle edizioni ariostee.* 2 vols. Bologna: Zanichelli, 1933.

Albini, Giuseppe. "I versi nell'*Erodoto* del Boiardo." *GSLI* 69 (1917): 307–40.

Albrecht, Michael von. *Die Parenthese in Ovids Met und ihre dichterische Funktion.* Hildesheim: Olms, 1964.

Alexander, Susan Perry. "The Poet's Craft: The Tapestry Metaphor for Poetry in Ariosto and Spenser." Diss. Columbia University, 1982.

Alpers, Paul. *The Singer of the* Eclogues: *A Study of Virgilian Pastoral.* Berkeley: U of California P, 1979.

Altman, Charles. "Medieval Narrative vs. Modern Assumptions: Revising Inadequate Typology." Rev. of *Structure in Medieval Narrative,* by William W. Ryding. *Diacritics* 4 (1974): 12–19.

Alton, E. H., and D. E. W. Wormell. "Ovid in the Medieval Schoolroom." *Hermathena* 94 (1960): 21–38; 95 (1961): 67–82.

Altrocchi, Rudolph. "Tasso's Holograph Annotations to Horace's *Ars Poetica.*" *PMLA* 43 (1928): 931–52.

Amis, Martin. "Don Juan in Hell." *The New Yorker* 12 July 1993: 74–82.

Anceschi, Giuseppe, ed. *Il Boiardo e la critica contemporanea: Atti del Convegno di Studi su M. M. Boiardo.* Scandiano-Reggio Emilia, 25–27 aprile 1969. Florence: Olschki, 1970.

Andrews, Richard. "The Canto as a Unit in Ariosto: *OF* 24." *Italianist* 3 (1983): 9–29.

Arnaldi, Francesco, Lucia Rosa, and Liliana Sabia, eds. *Poeti latini del Quattrocento.* Milan: Ricciardi, 1964.

Ascari, Tiziano. "Rassegna di studi ariosteschi: 1954–60." *Atti e memorie della Accademia Nazionale di Scienze, Lettere e Arti di Modena* 6th ser., vol. 3 (1961): 161–77.

Ascoli, Albert Russell. *Ariosto's Bitter Harmony: Crisis and Evasion in the Italian Renaissance.* Princeton: Princeton UP, 1987.

————. "Liberating the Tomb: Difference and Death in *GL*." *Annali d'italianistica* 12 (1994): 159–80.

————. Rev. of *L'OF e il romanzo cavalleresco medievale,* by Daniela Delcorno Branca. *Italica* 60 (1983): 278–81.

————. Rev. of *Le strutture narrative dell'*OF, by Giuseppe Dalla Palma. *Renaissance Quarterly* 38 (1985): 751–54.

Ascoli, Albert Russell, Dennis Looney, and Elissa Weaver, eds. *Ferrara: Cultural Change from Boiardo to Tasso.* (forthcoming)

Ashtor, Eliyahu. *Levant Trade in the Later Middle Ages.* Princeton: Princeton UP, 1983.

Badini, Caterina. "Rassegna ariostesca (1976–1985)." *Lettere Italiane* 38.1 (1986): 104–24.

Baldassarri, Guido. "Introduzione ai *Discorsi dell'arte poetica* del Tasso." *Studi tassiani* 26 (1977): 5–38.

————, ed. *Quasi un picciolo mondo. Tentativi di codificazione del genere epico nel Cinquecento.* Padua: Unicopi, 1982.

————. *Il sonno di Zeus: Sperimentazione narrativa del poema rinascimentale e tradizione omerica.* Rome: Bulzoni, 1982.

Baldini, Gino, ed. *Ludovico Ariosto: Documenti, Immagini, Fortuna critica.* Rome: Istituto Poligrafico e Zecca dello Stato, n.d. [1992].

Baldwin, Marshall W., ed. *The First Hundred Years.* 2nd ed. Madison: U of Wisconsin P, 1969. Vol. 1 of *A History of the Crusades.* Kenneth M. Setton, gen. ed. 6 vols. 1969–85.

Balsamo, Luigi. "L'industria tipografico-editoriale nel ducato estense all'epoca dell'Ariosto." *Il Rinascimento nelle corti padane: Società e cultura.* Ed. Paolo Rossi et al. Bari: De Donato, 1977. 277–98.

Bàrberi Squarotti, Giorgio. *L'artificio dell'eternità.* Verona: Fiorini, 1972.

Barkan, Leonard. *The Gods Made Flesh: Metamorphosis and the Pursuit of Paganism.* New Haven: Yale UP, 1986.

Baruzzo, Elisabetta. *Niccolò degli Agostini: Continuatore del Boiardo.* Pisa: Giardini, 1983.

Basile, Jose. "Premessa a uno studio della poetica ariostesca." *Forma simbolica et allegorica nei 'Rerum vulgarium fragmenta' ed altre cose.* Assisi: B. Carucci, 1971. 27–47.

Bastiaensen, Michel. "La ripetizione contrastata nel *Furioso*." *Rassegna della Letteratura Italiana* 74.1 (1970): 112–33.

Beer, Marina. *Romanzi di cavalleria. Il* Furioso *e il romanzo italiano del primo Cinquecento.* Rome: Bulzoni, 1987.

Bennett, Josephine Waters. "Genre, Milieu and Epic-Romance." *English Institute Essays (1951).* Ed. Alan S. Downer. New York: Columbia UP, 1952. 95–125.

Benson, Pamela Joseph. *The Invention of the Renaissance Woman.* University Park, PA: The Pennsylvania State UP, 1992.

Bernbeck, Ernst Jurgen. *Beobachtungen zur Darstellungsart in Ovids Met.* Munich: C. H. Beck, 1967.

Berrigan, Joseph R. "The Latin Aesop of Ermolao Barbaro." *Manuscripta* 22.3 (1978): 141–48.

Bertelli, Sergio, Franco Cardini, and Elvira Garbero Zorzi, eds. *Italian Renaissance Courts.* London: Sidgwick & Jackson, 1986.

Bertino, Francesco. "Giuseppe Ferrari." *Grande Dizionario Enciclopedico UTET.* Vol. 7 (1968): 720–21.

Bertoni, Giulio. "La biblioteca di Borso d'Este." *Atti della R. Accademia delle Scienze di Torino* 41 (1925–26): 705–28.

———. *La biblioteca estense e la coltura ferrarese ai tempi del Duca Ercole I (1471–1505).* Turin: Loescher, 1903.

———. *Guarino da Verona fra letterati e cortigiani a Ferrara (1429–1460).* Geneva: Olschki, 1921.

———. "Il linguaggio poetico di L. Ariosto." *Lingua e pensiero.* Florence: Olschki, 1932. 121–51.

———. *Nuovi studi su Matteo Maria Boiardo.* Bologna: Zanichelli, 1904.

———. *L'OF e la Rinascenza a Ferrara.* Modena: Orlandini, 1919.

Bestor, Jane. "The Problem of Bastardy in the Estense Succession." Ascoli, Looney, and Weaver.

Bigi, Emilio. "Appunti sulla lingua e sulla metrica del *Furioso*." *La cultura del Poliziano e altri saggi umanistici.* Pisa: Nistri-Lischi, 1967. 164–86.

———. "Ariosto." *Enciclopedia Virgiliana.* Vol. 1. Rome: Treccani, 1984. 314–17.

———. "Petarchismo ariostesco." *Dal Petrarca al Leopardi.* Milan: Ricciardi, 1954. 47–76.

———. *La poesia del Boiardo.* Florence: Sansoni, 1941.

Billanovich, Guido. "*Vetera vestigia vatum* nei carmi dei preumanisti padovani." *Italia Medioevale e Umanistica* 1 (1958): 155–243.

Binni, Walter, ed. *I classici italiani nella storia della critica.* Florence: La Nuova Italia, 1967.

———. *Metodo e poesia di Ludovico Ariosto.* Messina: D'Anna, 1961.

Binns, J. W., ed. *Ovid.* London: Routledge and Kegan Paul, 1973.

Boillat, Michel. *Les Mét d'Ovide: Thèmes majeurs et problèmes de composition.* Bern: Lang, 1976.

Bolgar, R. R. *The Classical Heritage and Its Beneficiaries from the Carolingian Age to the End of the Renaissance.* Cambridge: Cambridge UP, 1954.

Bolza, G. B. *Manuale ariostesco.* Venice: Munster, 1866.

Bondanella, Peter and Julia Conway Bondanella, eds. *The Macmillan Dictionary of Italian Literature.* Westport, CT: Greenwood P, 1979.

Borlenghi, Aldo. *Ariosto.* Storia della critica 9. Palermo: Palumbo, 1961.

Borsetto, Luciana. *Il furto di Prometeo. Imitazione, scrittura, riscrittura nel Rinascimento.* Alessandria: Edizioni dell'Orso, 1990.

Branca, Vittore. *Poliziano e l'umanesimo della parola.* Turin: Einaudi, 1983.

———, ed. *Il Rinascimento: Aspetti e problemi attuali.* Florence: Olschki, 1982.

Brand, C. P. "L'entrelacement nell'*OF.*" *GSLI* 154 (1977): 509–32.

———. *Ludovico Ariosto.* Edinburgh: Edinburgh UP, 1970.

———. *Torquato Tasso.* Cambridge: Cambridge UP, 1965.

Bregoli-Russo, Mauda. "Boiardo, Arisoto e i commentatori del Cinquecento." *Annali Istituto Universitario Orientale, Napoli, Sezione Romanza* 29.1 (1987): 77–86.

———. "Rassegna della critica boiardesca." *Annali d'italianistica* 1 (1983): 159–73.

———. "Rassegna della critica boiardesca: 1983–1994." *Annali d'italianistica* 12 (1994): 267–97.

Brewer, Wilmon. *Ovid's Met in European Culture.* 3 vols. Boston: Cornhill, 1933.

Brownlee, Kevin, and Marina Scordilis Brownlee, eds. *Romance-Generic Transformation from Chrétien de Troyes to Cervantes.* Hanover, NH: UP of New England, 1985.

Bruscagli, Riccardo. "Prove di un commento." *Studi Italiani* 1 (1989): 1–25.

———. *Stagioni della civiltà estense.* Pisa: Nistri-Lischi, 1983.

———. "Vita d'eroe: l'*Ercole.*" *Schifanoia* 12 (1991): 9–19.

———., ed. *I libri di* OI. Modena: Panini, 1987.

Bullock, Walter Llewellyn. "Italian Sixteenth-Century Criticism." *MLN* 41 (1926): 254–63.

Burckhardt, Jacob. *The Civilization of the Renaissance in Italy.* Trans. S. G. C. Middlemore. 3rd ed. London: Phaidon, 1950.

Burrow, Colin. *Epic Romance: Homer to Milton.* Oxford: Clarendon P, 1993.

Cabani, Maria Cristina. *Costanti ariostesche. Tecniche di ripresa e memoria interna nell'*OF. Pisa: Scuola Normale Superiore, 1990.

Campanini, N., ed. *Studi su Matteo Maria Boiardo.* Bologna: Zanichelli, 1894.

Cappellani, M. *La sintassi narrativa dell'Ariosto.* Florence: La Nuova Italia, 1952.

Carducci, Giosuè. "La gioventù dell'Ariosto e la poesia latina a Ferrara." *Edizione nazionale delle opere.* Vol. 13. Bologna: Zanichelli, 1942. 115–374.

Caretti, Lanfranco. *Antichi e moderni: Studi di letteratura italiana.* Turin: Einaudi, 1976.

———. *Ariosto e Tasso.* Turin: Einaudi, 1961.

Carne Ross, D. S. "The One and the Many: A Reading of the *OF.*" *Arion* ns 3.2 (1976): 146–219.

———. "The One and the Many: A Reading of *OF,* Cantos 1 and 8." *Arion* 5.2 (1966): 195–234.

Carrara, Enrico. "Dall'*Innamorato* al *Furioso.*" *Studi petrarcheschi ed altri scritti.* Turin: Bottega d'Erasmo, 1959. 243–76.

Carroll, Clare. OF: *A Stoic Comedy.* Binghamton: Medieval Renaissance Texts and Studies, 1996.

Casadei, Alberto. *Il percorso del* Furioso. *Ricerche intorno alle redazioni del 1516 e del 1521.* Bologna: Il Mulino, 1993.

———. *La strategia delle varianti. Le correzioni storiche del terzo* Furioso. Lucca: Pacini Fazzi, 1988.

Castiglione, Luigi. *Studi intorno alle fonti e alla composizione delle* Met *di Ovidio.* Rome: L'Erma, 1964.

Catalano, Michele. *Vita di Lodovico Ariosto.* 2 vols. Geneva: Olschki, 1930–31.

Cavallo, Jo Ann. *Boiardo's* OI: *An Ethics of Desire.* Rutherford: Associated U Presses, 1993.

———. "L'*OF* nella critica anglo-americana (1986–1991)." *Lettere Italiane* 45 (1993): 129–49.

Cave, Terence. *The Cornucopian Text: Problems of Writing in the French Renaissance.* Oxford: Clarendon P, 1979.

———. *Recognitions: A Study in Poetics.* Oxford: Clarendon P, 1988.

Cecchi, Emilio, and Natalino Sapegno, gen. eds. *Storia della letteratura italiana.* 8 vols. Milano: Garzanti, 1966. Vol. 3: *Il Quattrocento e l'Ariosto.* Ed. Lanfranco Caretti, Domenico de Robertis, and Eugenio Garin.

Cecchini, Augusto. "Positivismo." *Grande Dizionario Enciclopedico UTET.* Vol. 15. Turin: UTET, 1971. 89–92.

Cent'anni di GSLI. *Atti del convegno, Torino, 5, 6, 7 dicembre 1983.* Turin: Loescher, 1985.

Cerulli, Enrico, ed. *Ludovico Ariosto.* Rome: Accademia Nazionale dei Lincei, 1975.

Ceserani, Remo. "Ariosto in America." *Forum Italicum* 19 (1985): 322–32.

———. "Due modelli culturali e narrativi nell'*OF.*" *GSLI* 161 (1984): 481–506.

Charlton, D. G. *Positivist Thought in France during the Second Empire, 1852–1870.* Oxford: Oxford UP, 1959.

Chiampi, James T. "Angelica's Flight and the Reduction of the Quest in the *OF.*" *Canadian Journal of Italian Studies* 4 (1980–81): 1–25.

———. "Between Voice and Writing: Ariosto's Irony According to St. John." *Italica* 60.4 (1983): 340–50.

Chiappini, Luciano. *Gli Estensi.* Milan: Dall'Oglio, 1967.

Clayton, Jay, and Eric Rothstein, eds. *Influence and Intertextuality in Literary History.* Madison: U of Wisconsin P, 1991.

Coleman, Arthur. "*OF.*" *Epic and Romance Criticism: A Checklist of Interpretations, 1940–72.* 2 vols. New York: Watermill, 1973–74. 2: 266–69.

Coleman, Robert. "Structure and Intention in the *Met.*" *Classical Quarterly* 21 (1971): 461–76.

Colie, Rosalie L. *The Resources of Kind: Genre-Theory in the Renaissance.* Ed. Barbara K. Lewalski. Berkeley: U of California P, 1973.

Colomer, José Luis. "Translation and Imitation: *Amplificatio* as a means of adapting the Spanish Picaresque Novel." *Revue de Littérature Comparée* 251.3 (1989): 369–76.

Conner, W. R., Ruth B. Edwards, Simon Tidworth, and Anne G. Ward, eds. *The Quest for Theseus.* New York: Praeger, 1970.

Conte, Gian Biagio. *Memoria dei poeti e sistema letterario.* 1974. Turin: Einaudi, 1985.

———. *The Rhetoric of Imitation: Genre and Poetic Memory in Virgil and Other Latin Poets.* Trans. Susan George et al. Ed. Charles Segal. Ithaca: Cornell UP, 1986.

———. *Virgilio. Il genere e i suoi confini.* Milan: Garzanti, 1984.

Contini, Gianfranco. "Come lavorava l'Ariosto." *Esercizi di lettura.* Florence: Parenti, 1939. 247–57.

Coon, Raymond H. "The Vogue of Ovid since the Renaissance." *Classical Journal* 25 (1929–30): 277–89.

Corti, Maria. *La felicità mentale.* Turin: Einaudi, 1983.

Cosenza, Mario. *Biographical and Bibliographical Dictionary of the Italian Humanists and of the World of Classical Scholarship in Italy, 1300–1800.* 5 vols. Boston: G. K. Hall, 1962.

Costa, Gustavo. "Arcadia" 17–19; "Enlightenment" 194–97; "Gravina" 261–62; and "Neoclassicism" 351–52. *Dictionary of Italian Literature.*

Coulson, Frank T. "Mss. of the 'Vulgate' Commentary on Ovid's *Met:* A Checklist." *Scriptorium* 39 (1985): 118–29.

Courtney, Susan. Jacket notes. Guarnieri Quartet. *Debussy/Ravel Quartets.* RCA, ARL1–0187, 1974.

Cremante, Enzo. Rev. of *Lodovico Ariosto: il suo tempo la sua terra la sua gente,* by various authors. *Studi e problemi di critica testuale* 18 (1979): 229–44.

Croce, Benedetto. *Ariosto, Shakespeare and Corneille.* Trans. Douglas Ainslie. New York: Holt, 1920.

———. *Ariosto, Shakespeare e Corneille.* 3rd ed. rev. Bari: Laterza, 1944.

———. *Problemi di estetica.* Bari: Laterza, 1923.

Crocetti, Camillo Guerrieri. *G. B. Giraldi ed il pensiero critico del secolo XVI.* Milan: Albrighi e Segati, 1932.

Crump, Mary Marjorie. *The Epyllion from Theocritus to Ovid.* Oxford: Basil Blackwell, 1931.

Crusca. *Vocabolario degli Accademici della Crusca.* 11 vols. Florence: Cellini, 1863–1923.

Curran, Leo C. "Transformation and Anti-Augustanism in Ovid's *Met.*" *Arethusa* 5 (1972): 71–91.

Dalla Palma, Giuseppe. *Le strutture narrative nell'*OF. Florence: Olschki, 1984.

D'Andrea, Antonio. "Il 'metodo storico.'" *Cent'anni di* GSLI. Turin: Loescher, 1985. 440–54.

———. "Per una teoria pluralistica della storiografia. Ricostruzioni storico-letterarie: Fonti e Strutture." *Lettere Italiane* 40 (1988): 465–85.

Dasenbrock, Reed Way. *Imitating the Italians: Wyatt, Spencer, Synge, Pound, Joyce.* Baltimore: Johns Hopkins UP, 1991.

Davis, Gregson. "Problem of Closure in a *Carmen Perpetuum:* Aspects of Thematic Recapitulation in Ovid, *Met* 15." *Grazer Beiträge* 9 (1980): 123–32.

Dean, Trevor. *Land and Power in Late Medieval Ferrara: The Rule of the Este, 1350–1450.* Cambridge: Cambridge UP, 1988.

Debenedetti, Santorre, ed. "Tavola comparativa delle tre edizioni originali del *Furioso.*" *I frammenti autografi dell'*OF. Turin: Chiantore, 1937. 155–60.

Delcorno Branca, Daniela. "Il cavaliere delle armi incantate: Circolazione di un modello narrativo arturiano." *GSLI* 159 (1982): 353–82.

———. *L'*OF *e il romanzo cavalleresco medievale.* Florence: Olschki, 1973.

De Robertis, Domenico. *L'esperienza poetica del Quattrocento. Storia della letteratura italiana.* Vol. 3. Milan: Garzanti, 1966.

Di Cesare, Mario A. "Isabella and Her Hermit: Stillness at the Center of the *OF.*" *Medievalia* 6 (1980): 311–32.

Di Girolamo, Costanzo, and Ivano Paccagnella, eds. *La parola ritrovata: Fonti e analisi letteraria.* Palermo: Sellerio, 1982.

Dionisotti, Carlo. "Appunti sui *Cinque Canti* e sugli studi ariosteschi."

Studi e problemi di critica testuale. Bologna: Commissione peri testi di lingua, 1960. 369–82.

———. "Regioni e letteratura." *Storia d'Italia.* Vol. 5. Turin: Einaudi, 1973. 1391–95.

———. "Tradizione classica e volgarizzamenti." *Geografia e storia della letteratura italiana.* Turin: Einaudi, 1967. 25–54.

Di Tommaso, Andrea. *Structure and Ideology in Boiardo's* OI. Chapel Hill: U of North Carolina P, 1972.

Donato, Eugenio. "Per selve e boscherecci labirinti: Desire and Narrative Structure in Ariosto's *OF.*" *Barocco* 4 (1972): 17–34. Rpt. in *Literary Theory/Renaissance Texts.* Ed. Patricia Parker and David Quint. Baltimore: Johns Hopkins UP, 1986. 33–62.

Doran, Madeleine. "Some Renaissance 'Ovids.' " *Literature and Society.* Ed. B. Slote. Lincoln: U of Nebraska P, 1964. 44–62.

Due, Otto Steen. *Changing Forms: Studies in the* Met *of Ovid.* Copenhagen: Gyldendal, 1974.

Durling, Robert M. "The Epic Ideal." *The Old World: Discovery and Rebirth.* Vol. 3: 105–46. *Literature and Western Civilization.* Ed. David Daiches and Anthony Thorlby. 5 vols. London: Aldus Books, 1972–75.

———. *The Figure of the Poet in Renaissance Epic.* Cambridge: Harvard UP, 1965.

DuRocher, Richard J. *Milton and Ovid.* Ithaca: Cornell UP, 1985.

Edbury, Peter W., and John Gordon Rowe. *William of Tyre: Historian of the Latin East.* Cambridge: Cambridge UP, 1988.

Engels, J. "Les commentaires d'Ovide au XVIe siècle." *Vivarium* 12 (1974): 3–13.

Evans, J. A. S. "Father of History or Father of Lies: The Reputation of Herodotus." *Classical Journal* 64 (1968): 11–17.

Fahy, Conor. *L'OF del 1532. Profilo di una edizione.* Milan: Vita e Pensiero, 1989.

Farrell, Joseph. *Vergil's* Georgics *and the Traditions of Ancient Epic: The Art of Allusion in Literary History.* New York: Oxford UP, 1991.

Fatini, Giuseppe. *Bibliografia della critica ariostea (1510–1956).* Florence: Le Monnier, 1958.

Fava, Domenico. *La biblioteca estense nel suo sviluppo storico.* Modena: Vincenzi, 1925.

Fehling, Detlev. *Herodotus and His "Sources": Citation, Invention and Narrative Art.* Trans. J. G. Howie. Leeds: Francis Cairns, 1989.

Ferguson, Margaret. *Trials of Desire.* New Haven: Yale UP, 1983.

Ferrante, Joan. "Good Thieves and Bad Thieves: A Reading of *Inferno* XXIV." *Dante Studies* 104 (1986): 83–98.

Ferrari, Virgilio. "Le case degli Ariosti in Ferrara." *Ferrara e l'Ariosto.* Ed. Raffaele Belvederi et al. Ferrara: SATE, 1974. 41–78.

Ferroni, Giulio. "Da Bradamante a Ricciardetto. Interferenze testuali e scambi di sesso." Di Girolamo and Paccagnella 137–59.

Fichter, Andrew John. *Poets Historical: Dynastic Epic in the Renaissance.* New Haven: Yale UP, 1982.

Finucci, Valeria. *The Lady Vanishes: Subjectivity and Representation in Castiglione and Ariosto.* Palo Alto: Stanford UP, 1992.

Flodr, Miroslav. *Incunabula Classicorum.* Amsterdam: Hakkert, 1973.

Forti, Franco. "Boiardo." *DBI.* Vol. 11. Rome: Istituto della Enciclopedia Italiana, 1969. 211–23.

Franceschetti, Antonio. "Struttura e compiutezza dell'*OI*." Anceschi 281–94.

Frappier, Jean. *Etude sur* La mort le Roi Artu. 3rd ed. Geneva: Droz, 1972.

Frasso, Giuseppe. "Un poeta improvvisatore nella 'familia' del cardinale Francesco Gonzaga: Francesco Cieco da Firenze." *Italia Medioevale e Umanistica* 20 (1977): 395–400.

Frati, Carlo. "Un nuovo codice del volgarizzamento di Erodoto di M. M. Boiardo." *La Bibliofilia* 20 (1918–19): 265–67.

———. "Il volgarizzamento di Erodoto, di M. M. Boiardo e un codice che lo contiene." *La Bibliofilia* 19 (1917–18): 114–17.

Frécaut, J.-M. "Les transitions dans les *Mét* d'Ovide." *Revue des études latines* 46 (1968): 247–63.

Freeman, Michelle. "Problems in Romance Composition: Ovid, Chrétien de Troyes and the *Romance of the Rose*." *Romance Philology* 30 (1976): 158–68.

Freudenburg, Kirk. *The Walking Muse: Horace on the Theory of Satire.* Princeton: Princeton UP, 1993.

Fumagalli, Edoardo. *Matteo Maria Boiardo volgarizzatore dell'*Asino d'oro: *Contributo allo studio della fortuna di Apuleio nell'umanesimo.* Padua: Antenore, 1988.

———, ed. *Nascita, infanzia e prime imprese di Ciro il Grande. Volgarizzamento di Matteo Maria Boiardo.* Fribourg, Switz.: privately printed, 1994.

Fumagalli, Giuseppina. *La fortuna dell'*OF. Ferrara: Zuffi, 1910.

Fusinato, Guido. "Un cantastorie chioggiotto." *Giornale di filologia romanza.* 2nd ser. 4, fasc. 3–4, no. 9 (1883): 170–83.

Fyler, John M. *Chaucer and Ovid.* New Haven: Yale UP, 1979.

Galinsky, G. Karl. "Hercules Ovidianus (*Met* 9, 1–272)." *Wiener Studien* 85 (1972): 93–116.

————. *Ovid's* Met: *An Introduction to the Basic Aspects*. Berkeley: U of California P, 1975.

Gardner, Edmund G. *Dukes and Poets in Ferrara*. London: Constable, 1904.

————. *King of Court Poets: A Study of the Life, Work, and Times of Lodovico Ariosto*. 1906. New York: Haskell, 1968.

Gareffi, Andrea. *Figure dell'immaginario nell'*OF. Rome: Bulzoni, 1984.

Garin, Eugenio. *L'educazione in Europa 1400/1600*. 1957. Bari: Laterza, 1976.

————. "Guarino Veronese e la cultura a Ferrara." *Ritratti di umanisti*. Florence: Sansoni, 1967. 69–106.

Geanakoplos, Deno John. *Greek Scholars in Venice*. Cambridge: Harvard UP, 1962.

Gennari, Aldo. "Progetto di raccogliere tutti gli oggetti appartenenti all'Ariosto in una sala della biblioteca." *Gazzetta Ferrarese* 5–6 Nov. 1881, bound in an untitled vol. of *Tracts 1790–1882* in the British Library (820.F.43), p. 3.

Giamatti, A. Bartlett. "Sfrenatura: Restraint and Release in the *OF*." Scaglione, *Ariosto* 31–39.

Gibbons, Felton. *Dosso and Battista Dossi: Court Painters at Ferrara*. Princeton: Princeton UP, 1968.

————. "Ferrarese Tapestries of Metamorphosis." *Art Bulletin* 47 (1966): 408–13.

Gilbert, Allan H. "The Sea-monster in Ariosto's *Cinque Canti*." *Italica* 33 (1956): 260–63.

Gilbert, C. D. "Ovid, *Met* 1.4." *Classical Quarterly* ns 26 (1976): 111–12.

Ginzburg, C. "Tiziano, Ovidio e i codici della figurazione erotica nel Cinquecento." *Paragone-Arte* 29 (maggio 1978): 12–17.

Gordon, G. S., ed. *English Literature and the Classics*. Oxford: Clarendon P, 1912.

Grafton, Anthony, and Lisa Jardine. *From Humanism to the Humanities*. Cambridge: Harvard UP, 1986.

Gransden, K. W. *Virgil's* Iliad: *An Essay on Epic Narrative*. Cambridge: Cambridge UP, 1984.

Green, D. H. *Irony in the Medieval Romance*. Cambridge: Cambridge UP, 1979.

Greenblatt, Stephen. "Shakespeare and the Exorcists." *Shakespeare and the Question of Theory*. Ed. Patricia Parker and Geoffrey Hartman. New York: Methuen, 1985. 163–87.

Greene, Thomas M. *The Descent from Heaven: A Study in Epic Continuity*. New Haven: Yale UP, 1963.

————. *The Light in Troy: Imitation and Discovery in Renaissance Poetry.* New Haven: Yale UP, 1982.

Grendler, Paul F. *Schooling in Renaissance Italy: Literacy and Learning, 1300–1600.* Baltimore: Johns Hopkins UP, 1989.

Griffin, Robert. *Ludovico Ariosto.* New York: Twayne, 1974.

Gundersheimer, Werner L. *Ferrara: The Style of a Renaissance Despotism.* Princeton: Princeton UP, 1973. Trans. with a new introduction by the author, *Ferrara Estense. Lo stile del potere.* Modena: Panini, 1990.

Guthmuller, H. Bodo. "Literarische Uebersetzung im Bezugsfeld Original-Leser (Am Beispeil italienischen Uebersetzungen der Metamorphosen Ovids im 16. Jahrhundert)." *Bibliothèque d'Humanisme et Renaissance* 36 (1974): 233–51.

————. *Ovidio* Met *Vulgare: Formen und Funktionen der volkssprachlichen Wiedergabe klassischer Dichtung in der italienischen Renaissance.* Boppard am Rhein: Boldt, 1981.

Guyard, M.-F., and Ulrich Weisstein. "Stoffgeschichte." *Comparative Literature and Literary Theory.* Bloomington: Indiana UP, 1968. 124–49.

Haddad, Miranda Johnson. "Ovid's Medusa in Dante and Ariosto: The poetics of self-confrontation." *JMRS* 19 (1989): 211–25.

Hampton, Timothy. *Writing from History: The Rhetoric of Exemplarity in Renaissance Literature.* Ithaca: Cornell UP, 1990.

Hanning, R. W. "Ariosto, Ovid, and the Painters." Scaglione, *Ariosto* 99–116.

Harding, Davis P. *Milton and the Renaissance Ovid.* Urbana: U of Illinois P, 1946.

Hare, Augustus. *Augustus Hare in Italy.* Ed. Gavin Henderson. New York: Ecco P, 1988.

Harris, William V. *Ancient Literacy.* Cambridge: Harvard UP, 1989.

Hart, Thomas R. *Cervantes and Ariosto: Renewing Fiction.* Princeton: Princeton UP, 1989.

Hauvette, Henri. *L'Arioste et la Poésie chevaleresque a Ferrare au Début du XVIe Siècle.* Paris: Champion, 1927.

Hay, Denys. "1500–1700: the bibliographical problem. A continental S.T.C.?" *Classical Influences on European Culture, A.D. 1500–1700.* Ed. R. R. Bolgar. Cambridge: Cambridge UP, 1976. 33–39.

Hempfer, Klaus W. *Diskrepante Lektüren: Die Orlando-Furioso-Rezeption im Cinquecento.* Stuttgart: Franz Steiner, 1987.

Herescu, N. I., ed. *Ovidiana: Recherches sur Ovide.* Paris: Les Belles Lettres, 1958.

Herington, John. "The Poem of Herodotus." *Arion.* 3rd ser. 1/3 (1991): 5–16.

Herter, Haus. *Theseus.* Munich: Druckenmuller, 1973.

Hyde, Thomas. "Boccaccio: The Genealogies of Myth." *PMLA* 100 (1985): 737–45.

Iannucci, Amilcare A. "Ariosto umanista: l'educazione di Virginio." Branca, *Il Rinascimento* 485–98.

Immerwahr, Henry R. *Form and Thought in Herodotus.* Cleveland: Western Reserve UP, 1966.

Isella, Dante. "La critica stilistica." *I metodi attuali della critica in Italia.* Ed. Maria Corti and Cesare Segre. Turin: ERI, 1980. 138–51.

Jacoff, Rachel, and Jeffrey T. Schnapp, eds. *The Poetry of Allusion: Virgil and Ovid in Dante's* Commedia. Stanford: Stanford UP, 1991.

Jameson, Caroline. "Ovid in the Sixteenth Century." Binns 210–42.

Javitch, Daniel. "Cantus Interruptus in the *OF.*" *MLN* 95 (1980): 66–80.

———. "The Imitation of Imitations in the *OF.*" *Renaissance Quarterly* 2 (1985): 215–39.

———. "The *OF* and Ovid's Revision of the *Aeneid.*" *MLN* 99 (1984): 1023–36.

———. *Proclaiming a Classic: The Canonization of* OF. Princeton: Princeton UP, 1991.

———. "Rescuing Ovid from the Allegorizers: The Liberation of Angelica, *Furioso* X." Scaglione, *Ariosto* 85–98.

———. "Sixteenth-Century Commentaries on Imitations in the *OF.*" *Harvard Library Bulletin* 34 (1986): 221–50.

Kallendorf, Craig. *In Praise of Aeneas: Virgil and Epideictic Rhetoric in the Early Italian Renaissance.* Hanover, NH: UP of New England, 1989.

Kellett, E. E. *Literary Quotation and Allusion.* 1933. Port Washington, NY: Kennikat P, 1969.

Kennedy, George A. *Classical Rhetoric and Its Christian and Secular Tradition from Ancient to Modern Times.* Chapel Hill: U of North Carolina P, 1980.

Kennedy, William J. *Rhetorical Norms in Renaissance Literature.* New Haven: Yale UP, 1978.

Kenney, E. J. *The Classical Text: Aspects of Editing in the Age of the Printed Book.* Berkeley: U of California P, 1974.

———. "Ovid." *Latin Literature.* Ed. E. J. Kenney. 2 vols. Cambridge History of Classical Literature. Cambridge: Cambridge UP, 1982. 2: 420–57.

———. "The Style of the *Met.*" Binns 116–53.

Knauer, G. N. "Vergil's *Aeneid* and Homer." *Oxford Readings in Vergil's* Aeneid. Ed. S. J. Harrison. Oxford: Oxford UP, 1990. 390–412.

Kolodny, Annette. "A Map for Rereading: Gender and the Interpretation of Literary Texts." *The New Feminist Criticism: Essays on Women, Literature, and Theory.* Ed. Elaine Showalter. New York: Pantheon, 1985. 46–62.

Kraus, Walther. "P. Ovidius Naso, der Dichter." *Paulys Real-Encyclo-padie der Classischen Altertumswissenschaft.* Stuttgart: Metzler-sche, 1942. Vol. 18, pt. 2: 1910–86.

Kwintner, Michelle. Rev. of *The Liar School of Herodotus,* by W. Kend-rick Pritchett. *Bryn Mawr Classical Review* 94.4.10 (electronic version).

Lafaye, Georges. *Les* Met *d'Ovide et leurs modèles grecs.* Paris: Alcan, 1904.

Laidlaw, William Addison. "Crete." *Oxford Classical Dictionary.* Ox-ford: Oxford UP 1949.

Lamarque, Henri, and G. Soubeille, eds. *Ovide en France dans la Re-naissance.* Toulouse: U de Toulouse-Le Mirail, 1981.

Lansing, Richard H. "Ariosto's *OF* and the Homeric Model." *Compara-tive Literature Studies* 24 (1987): 311–25.

La Penna, Antonio. "La teoria dell' 'arte allusiva' nel *De arte poetica* di Girolamo Vida." *Tradizione classica e letteratura umanistica. Per Alessandro Perosa.* Ed. Roberto Cardini et al. 2 vols. Rome: Bulzoni, 1985. 2: 643–50.

Lascu, N. "La fortuna di Ovidio dal Rinascimento ai tempi nostri." *Studi Ovidiani.* Rome, 1979. 79–112.

Lateiner, Donald. *The Historical Method of Herodotus.* Toronto: U of Toronto P, 1989.

Lausberg, Heinrich. *Handbuch der Literarischen Rhetorik.* 2 vols. Mu-nich: Max Hueber, 1960.

Lazzari, Alfonso. "Un improvvisatore alla corte del duca Ercole II d'Este Silvio Antoniani." *Attraverso la storia di Ferrara: Profili e scorci.* Rovigo: Modernografica, 1954. 333–37.

Leach, Eleanor Winsor. "Ekphrasis and the Theme of Artistic Failure in Ovid's *Met.*" *Ramus* 3 (1974): 102–42.

Lee, Vernon. [Violet Paget] "The School of Boiardo." *Euphorion: Being Studies of the Antique and the Mediaeval in the Renaissance.* London: Unwin, 1899. 263–333.

Lentricchia, Frank, and Thomas McLaughlin, eds. *Critical Terms for Literary Study.* Chicago: U of Chicago P, 1987.

Lenz, Federico W. "Parerga Ovidiana." *Rendiconti della R. Accademia dei Lincei: Classe di scienze morali, storiche e filologiche* 13 (1938): 320–410.

Lettere, Vera. "Ciofano, Ercole." *DBI.* Vol. 25. Rome: Instituto della Enciclopedia Italiana, 1981. 661–63.

Lewis, C. S. *Major British Writers.* Ed. G. B. Harrison. New York: Harcourt, 1954.

Limentani, Alberto. "Casella, Palinuro e Orfeo: 'Modello narrativo' e 'rimozione della fonte.'" Di Girolamo and Paccagnella 82–98.

Little, Douglas A. "The Structural Character of Ovid's *Met.*" Diss. U of Texas at Austin, 1972.

Lizzi, Rita. "La memoria selettiva." *Lo spazio letterario di Roma antica.* Vol. 3: *La ricezione del testo.* Ed. Guglielmo Cavallo et al. Rome: Salerno, 1992. 647–76.

Looney, Dennis. "Ariosto and the Classics." *Major Italian Authors: Ariosto.* Ed. Massimo Ciavolella and Roberto Fedi. Toronto: U of Toronto P, 1996.

———. "Ariosto's Ferrara: A National Identity between Fact and Fiction." *Yearbook of Comparative and General Literature* 39 (1990–91): 25–34.

———. "Ariosto the Ferrarese Rhapsode: A Compromise in the Critical Terminology for Narrative in the Mid-Cinquecento." *Interpreting the Italian Renaissance: Literary Perspectives.* Ed. A. Toscano. Stony Brook, NY: Forum Italicum, 1991. 139–50.

———. "Ludovico Ariosto." *Macmillan Dictionary of Art* (forthcoming).

———. "The Misshapen Beast: The *Furioso*'s Serpentine Narrative." *Countercurrents: The Primacy of the Text in Literary Criticism.* Ed. R. A. Prier. Albany: SUNY P, 1992. 73–97.

———. "Ovidian Influence on the Narrative of the *OF.*" Diss. U of North Carolina at Chapel Hill, 1987. Ann Arbor: UMI, 1987. 8722318.

———. "Recent Trends in Ariosto Criticism: Intricati rami e aer fosco." *Modern Philology* 88:2 (1990): 153–65.

———. "Torquato Tasso." *Macmillan Dictionary of Art* (forthcoming).

Lot, Ferdinand. *Etude sur le* Lancelot en prose. 1918. Paris: Champion, 1954.

Ludwig, Walther. *Struktur und Einheit der* Met Ovids. Berlin: W. de Gruyther, 1965.

Luzio, Alessandro and Rudolfo Renier. "La coltura e le relazioni letterarie di Isabella d'Este Gonzaga." *GSLI* 150 (1902): 289–334.

Lyne, R. O. A. M. *Words and the Poet: Characteristic Techniques of Style in Vergil's* Aeneid. Oxford: Oxford UP, 1989.

Mack, Sara. *Ovid.* New Haven: Yale UP, 1988.

Maldè, Ettore de. *Le fonti della* GL. Parma: Tipografia Cooperativa, 1910.

Malkiel-Jirmounsky, Myron. "Notes sur les trois rédactions du *Roland Furieux* de l'Arioste." *Humanisme et Renaissance* 3 (1936): 429–46.

Mancini, Albert N. *I Capitoli letterari di Francesco Bolognetti: Tempi e modi della letteratura epica fra l'Ariosto e il Tasso.* Naples: Federico & Ardia, 1989.

———. "Personaggi della poesia cavalleresca: Cavalieri e villani nell' *OF.*" *Civiltà della parola.* Ed. Italo Bertoni. Milan: Marzorati, 1989. 171–88.

Manica, Raffaele. *Preliminari sull'OF.* Rome: Bulzoni, 1983.

Marcus, Millicent. "Angelica's Loveknots: The Poetics of Requited Desire in *OF* 19 and 23." *Philological Quarterly* 72 (1993): 33–51.

Marinelli, Peter V. *Ariosto and Boiardo: The Origins of the* OF. Columbia: U of Missouri P, 1987.

———. *Pastoral.* London: Methuen, 1971.

———. "Shaping the Ore: Image and Design in Canto I of *OF.*" *MLN* 103.1 (1988): 31–49.

Marsh, David. "Lorenzo Valla: The Translation from Xenophon's *Cyropaedia.*" *Bibliothèque d'Humanisme et Renaissance* 46.2 (1984): 407–20.

Martindale, Charles. *John Milton and the Transformation of Ancient Epic.* London: Croom Helm, 1986.

Martinez, Ronald L. "Ricciardetto's Sex and the Castration of Orlando: Anatomy of an Episode from the *OF.*" Unpublished essay.

Mattioli, Emilio. *Luciano e l'umanesimo.* Naples: Istituto italiano per gli studi storici, 1980.

Maylender, Michele. *Storia delle Accademie d'Italia.* 5 vols. Bologna: Cappelli, 1926–30.

Mazzacurati, Giancarlo. *Il problema storico del petrarchismo italiano (dal Boiardo a Lorenzo).* Naples: Liguori, 1963.

Mazzotta, Giuseppe. *Dante, Poet of the Desert.* Princeton: Princeton UP, 1979.

———. "Power and Play: Machiavelli and Ariosto." *Western Pennsylvania Symposium on World Literatures: Selected Proceedings 1974–1991.* Greensburg: Eadmer P, 1992. 151–70.

Medici, Domenico. "La bibliografia della critica ariostesca dal Fatini ad oggi (1957–74)." *Ludovico Ariosto: Il suo tempo, la sua terra, la sua gente.* 3 vols. Reggio Emilia: Bollettino Storico Reggiano, 1974. 3: 63–150.

———. "La critica boiardesca dal 1800 al 1976: Bibliografia ragionata." Xerographic reproduction in the Newberry Library, OZ 8107.36 M43.

Micheli, Pietro. *Dal Boiardo all'Ariosto.* Conegliano: Cagnoni, 1898.

Migiel, Marilyn and Juliana Schiesari, eds. *Refiguring Woman: Perspectives on Gender and the Italian Renaissance.* Ithaca: Cornell UP, 1991.

Milani, Marisa. "Sonetti ferraresi del '400 in una raccolta di poeti cortigiani." *GSLI* 150 (1973): 292–322.

Miller, Frank J. "Some Features of Ovid's Style: Ovid's Methods of Ordering and Transition in the *Met.*" *Classical Journal* 16 (1920–21): 464–76.

Mitchell, Bonner. *1598: A Year of Pageantry in Late Renaissance Ferrara.* Binghamton: MRTS, 1990.

Momigliano, Arnaldo. "The Place of Herodotus in the History of Historiography." *History* 43 (1958): 1–13.

Monteverdi, Angelo. "A proposito delle fonti dell'*OF.*" *Cultura Neolatina* 21 (1961): 259–67.

Moog-Grunewald, Maria. *Metamorphosen der* Met: *Rezeptionsarten der Ovidischen Verwandlungsgeschichten in Italien und Frankreich im XVI und XVII Jahrhundert.* Heidelberg: Winter, 1979.

Moretti, Walter. "La bontà di cuore nell'*OF.*" *Cortesia e furore nel Rinascimento italiano.* Bologna: Pàtron, 1970. 19–33.

———. *L'ultimo Ariosto.* Bologna: Pàtron, 1977.

Moss, Ann. *Ovid in Renaissance France: A Survey of the Latin Editions of Ovid and Commentaries Printed in France before 1600.* London: Warburg Institute and U of London, 1982.

———. *Poetry and Fable: Studies in Mythological Narrative in Sixteenth-Century France.* Cambridge: Cambridge UP, 1984.

Multineddu, Salvatore. *Le fonti della* GL. Turin: Clausen, 1895.

Munari, Franco. *Ovid in Mittelalter.* Zurich: Artemis, 1960.

Müntz, Eugene. *La Tapisserie.* Paris: Quantin, n.d. [1891?].

Murrin, Michael. "Agramante's War." *Annali d'italianistica* 1 (1983): 107–28.

———. *The Allegorical Epic: Essays in Its Rise and Decline.* Chicago: U of Chicago P, 1980.

———. *History and Warfare in Renaissance Epic.* Chicago: U of Chicago P, 1994.

Murtaugh, Kristen Olson. *Ariosto and the Classical Simile.* Cambridge: Harvard UP, 1980.

Natali, Giulio. *Ludovico Ariosto.* Florence: La Nuova Italia, 1966.

Navarrete, Ignacio. "Boiardo's *Pastorali* as a Macrotext." *Stanford Italian Review* 5 (1985): 37–53.

Nohrnberg, James. *The Analogy of* The Fairie Queen. Princeton: Princeton UP, 1976.

————. Lecture. NEH Summer Institute on Ariosto and Tasso at Northwestern University. Evanston, 26 July 1990.

————. "Orlando's Opportunity." American Boiardo Quincentennial Conference. New York, 8 Oct. 1994.

Norwich, John Julius. *A History of Venice.* New York: Knopf, 1982.

Novati, Francesco. "I codici francesi de' Gonzaga secondo nuovi documenti." *Romania* 19 (1890): 160–200.

Orlandi, Mary-Kay Gamel. "Ovid True and False in Renaissance Poetry." *Pacific Coast Philology* 13 (1978): 60–70.

Otis, Brooks. *Ovid as an Epic Poet.* 2nd ed. Cambridge: Cambridge UP, 1975.

————. *Virgil: A Study in Civilized Poetry.* Oxford: Oxford UP, 1963.

Owen, S. G. "Ovid and Romance." Gordon 167–95.

Pampaloni, L. "Per una analisi narrativa del *Furioso.*" *Belfagor* 26 (1971): 133–150.

Paoletti, Lao. "Cultura ed attività letteraria dal XII al XV secolo." *Storia della Emilia Romagna.* Ed. Aldo Berselli. 3 vols. Bologna: UP Bologna, 1976. 1: 581–613.

Paolini, Paolo. "Situazione della critica ariostesca." *Italianistica* 3.3 (1974): 3–22.

Papponetti, Giuseppe. "Geminazione della memoria: L'*Ovidio* di Hercole Ciofano." *Ovidio: Poeta della Memoria.* Ed. G. Papponetti. Sulmona: Herder, 1991. 143–79.

Papponetti, Giuseppe, and Adriano Ghisetti Giavarina. "Un'effige quattrocentesca di Ovidio." *Italia Medioevale e Umanistica* 29 (1986): 283–97.

Paratore, Ettore. *Bibliografia ovidiana.* Sulmona: Comitato per le celebrazioni del bimillenario, 1958.

————. "Ercole Ciofano." *Dal Petrarca all'Alfieri: Saggi di letteratura comparata.* Florence: Olschki, 1975. 263–90.

————. "L'*OI* e l'*Eneide.*" Anceschi 347–75.

Pardi, Giuseppe. *Lo studio di Ferrara nei secoli XV e XVI con documenti inediti.* Ferrara: Zuffi, 1903. Bologna: Forni, 1972.

Parker, Patricia. *Inescapable Romance: Studies in the Poetics of a Mode.* Princeton: Princeton UP, 1979.

Parry, Hugh. "Ovid's *Met:* Violence in a Pastoral Landscape." *TAPA* 95 (1964): 268–82.

Paschall, D. M. "The Vocabulary of Mental Aberration in Roman Comedy and Petronius." Supplement to *Language* 15.1 (1939).

Pasini, Gian Franco. *Dossier sulla critica delle fonti (1896–1909).* Bologna: Pàtron, 1988.

Pasquali, Giorgio. "Arte allusiva." *Italia che scrive* 5 (1942): 185–87.

————. *Storia della tradizione e critica del testo.* 1952. Milan: Mondadori, 1974.

Pasquazi, Silvio. *Poeti estensi del Rinascimento.* Florence, 1966.

Patroni, Giovanni. "Rileggendo le *Metamorfosi.*" *Athenaeum* 1 (1929): 145–72; *Athenaeum* 3 (1929): 289–315.

Patterson, Annabel. "Intention." Lentricchia and McLaughlin 135–46.

————. "Tasso and Neoplatonism." *Studies in the Renaissance* 18 (1971): 105–33.

Pavlock, Barbara. *Eros, Imitation, and the Epic Tradition.* Ithaca: Cornell UP, 1990.

Perez, Louis C. "The Theme of Tapestry in Ariosto and Cervantes." *Revista de Estudios Hispanicos* 7.2 (1973): 289–98.

Pettinelli, Rosanna Alhaique. "Di alcune fonti del Boiardo." Anceschi 1–10.

————. *L'immaginario cavalleresco nel Rinascimento ferrarese.* Rome: Bonacci, 1983.

Phillimore, J. S. "The Greek Romances." Gordon 87–117.

Pieri, Marzia. "La scena pastorale." *La Corte e lo spazio: Ferrara estense.* Ed. Giuseppe Papagno e Amedeo Quondam. 3 vols. Rome: Bulzoni, 1982. 2: 489–525.

Piromalli, Antonio. *Ariosto.* Padua: R.A.D.A.R., 1969.

————. *La cultura a Ferrara al tempo dell'Ariosto.* Florence: La Nuova Italia, 1953.

Pischedda, Giovanni. "Conclusioni sul classicismo ariosteo." *Classicità provinciale.* L'Aquila: La Bodoniana Tipografica, 1956. 195–210.

Ponte, Giovanni. "La fortuna e la critica del Boiardo." *La Rassegna della letteratura italiana* 57.3 (1953): 275–90; 57.4 (1953): 420–37.

————. *La personalità e l'opera del Boiardo.* Genoa: Tilgher, 1972.

Pöschl, Viktor. *The Art of the* Aeneid. Trans. Gerda Seligson. Ann Arbor: U of Michigan P, 1970.

Powell, J. Enoch. *A Lexicon to Herodotus.* Hildesheim: Olms, 1960.

Pozzi, Giovanni. "Ludicra Mariniana." *Studi e problemi di critica testuale* 6 (1973): 132–62.

Pritchett, W. Kendrick. *The Liar School of Herodotus.* Amsterdam: Gieben, 1993.

Quinn, Kenneth. *Latin Explorations.* London: Routledge and Kegan Paul, 1963.

————. *Virgil's* Aeneid: *A Critical Description.* 1968. Ann Arbor: U of Michigan P, 1969.

Quint, David. "The Boat of Romance and Renaissance Epic." Brownlee and Brownlee 178–202.

————. *Epic and Empire: Politics and Generic Form from Virgil to Milton*. Princeton: Princeton UP, 1993.

————. "The Figure of Atlante: Ariosto and Boiardo's Poem." *MLN* 94 (1979): 77–91.

————. *Origin and Originality in Renaissance Literature*. New Haven: Yale UP, 1983.

————. "Political Allegory in the *GL*." *Renaissance Quarterly* 43 (1990): 1–29.

Quondam, Amedeo. *Cultura e ideologia di Gianvincenzo Gravina*. Milan: Mursia, 1968.

Ragni, Eugenio. "Boiardo." *Enciclopedia Virgiliana*. Rome: Istituto della Enciclopedia Italiana, 1984. 1: 518–21.

————. "Il 'Lucio Apulegio Volgare.' " Anceschi 427–36.

Raimondi, Ezio. *Intertestualità e storia letteraria: Da Dante a Montale*. Bologna: CUSL, 1991.

Rajna, Pio. *Le fonti dell'OF*. 1876. 1900. Florence: Sansoni, 1975.

————. "L'*OI* di Matteo Maria Boiardo." Campanini 117–46.

————. "Ricordi di codici francesi posseduti dagli Estensi nel Secolo XV." *Romania* 2 (1873): 49–58.

————. "I 'Rinaldi' o i cantastorie di Napoli." *Nuova Antologia* 12.24 (1878): 557–79.

Ramat, Raffaello. *La critica ariostesca dal secolo XVI ad oggi*. Florence: La Nuova Italia, 1954.

Rand, Edward Kennard. *Ovid and His Influence*. New York: Cooper Square, 1963.

Rasi, Donatella. "Breve ricognizione di un carteggio cinquecentesco: Bernardo Tasso e G. B. Giraldi." *Studi Tassiani* 28 (1980): 5–24.

Razzoli, G. *Per le fonti dell' OI di Matteo Maria Boiardo: I primi trenta canti del poema*. Milan: Albrighi e Segati, 1901.

Reichenbach, Giulio. "Il codice della traduzione boiardesca di Erodoto." *La Bibliofilia* 31 (1929): 281–84.

————. *Matteo Maria Boiardo*. Bologna: Zanichelli, 1929.

————. *L'OI di M. M. Boiardo*. Florence: La Nuova Italia, 1936.

Rhu, Lawrence F. *The Genesis of Tasso's Narrative Theory*. Detroit: Wayne State UP, 1993.

Robathan, Dorothy M. "Ovid in the Middle Ages." Binns 191–209.

Rodini, Robert J. "Selected Bibliography of Ariosto Criticism, 1980–87." *MLN* 103.1 (1988): 187–203.

————. "Selected Bibliography of Ariosto Criticism, 1986–1993." *Annali di italianistica* 12 (1994): 299–317.

Rodini, Robert J., and Salvatore Di Maria. *Ludovico Ariosto: An An-*

notated Bibliography of Criticism, 1956–1980. Columbia: U of Missouri P, 1984.

Romizi, Augusto. "L'Ariosto in gara con Virgilio e Ovidio." *Bollettino Filologia Classica* 1 (1894–95): 259–60.

———. *Le fonti latine dell'OF.* Turin: Paravia, 1896.

———. *Paralleli letterari tra poeti greci, latini e italiani.* 2nd ed. Livorno: Giusti, 1892.

Rose, Linda. "Crete." *Dictionary of the Middle Ages.* 13 vols. New York: Scribner's, 1982–89. 3: 678.

Rosenmeyer, Thomas G. *The Green Cabinet: Theocritus and the European Pastoral Lyric.* Berkeley: U of California P, 1969.

Ross, Charles S. "Boiardo." *The Spenser Encyclopedia.* Toronto: U of Toronto P, 1990. 100–101.

Rossi, Ermete. "Nota bibliografica circa il Boiardo traduttore." *La Bibliofilia* 39 (1937): 360–69.

———. "Un plagio del Boiardo traduttore?" *GSLI* 114 (1939): 1–25.

Rossi, Vittorio. *Il Quattrocento.* Milan: Vallardi, 1938.

Rudd, Niall. *The Satires of Horace.* Cambridge: Cambridge UP, 1966.

Russo, Luigi. "La dissoluzione del mondo cavelleresco: Il *Morgante* di Luigi Pulci." *Belfagor* 7 (1952): 36–54.

———. "La letteratura cavalleresca dal *Tristano* ai *Reali di Francia*." *Belfagor* 6 (1951): 40–59.

———. *L'OI di M.M. Boiardo.* Pisa: Goliardica, 1952.

Ryding, William W. *Structure in Medieval Narrative.* The Hague: Mouton, 1971.

Sabbadini, Remigio. *Epistolario* [of Guarino Veronese]. 3 vols. 1919. Turin: Bottega d'Erasmo, 1969.

———. *Guariniana: Vita di Guarino Veronese; La scuola e gli studi di Guarino Veronese.* 2 rpt. vols. bound in 1 with original pagination. Ed. Mario Sancipriano. 1891. 1896. Turin: Bottega d'Erasmo, 1964.

Saccone, Eduardo. "Il 'soggetto' del *Furioso*." *Il 'soggetto' del Furioso e altri saggi tra quattro e cinquecento.* Naples: Liguori, 1974. 201–47.

Santoro, Mario. *Ariosto e il Rinascimento.* Naples: Liguori, 1989.

———. "Introduzione." *OF.* Naples: Rondinella, 1945. v–lv.

Savarese, Gennaro. *Il Furioso e la cultura del Rinascimento.* Rome: Bulzoni, 1984.

Savoia, Francesca. "L'abito e la pazzia d'Orlando." *Forma e parola: Studi in memoria di Fredi Chiappelli.* Ed. Dennis J. Dutschke et al. Rome: Bulzoni, 1992. 255–70.

Scaglione, Aldo, ed. *Ariosto 1974 in America.* Ravenna: Longo, 1976.

————. "L'*Asino d'oro* e il Firenzuola." *GSLI* 126 (1949): 225–49.

————. "Chivalric and Idyllic Poetry in the Italian Renaissance." *Italica* 33 (1956): 252–60.

————. *Knights at Court.* Berkeley: U of California P, 1991.

Schama, Simon. "Clio Has a Problem." *New York Times Magazine* 8 September 1991: 30–34.

Schoeck, R. J. *Intertextuality and Renaissance Texts.* Bamberg: H. Kaiser, 1984.

Schweyen, Renate. *Guarino Veronese: Philosophie und humanistiche Pädagogik.* Munich: Fink, 1973.

Scolari, Antonio. "L'*OF* e la critica del secolo XVI." *Scritti di varia letteratura e di critica.* Bologna: Zanichelli, 1937.

Scott, Izora. *Controversies Over the Imitation of Cicero in the Renaissance.* 1910. Davis, CA: Hermagoras P, 1991.

Segre, Cesare. "Appunti sulle fonti dei *Cinque Canti.*" *Rassegna della Letteratura Italiana* 58 (1954): 413–20. Rpt. in *Esperienze* 97–109.

————. "La biblioteca dell'Ariosto." *Esperienze* 45–50.

————. *Esperienze ariostesche.* Pisa: Nistri-Lischi, 1966.

————. "Intertestuale-interdiscorsivo: Appunti per una fenomenologia delle fonti." Di Girolamo and Paccagnella 15–28.

————. "L'intertestualità." *L'interpretazione: Letteratura italiana.* Vol. 4. Turin: Einaudi, 1985. 83–86.

————, ed. *Ludovico Ariosto: Lingua, stile e tradizione.* Milan: Feltrinelli, 1976.

————. "Pio Rajna: le fonti e l'arte dell'*OF.*" *Strumenti critici* 64 ns 5.3 (1990): 315–27.

————. "La poesia dell'Ariosto." *Esperienze* 9–27.

————. "Un repertorio linguistico e stilistico dell'Ariosto: La *Commedia.*" *Esperienze* 51–83.

Sestan, Ernesto. "Cattaneo." *DBI.* Vol. 22. Rome: Instituto della Enciclopedia Italiana, 1979. 422–39.

Seznec, Jean. *The Survival of the Pagan Gods.* Trans. Barbara F. Sessions. 1940. 1953. Princeton: Princeton UP, 1972.

Shapiro, Marianne. *The Poetics of Ariosto.* Detroit: Wayne State UP, 1988.

Shemek, Deanna. "Circular Definitions: Configuring Gender in Italian Renaissance Festival." *Renaissance Quarterly* 48.1 (1995): 1–40.

————. "Of Women, Knights, Arms, and Love: The *Querelle des Femmes* in Ariosto's Poem." *MLN* 104.1 (1989): 68–97.

————. "That Elusive Object of Desire: Angelica in the *OF.*" *Annali d'italianistica* 7 (1989): 116–41.

Sherberg, Michael. *Rinaldo: Character and Intertext in Ariosto and Tasso.* Stanford: ANMI Libri, 1993.

———. "Text and Book in the *OI.*" American Boiardo Quincentennial Conference. New York, 8 Oct. 1994.

Simon, W. M. *European Positivism in the Nineteenth Century.* Ithaca: Cornell UP 1963.

Snell, Bruno. *The Discovery of the Mind in Greek Philosophy and Literature.* Trans. Thomas G. Rosenmeyer. 1946. 1953. New York: Dover, 1982.

Solerti, Angelo. "Ragguaglio della favola . . ." *Gerusalemme Conquistata.* Ed. Luigi Bonfigli. 2: 385–409.

Solodow, Joseph B. *The World of Ovid's* Met. Chapel Hill: U of North Carolina P, 1988.

Sorbelli, Tommaso. "Relazioni fra la letteratura italiana e le letterature classiche." *Problemi ed orientamenti critici di lingua e di letteratura italiana.* Milan: Marzorati, 1948.

Sowell, Madison U., ed. *Dante and Ovid: Essays in Intertextuality.* Binghamton: Medieval and Renaissance Texts and Studies, 1991.

———. "Dante's Nose and Publius Ovidius Naso: A Gloss on *Inferno* 25.45." *Quaderni d'italianistica* 10.1–2 (1989): 157–71.

Steiner, Grundy. "Ovid's *Carmen Perpetuum.*" *TAPA* 89 (1958): 218–36.

Stephens, Walter. Lecture. NEH Summer Institute on Ariosto and Tasso at Northwestern University. Evanston, 19 July 1990.

Stirrup, Barbara E. "Ovid's Narrative Technique: A Study in Duality." *Latomus* 35.1 (1976): 97–107.

Stroh, Wilfried. *Ovid im Urteil der Nachwelt.* Darmstadt: Wissenschaftliche Buchgesellschaft, 1969.

Sturm-Maddox, Sara. *Petrarch's Metamorphoses.* Columbia: U of Missouri P, 1985.

Tarditi, G. "Sull'origine e sul significato della parola 'rapsodo.' " *Maia* 20 (1968): 137–45.

Tarrant, R. J. "Ovid." *Texts and Transmission: A Survey of the Latin Classics.* Oxford: Clarendon P, 1983. 257–84.

Thomas, Richard F. "Virgil's *Georgics* and the Art of Reference." *Harvard Studies in Classical Philology* 90 (1986): 171–98.

Tincani, Carlo. "Matteo Maria Boiardo: Traduttore." Campanini 263–307.

Tissoni Benvenuti, Antonia. "Il mondo cavalleresco e la corte estense." Bruscagli, *I libri* 13–34.

———. *Il Quattrocento Settentrionale.* Bari: Laterza, 1951.

Toffanin, Giuseppe. *Il Cinquecento.* Milan: Vallardi, 1945.

Tolkiehn, J. "Die Bucheinteilung der *Met* Ovids." *Sokrates* 96 (1915): 315–19.

Tremoli, P. "Appunti sulla critica ovidiana nel Cinquecento." *Annali Triestini* 4.7 (1953): 267–94.

Tristano, Richard M. "Vassals, Fiefs, and Social Mobility in Ferrara during the Middle Ages and Renaissance." *Medievalia et Humanistica* ns 15 (1987): 43–64.

Truffi, Riccardo. "Erodoto tradotto da Guarino Veronese." *Studi italiani di filologia classica* 10 (1902): 73–94.

Turolla, Enzo. "Aristotele e le poetiche del Cinquecento." *Dizionario critico della letteratura italiana.* Ed. Vittore Branca. Turin: UTET, 1986. 1: 132–37.

Turri, Giuseppe. "Tre rogiti che furono celebrati in Ferrara nel 1801 per trasporto delle ossa di Lodovico Ariosto alla biblioteca di quella città si pubblicano in aggiunta alla descrizione del centenario ariosteo . . . da Giuseppe Turri." Reggio-Emilia: Calderini, 1876.

Tuve, Rosemond. *Allegorical Imagery: Some Medieval Books and Their Posterity.* Princeton: Princeton UP, 1966.

Ugolini, Francesco A. *I cantari d'argomento classico.* Florence: Olschki, 1933.

Ullman, Berthold L. "Classical Authors in the Medieval Florilegia." *Classical Philology* 27 (1932): 1–42.

Vinaver, Eugene. *The Rise of Romance.* Oxford: Clarendon P, 1971.

Vivaldi, Vincenzo. *La GL studiata nelle sue fonti.* Trani: Vecchi, 1907.

———. *Prolegomeni ad uno studio completo sulle fonti della GL.* Trani: Vecchi, 1904.

———. *Sulle fonti della GL.* 2 vols. Catanzaro: Caliò, 1893.

Weaver, Elissa B. "Lettura dell'intreccio dell'*OF:* Il caso delle tre pazzie d'amore." *Strumenti critici* 11 (1977): 384–406.

———. "Riformare l'*OI.*" Bruscagli, *I libri* 117–44.

Weinberg, Bernard. "Argomenti di discussione letteraria nell'Accademia degli Alterati (1570–1600)." *GSLI* 131 (1954): 175–94.

———. *A History of Literary Criticism in the Italian Renaissance.* 2 vols. Chicago: U of Chicago P, 1961.

———, ed. *Trattati di poetica e retorica del Cinquecento.* 4 vols. Bari: Laterza, 1970–72.

Weinberg, Florence M. *The Cave: The Evolution of a Metaphoric Field from Homer to Ariosto.* New York: Lang, 1986.

The Westminster Historical Atlas to the Bible. Ed. George Ernest Wright and Floyd Vivian Filson and intro. William Foxwell Albright. Philadelphia: Westminster, 1945.

Whitfield, J. H. "Leon Battista Alberti, Ariosto and Dosso Dossi." *Italian Studies* 21 (1966): 16–30.

Wiggins, Peter DeSa. *Figures in Ariosto's Tapestry: Character and Design in the* OF. Baltimore: Johns Hopkins UP, 1986.

Wilkinson, L. P., ed. *Ovid Recalled.* Cambridge: Cambridge UP, 1955.

———. "World of the *Met.*" *Ovidiana: Recherches sur Ovide.* Ed. N. I. Herescu. Paris: Les Belles Lettres, 1958.

Williamson, Edward. *Bernardo Tasso.* Rome: Edizioni di Storia e Letteratura, 1951.

Wimsatt, James I. "Theories of Intertextuality and Chaucer's Sources and Analogues." *Medievalia* 15 (1993): 231–39.

Woodward, William H. *Vittorino da Feltre and Other Humanist Educators.* Cambridge: Cambridge UP, 1921.

Worton, Michael, and Judith Still, eds. *Intertextuality: Theories and Practices.* Manchester: Manchester UP, 1990.

Zacchetti, Corrado. *L'imitazione classica nell'*OF. Bologna: Fava e Garagnani, 1891.

Zampese, Cristina. *Or si fa rossa or pallida la luna. La cultura classica nell'*OF. Lucca: Pacini Fazzi, 1994.

Zatti, Sergio. *Il* Furioso *fra epos e romanzo.* Lucca: Pacini Fazzi, 1990.

———. *L'uniforme cristiano e il multiforme pagano.* Milan: Il Saggiatore, 1983.

Zevi, Bruno. *Biagio Rossetti, architetto ferrarese, il primo urbanista moderno.* Turin: Einaudi, 1960.

Zumwalt, Nancy. "*Fama Subversa:* Theme and Structure in Ovid *Met* 12." *California Studies in Classical Antiquity* 10 (1977): 209–22.

Index

Acheron, 150–51
Achilles, 109
Acocella, Maria, 188 n. 47
Adonio, 139
Aeneas, 26, 77–88, 106
Agamemnon, 153
Agramante, 137–38
Agricola, Rodolphus, 64, 188 n. 33
Aladino, 147, 150–52, 163–64
Alcasto, 146
Alcina, 128, 134
Alexios I Komnenos, 143
Altrocchi, Rudolph, 201 n. 36
Amis, Martin, 15
amplification, 81–82, 88
Anchises, 78–79
Androgeos, 131–32, 139
Angelica, 19–26, 81–84, 102, 106, 116, 128–31, 134–35
Apollonius Rhodius, 78
Apuleius, 47, 66, 188 n. 43, 197 n. 44
Aquinas, St. Thomas, 166
Arachne, 102–3
Arcadia, the Roman Academy, 57–58
Argalia, 175 n. 7

Ariosto, Ludovico, Ferrarese Homer or Vergil, 17, 47; Ferrarese rhapsode, 53–54; *Furioso* and *Metamorphoses* compared, 193 n. 12, 194 n. 13; his tomb, 31–32, 180 n. 2; his tutors, 187 n. 32; narrator who must choose, 91–93, *Tragedia di Tisbe*, 107, 197 n. 38
Ariosto, Virginio, 97
ariostofili, 11
Aristotle, 46–48, 104, 142, 167–69, 182 n. 36
Armida, 127–29, 143, 147, 165
Arthurian cycle, 27, 29, 56, 100, 107, 166
Ascoli, Albert Russell, 40, 101, 175 n. 13, 176 n. 31, 179 n. 48, 194 n. 17, 197 n. 47, 199 nn. 15, 16, 202 n. 8
Astolfo, 192 n. 6
Athenaeus, 69

Baiardo, 81, 86–87, 89
Bakhtin, Mikhail, 40
Baldassarri, Guido, 40, 181 n. 24

Index